People in Places

Refuelling at sea

People in Places
——

WILLIAM
GLADSTONE

MICHAEL RUSSELL

© William Gladstone 2013

The right of Sir William Gladstone
to be identified as the author of this work
has been asserted by him in accordance with the
Copyright, Designs and Patents Act, 1988

First published in Great Britain 2013
by Michael Russell (Publishing) Ltd
Wilby Hall, Wilby, Norwich NR16 2JP

Page makeup in Sabon by Waveney Typesetters
Wymondham, Norfolk
Printed and bound in Great Britain
by Berforts Information Press

All rights reserved

ISBN 978-0-85955-325-4

IN HOMAGE TO
SIR THOMAS BROWNE

Contents

Preface		1
1 Scaitcliffe: A Preparatory School in the 1930s		5
2 Eton, 1938–43		17
3 The Navy, 1943–45		54
4 Post-War Oxford		93
5 Eton Again		107
6 Lancing		127
7 The Scouts 1972–82		149
1 A New Shape for Scouting		149
2 Organisation, Local and Central		154
3 Robert Baden-Powell		160
4 The Scout Group		164
5 Scoutreach		172
6 The Chief Scout		177
7 The World Organisation		186
8 The Church in Wales 1972–92		200
1 Disestablishment		200
2 Welsh Christianity		207
3 The New Province		211
4 A Modern Structure?		220
5 The Representative Body		222
6 When Things Went Wrong		226
7 Doctrine		227
8 Institutions		230

9	Some Local Institutions	237
	1 The Flintshire County Council 1970–74	237
	2 The Magistracy, 1976–2000	248
	3 The Lord-Lieutenant, 1985–2000	256
	Dramatis Personae	271

Preface

This book is not an autobiography, although it is avowedly autobiographical. It is a series of snapshots of the various institutions to which I have been attached, in both senses of the word, since I was eight years old. Much of my life has been lived within the framework of the institutions listed in the chapter headings. I proposed entitling this book 'Life in an Institution', but my publisher did not share my satirical frame of mind, suggesting that potential readers would assume that I had done my time in a prison or a mental hospital, and that they could not anticipate much pleasure or interest from reading about that.

I suggest in my first chapter that there are two sorts of people: those who like to live within the framework of institutions and those who don't. This includes institutions which govern individual as well as collective conduct – most notably marriage. There are people who wish to commit themselves to this institution, and people who don't. I am one of the former, but this book deals only with institutions which involve the collective activity of diverse ranges of individuals. In that sense again, then, this is not an autobiography. If I am spared, I may attempt a more autobiographical kind of book, not about private or personal matters but about my parents and my nanny and my uncles and aunts, and some of the experiences and adventures of our immediate family, and about friends and colleagues involved in the institutions which I describe in this volume, with a sprinkling of anecdotes about their habits and eccentricities. That, if ever it saw the light of day, would be a more self-indulgent book than this one. Self-indulgence is a characteristic of an autobiography. That is what makes it fun to write one.

History has been my lifelong interest: but this is not a history of the institutions which are my subject matter. Here and there I do touch on their origins and their development, but that is merely incidental to my snapshot of what they were like when I was involved in them. To that extent these descriptions might conceivably be a source of history, however modest: raw materials, but not the dish served up (I avoid the

Preface

word 'cooked') by a historian. I have left the reader to draw his or her own conclusions about the way in which these institutions fitted in to the culture of the times, and how they have changed since then.

During my lifetime – it is now almost eighty years since I entered my preparatory school – I have witnessed the end of the British Empire; the end of the Establishment which traces its history back to 1714 (or perhaps even 1689 when for the first time the King and Queen depended on an Act of Parliament rather than a Divine Right); the end of the Renaissance, with Latin as its universal language; and the emancipation of women. I have also seen Britain become what correct people call a multicultural society.

It is easy nowadays to underestimate the influence of Marxist thought (I might almost say the Marxist creed) on Western Europe from the Russian revolution in 1917 until the time of Gorbachev in the 1980s. It was a dominant feature in British intellectual and political life, at least from 1945, until Jim Callaghan, perhaps the most underrated of our Prime Ministers, recognised a 'sea change' for what it was, opening the door for the transformation of our economy masterminded by Margaret Thatcher and her lieutenant Keith Joseph.

I have witnessed the electronic or digital revolution. One of my last acts at Lancing in 1969 was to sanction the purchase of ten mechanical calculators, costing £50 each, to save the mathematical sixth form from having to do their own arithmetic and algebra or to use tables to find logarithms, sines and cosines. It was not long before these gadgets were to become museum pieces. Now we live in a world obsessed by instant global twenty-four-hour communication. Time will show whether or not the human frame can tolerate that.

Finally, and to me most significantly, Christian Britain has given way to Post-Christian Britain. This dismays and perplexes me, because the field of contention has been such a narrow one. I touch on this in my essay on the Church in Wales. But I detest and deplore judgemental history, and its scion political correctness, which is now the fashion for raucous polemicists and for some practitioners in the self-indulgent modern phenomenon known as 'The Media'. They require, for instance, that Britain must apologise for the British Empire, without the faintest understanding of its history or the wit to consider the motivation which created it; let alone to recognise its successor in the guise (or rather disguise) of modern colonialism.

Historians owe their interest in institutions, and the concept that a

Preface

culture is the sum of its institutions, to the Enlightenment of the eighteenth century, which transformed our way of thinking about history and society. The hotspots of the Enlightenment were Scotland, France and to a lesser degree Switzerland; perhaps, it has been suggested, because they had all shaken off the rigid puritan dominance of Calvinism, retaining nevertheless the questioning mindset of the protestant, and introducing the Age of Reason. The Scotsman David Hume was the first modern historian. He regarded history as more than a record, a mere chronicle of events. He looked for reasons why cultures change, examining the ideas of those who brought changes about. Another Scotsman, Adam Smith, recognised that the market itself actually created wealth: institutions were self-fuelling. Edward Gibbon, an Englishman whose first language was French, author of *The Decline and Fall of the Roman Empire* (he was asking himself why it happened), summed up in one sentence the whole concept of institutions as the driving force of history: 'The value of money has been settled by general consent to represent our wants and our property, as letters were invented to express our ideas; and both these institutions, by giving more active energy to the powers and passions of human nature, have contributed to multiply the objects they were designed to represent.'

For better or for worse the British Empire, the Establishment and Socialist Britain have been swept away. Each of us can look around and see how their objectives and functions are being approached and performed now. Ferdinand Mount has written an account of The New Few.

Thus my attachment to history as a way of thought led me to the study of institutions, in the wide sense of that word, and the reasons why they survive or disappear. Institutions, like animal species, survive if they evolve to cope with an ever-changing environment. If they do, they themselves change that environment, namely the culture within which we live. They are more complicated than they look at first sight. They depend on ways of thought which are difficult to analyse, and on customs and conventions which are not codified in rules and regulations. I have an idea that customs and conventions may be more important than rules and regulations in the evolution and survival of our institutions. They govern the kind of way we speak to and understand each other.

I admire British institutions for their extraordinary, indeed unique,

Preface

capacity to evolve and survive. This is due to two national characteristics. The first is a pragmatic approach: an insistence on what works rather than what ought to work in theory. The second is our ingenuity and our willingness to improvise in order to solve a problem, regardless of anomalies. Heading the list of our ancient national institutions is the Crown in Parliament, a typically strange and subtle label which, I suspect, is less easily understood nowadays than it was fifty years ago. It has taken us about eight hundred years to get where we are in terms of parliamentary government. People say that in recent years the House of Commons has failed to evolve with the times. I don't know whether they are right, but if they are I think the reason may be in its failure to nurture its conventions – and hence, incidentally, to be less captivating to its members than it was. Many a member used to be sucked into the ethos of the Palace of Westminster in a way that does not seem to happen nowadays.

We need not deny the part played by individual geniuses in order to accept that it has been the institutions created by their ideas which are the driving force of history. We confer on these institutions the ending '-ism': puritanism, protestantism, rationalism, socialism; Bonapartism, Marxism, and now even Thatcherism. Strict teachers (and cynics) say that these '-isms' do no more than save us from defining what we mean. That is valuable cautionary advice; yet perhaps an '-ism' confers a sort of recognition that an institution has achieved the status which has made it a notable influence in our lives.

I
Scaitcliffe: A Preparatory School in the 1930s

In September 1934, just before my ninth birthday, I joined my preparatory school, Scaitcliffe, at Englefield Green in Surrey. Throughout the summer I had been asked by well-meaning people whether I was looking forward to going to boarding school; alternatively the question had been asked in my presence in the third person, on the grounds presumably (and correctly) that I was incapable of answering it myself: 'And is Billy looking forward to boarding school?' Although I vaguely felt that I was not – I had no complaints about the status quo – I felt equally vaguely that this was not the expected answer.

I had no concept of what lay ahead, but I realised that it was inevitable. When I got to Scaitcliffe, I accepted everything that happened as inevitable. There were things I enjoyed, and things I hated, but almost all of them were part of an experience which was going to happen anyway. It never occurred to me to express my feelings, let alone my objections.

I wonder if acceptance of the inevitable is the reaction of the great majority of us throughout our lives. I suspect that it is, but I also suspect that there are two sorts of people, those who like to fit in and those – the misfits – who don't. There are of course infinite gradations of conformity and nonconformity, but we all belong to one type or the other. I am emphatically a conformist. I like to live my life within a framework. I may not like the rules, and indeed I may object to them and try to get them changed. I may, and frequently do, disobey them or, more cunningly, try to find a way round them; but I like the structure to be there. It is an essential feature of order and civilisation. The other sort of person prefers to live in as loose a framework as possible, since it is difficult if not impossible not to be caught by it in one way or another.

People like me, who like to live within a framework, actually live within a series of frameworks. They need the general rules of society, which is a negative attitude, but they also like a clearly designed structure within it, in which to earn their daily bread, play their games and build their families. They are institutional, and become institutionalised. They like to be members of a team, and they get married. This is tribalism, I suppose.

Boys at preparatory schools wear their tribalism on their sleeves, as do grown-up children at football matches. Yet tribalism is the nursery of all culture, and its modern manifestation in the form of reverence for the past is far more sophisticated than the desire to be rid of it, which is to prefer the path towards anarchy, or at least towards nihilism. These thoughts did not colour my attitude to Scaitcliffe. They came later.

There were just over forty boys at Scaitcliffe when I arrived. Times were hard for our parents, and indeed for the school. Neither the professional classes nor the idle rich had recovered from the economic collapse of 1929–30. The fees were £50 a term, roughly the equivalent of £5,000 now. However, for some reason I have never discovered, most of the schools against whom we played cricket or football matches were larger. Scaitcliffe had five forms, so the average class size was only eight or nine. The most important activities were Latin and cricket.

Latin began with nouns of the first declension in *Kennedy's Shorter Latin Primer*. All the preliminary blurb about vowels and consonants, inflexion, parts of speech, declension, and gender were sensibly skipped so that we could get straight ahead with the vocative case of *mensa*, a table. Unlike Winston Churchill, none of us was bold enough to ask why we should begin by learning how to speak to a table, although I did wonder. Winston became a politician, and he should have had the wit to realise, before he committed to paper a record of his early life, that this was his first lesson in the political dictum enunciated by Disraeli: 'Never excuse, never explain.' I admit that on the whole my education encouraged me to question things – which later got me into trouble, in the Navy. But at the age of eight we tried to learn what we were told to learn, without asking why. I have no doubt that it is still the best way of starting Latin, for the few who are still privileged to do so.

Cricket was approached in a similar way. You did what you were told. We had no preaching about team spirit or not questioning the umpire's decision. We knew that if we threw our wicket away, or worse still threw away someone else's, or if we did question the umpire, we would be punished, and that was the beginning and end of it. Just as the learning by rote of *mensa*, a table, was the best start along the road of questioning what we were ordered to do, so Scaitcliffe's approach to cricket taught us that certain things were Not Done. This is the essence of the tribal framework. The notion that some things were Done and other things were Not Done was my sheet anchor. When eventually it started to drag in the storms of the 1960s this was something I was not happy about.

The headmaster and proprietor, Ronald Vickers, then in his sixties, was a brilliant but ruthless teacher of the boys in the top form, aged eleven to thirteen, who were being prepared for Common Entrance or for scholarships to public schools, mostly leading schools, something like half the boys going on to Eton. We all lived in fear of him, although we did not encounter him in class until we reached the second form. Here we underwent our baptism of fire in the form of Latin 'unseens' (translations from Latin) and 'proses' (compositions into Latin) twice a week, on Tuesdays and Thursdays, during the last sessions of the day. If our written efforts did not come up to standard they were mercilessly torn up ('ripped') and thrown off his desk, a few going through the window and having to be retrieved from the garden.

Vickers taught me to read through my work carefully in order to correct mistakes, a lesson I have never forgotten – principally because it was purchased at the price of nine strokes of the cane (though I had transgressed in one or two other minor ways, such as fooling about in the dormitory). Vickers knew what he was about when it came to a beating. He was an accurate shot and with nine strokes he could be sure to hit the same spots several times. His mastery however depended on timing – a pause between each stroke just long enough to let the pain reach its peak, but not long enough to allow it to subside. I had never been hurt like that before. Not surprisingly I resolved to keep out of trouble in the future. This I achieved, at both Scaitcliffe and Eton, by careful tactics and cunning. The skill was to learn how to play the system. I think I was a more canny practitioner than many. Some of my friends and contemporaries were simply too careless to avoid being caught. When accused, they did not know how to be economical with the truth. For all that there was honour among thieves: you could cheat in order to save your own skin, but not in order to gain an advantage over others. This was one of the salient rules of what was Done and what was Not Done.

Vickers was an excellent French teacher. Once we had started to learn the basic grammar, he moved quickly through the textbook, enabling us to become familiar with the shape of the sentences. He used Scripture, as Religious Instruction was then known, to teach us the beauty of the language of the Authorised Version of 1611, mainly from the Old Testament. We had already some acquaintance with the Gospels and now we came to know the great stories and some of the noblest passages from Genesis to Kings. Vickers knew the Bible well, skipping the boring or difficult chapters so that we got along quickly. We thought that he was skipping in order to avoid the dirty bits, and did our best to skim through them for salacious material unless we were actually reading aloud, but without much success. We were taught English by Denis Owen, of whom later, and introduced to some poetry and to Shakespeare. We read *Coriolanus* – an odd choice – and acted *The Merchant of Venice*. But it was at Latin, which we did at least once every day, that Vickers excelled.

By the time we reached the top form we were well versed in the basics of Latin grammar, and were beginning to cope with compound sentences. Julius Caesar might have written his text on the Gallic War for the benefit of boys like us. This was fairly simple narrative prose on a subject that was likely to appeal to us if anything did. Our very first Latin sentences (subject, verb and object) required a first declension general, one whose name declined like *mensa*, a table. This was Cotta, whose fame is more or less confined to those who had not got as far as the second declension. Here the general was Labienus, whose name declined like *annus*, a year. Then we graduated to Caesar, third declension, with his infantry, his cavalry – but with simple names, foot and horse. Cohorts, legions and centurions needed little translation. His vocabulary repeated itself in each campaign. He fought battles and wars, he made camps and ramparts and went into winter quarters. He threw bridges across rivers and laid waste the countryside. To meet him was our first experience of the sunlit uplands, after a long struggle in distinguishing between perfect, imperfect and pluperfect tenses in the grammar. Latin was still unpleasant, but less so.

The one thing you had to grasp with Caesar was the ablative absolute. You could not have a narrative without being able to write 'when he had done this he did that', and Caesar insisted on complicating the process by writing 'this having been done…'. This involved us in the passive voice, but only in a very small part of it – the past participle.

Scaitcliffe: A Preparatory School in the 1930s

...il and on Greek. In three of the four years I was at Scaitcliffe we ... a first, a second and a third scholarship to Eton, a fine record for ... prep school, let alone one as small as Scaitcliffe; but to the two of ...m whom I knew, the process was almost unbearable: it was not all ...ne by kindness. Besides, Latin did not suit those who had no aptitude ... languages, and there was no alternative.

...ickers's approach to cricket was similar to his approach to Latin, with ...uch more emphasis on what to do than why. The refinements of the ...ame were interesting to us in themselves, with first and second slips and gully and third man and backward point and point and cover point and extra cover all occupying one sector of the field, not to mention silly mid-on and silly mid-off and long leg and fine leg and square leg and short leg and all the rest; leg breaks, off breaks, googlies and yorkers, they were all part of our pleasure. But as with Latin, so with cricket, Vickers simplified the code to its essentials. When it came to playing a correct shot, you did what you were told (as far as you were able) without asking questions.

Only three shots were allowed: a forward shot or off-drive, with your left leg close to the line of the ball and a straight bat, whether this shot was defensive or offensive; secondly, a square cut towards cover and thirdly, for a short ball (a long hop), a sweep to leg. In bowling, you bowled straight and to a length, practising landing the ball on a handkerchief. These were ideal rules for winning a prep school cricket match. If indeed you could bowl straight and to a length (this was good enough to take any number of prep school wickets), Vickers had no objection to your trying to bowl breaks; but it was no good trying to bowl breaks which ended up as full tosses or long-hops, which brought down his wrath. Fast bowling was not allowed, except by a very few large boys, certainly fewer than one a year, who could do it properly. Vickers would not have his beloved square mown short, so the pitch was slow and there was not much scope for fast bowlers anyway. The school was divided into four sections, appropriately named after Kitchener, Haig, Jellicoe and Beatty. Every morning one section did the duty of pushing and pulling the huge roller, designed for a horse with rubber shoes, slowly up and down the pitch.

There were fierce rules as to who should call a run, and how; and for completing a run with the correct corner of your bat along the ground: woe betide the transgressor, or anyone who ran down the middle of the

Scaitcliffe: A Preparatory School in

'This having been done' was simply *hoc facto* as [...] *hoc facio*. Once you got the hang of it, you cou[ld ...] Caesar did.

Of course you did have to know the construction[s ...] nate clauses, and the subjunctive tenses which they [...] not as difficult as it sounds. '*Ut*' clauses ('in order tha[t...] but for the most part you could string quite long se[ntences ...] once you had got hold of the dreaded ablative absolute[...] not only mercifully easy, but enabled one to show style, [...] *itaque*, which came first in the sentence, or *igitur* which [...] Vickers taught us how to construct the Caesarian sen[tence ...] assured us a good place in Common Entrance and a usef[ul ...] tion, if we were otherwise considered worthy, to a scholars[hip ...]

Towards the end of our Scaitcliffe careers our Latin beg[an ...] with some quite sophisticated words, including deponent ver[bs ...] have a passive form but an active meaning). *Loquor*, 'I spe[ak' ...] comparatively simple. *Utor*, 'I use', involved a much more com[plex] idea which has survived in the form of 'I am used to' in Englis[h ...] even took the dative, by the way), which fortunately did not da[unt] us. *Nanciscor*, 'I obtain' (what a lovely word), was essential fo[r the] invasion of England, clearly the most interesting of Caesar's campa[igns,] because without obtaining ideal weather Caesar could no more mo[unt] a cross-Channel invasion than Eisenhower and Montgomery cou[ld.] Presumably Caesar could not forecast the weather, so he had to obta[in] it. He therefore had to write 'When he had obtained' rather than 'Whe[n] he expected', but he couldn't use an ablative absolute because the past participle of *nanciscor* had an active meaning. A further refinement was the evident difficulty which Romans encountered trying to pronounce the consonants 'nct' as in *nanctus*; so it had tended to be shortened to *nactus*. These ideas, which seem quite complicated to adults, were by no means beyond the powers of twelve-year-olds, provided that they were clearly explained without resort to the reasons which might have led to them. We could also use gerunds, by the simple expedient of imitating a model phrase (the art of writing), without having to try to understand that gerunds were active nouns whereas gerundives were passive adjectives.

Caesar did have to be simplified for our benefit. All the same, this was the real thing, and the cleverer boys could compose a tolerable imitation of genuine Latin prose. The scholarship boys were started on pitch. Fielding was practised regularly. Correct methods had to be employed to prevent the ball from going between your legs, and to ensure that you did not york the wicketkeeper.

We had one phenomenal player, Luke White, who later played in some wartime test matches and who, no doubt, would have had a distinguished first-class career as an amateur but for the war. He won us all our matches almost single-handed. As Roger Pemberton put it, we were 'Luke White and ten rabbits'. Luke alone was allowed to play any shots he liked, and he was several times caught on the mid-wicket boundary trying to bring up the century (for no wicket) with what in anyone else's locker would have been called a cow-shot.

It was claimed among our opponent schools that if we lost a match we all got beaten by Vickers. This of course was not true, although I think we once or twice lost a half-holiday after having lost a match as a result of slackness or stupidity, and he made the evening's lessons hellish if he was displeased. But for all his harshness (and even his cruelty and bullying) Vickers was a gentleman. He did not mind if we lost a match, provided that we had gone about it properly. He liked us to do things well, not shoddily.

French started as Latin did, with the singular and plural of nouns in a grammar by one Henri Bué. By the second page we had got as far as plurals in 'x', including *hiboux*, *genoux* and *choux* (owls, knees and cabbages) and, more interestingly, *cieux* for skies but *ciels* for skies-in-pictures. I don't think we made much use of these words, at least for a few years, but the fact that I have remembered them perhaps vindicates the method.

There was a tiny purpose-built chapel with all the correct furnishings, and here we were thrown in at the deep end even more than in Latin or French, Vickers reading Mattins from the Prayer Book without compromise. The first words I remember hearing were 'Who desireth not the death of a sinner but rather that he should turn from his wickedness and live': strong meat for an eight-year-old. We did all the Canticles and the Psalms, and were taught the pointing of Anglican chants by Mr Surplice, the assistant organist at St George's Chapel, who came once a week and also taught us many of the best-known hymns. Here, as in Latin, French and cricket, the Vickers method worked wonders. As in Latin a word is either right or wrong, so with a note in music. We quickly picked up a few chants, and we could soon read the bars and the dotted notes. So we soaked up tunes and rhythms and wonderful language and at the same time we learnt accuracy. These music lessons were enjoyable.

Mathematics was well taught, with insistence on our learning our tables in the early stages. We had the good fortune to be taught by John Corlett in the upper forms. He was a young Cambridge exhibitioner, a man of the world and an interesting personality, who like many of his contemporaries in the 1930s could not find a job to match his talents. He was a breath of fresh air in the confined atmosphere of the school, and without ever being wild or even indiscreet he opened our eyes in several respects. He taught very well, but (for whatever reason) he told us what to do rather than trying to explain why. I did not understand factorising, nor what lay behind the process, but we knew the rules and we did hundreds of examples. We got quite a long way with arithmetic and algebra, but the ideal subject for the preparatory school was Euclidean geometry, where we really could see for ourselves the logic of the propositions without an explanation being required. This was the only subject in which it was not unusual to score 100% in Common Entrance: but there were plenty of other subjects to sort out the best from the also-rans.

Yet another activity which contributed to the Vickers system was air-rifle shooting. Everyone had five shots once a week under the eagle eyes (one was blue, the other brown) of Sergeant Fagents. Here again it was possible to achieve five bullseyes if, and only if, one did what one was told and concentrated on accuracy. During my last term the runner-up lost only one point in the whole ten or twelve weeks, the winner none.

The mainstay of the school's music was in Mr Surplice's lessons in chapel, but there was also a percussion band for the lower forms. This provided almost the only light relief of the week, since nobody but the teacher, a severe lady with a weather-beaten complexion, (and of course the powers that be, who were not present) took it seriously. The sessions were held in the sanatorium. Every boarding school in the land had been required after the First World War to construct a separate building where pupils with infectious or contagious diseases could be isolated. These buildings were expensive white elephants, hardly ever used, because seriously ill pupils were at once sent to a hospital, and if necessary an isolation ward. Scaitcliffe's unused sanatorium was suitably isolated for sound as well as bacteria. It had its full complement of chamber pots, which we used to the best advantage after we had

Scaitcliffe: A Preparatory School in the 1930s

switched off the electric lights, leaving our unfortunate teacher to try to restore order in pitch darkness. She wore a rather tight cotton dress and one of our ploys was to write rude messages in chalk in mirror writing on her chair.

There were piano lessons for individuals in the Sardine Tin. This was an extremely small unventilated room in the main lobby outside the classrooms, which was quite well insulated for sound in spite of having glass windows all round. There was just room for the upright piano, the teacher and the pupil. The teacher, who was known as Fishy, was small of stature and had extremely bad breath, which must have made the lessons insufferable to anybody without a severe head-cold. It was never known whether Fishy was so called because he worked in the Sardine Tin, or because his breath smelt similar to the fish which had meandered by goods train from Grimsby to Egham for our Friday lunches. At the end of a lesson, when the pupil was released, the atmosphere was released also.

The person who held the whole thing together was Denis Owen, the archetype preparatory school master. Small of stature, a pipe-smoking bachelor, a versatile, gifted, imaginative and witty teacher, he was liked and respected by all. He taught Latin, French and English and History and Geography as well. He coached the first eleven in both football and cricket (Vickers exercised his influence from the touchline or the boundary), exercised a universal benign influence and appeared to be in charge of most of the organisation and discipline. He had as sure a touch as Vickers with boys of our age, but a gentler one. Much of his holiday time was devoted to taking boys abroad, where at their parents' request he continued to contribute to their education. Paid presumably a pittance, he was always cheerful and gave his whole life to his Scaitcliffe pupils.

I have already mentioned John Corlett. Another master of some distinction was Alan Hilder, who played the occasional game of cricket for Kent, and hit the headlines as a batsman. He toed the Vickers line, teaching us to play forward and to bowl to a length, and was obviously something of a hero as well as being a competent teacher in the lower reaches. Our geography was mainly topography, and I learnt from Alan the rivers, inlets and counties of Britain, which was more useful than learning the exports of Wongobongoland as later became fashionable. Alan was offered a job on the Stock Exchange by Luke White's father in order that he could play cricket more often for Kent; but it turned out to be a clerk's job, boring and ill-paid, with the sole advantage of leave of absence when required by his county. Later he ran his own prep school for some years, but it was not really a success. He had never quite recovered from having been lionised as one of Lancing's finest ever athletes (he was a superb goalkeeper) and I met him there thirty years later, at an Old Boys' event, a disappointed man.

The rest of the teaching staff came and went, for reasons good or bad. One summer a master called Martin arrived, complete with his MG sports car, which impressed us. But somehow we at once detected what Vickers hadn't, that he was bogus. He did not last very long. I met him, too, thirty years later, when I was at Lancing. He was a more or less permanent resident at Ford Open Prison. It was extraordinary how, after thirty years, I recognised a person of no distinction whom I had only seen for a few weeks. I asked the Governor, who was kindly showing me round, 'What is that man's name?' 'Martin,' he replied. 'I know him,' I said.

Sergeant Fagents did the PT and the boxing as well as the shooting. The PT always seemed to begin with picking teams. They were named after the leading football teams, of which I had never heard, including Portsmouth, Arsenal and Preston North End. A highly imitable lean and wiry cockney ('What are you a'doing-of?'), he used a square two-handled canvas target to teach us boxing – 'Come on, 'it me, 'it me, left 'ook, right 'ook, uppercut, straight left, come on, 'it me', followed by a gentle but painful tap on the nose. I hated boxing and it always seemed to hurt me more than my opponent, with the merciful exception of Tommy Buxton, whom I could beat. However, if I let Tommy off lightly, this was immediately detected, and I was compelled by the system to hit him harder than I would have wished.

Two sisters were matrons, Nurse Minor and Nurse Minima, Nurse Major having disappeared from the scene before my arrival. They ran bath nights with a rod of iron and checked (cursorily, if methodically) that we had washed our ears and brushed our teeth, They dispensed malt every morning (to fatten us against catching cold), and syrup of figs (to loosen us) every few weeks.

In the background, emerging only when we were in the sickroom, was the severe figure of Starchy Ethel, who wore a white maid's hat and starched cuffs the size of gaiters, and looked after the linen. The gentler female side was represented only by the cuddly Ma Bub and her pretty

Scaitcliffe: A Preparatory School in the 1930s

daughter Rosie. Ma Bub was the widowed Ronald Vickers's second wife, his first leaving as testimony to her fine looks two elegant daughters who appeared occasionally. Ma Bub used to invite the new boys in to Sunday tea in her drawing room, a kindly act which however only emphasised the return to sparser surroundings immediately afterwards. We supposed that the three sisters known as Nurse, and Starchy Ethel, had started as members of the Vickers family domestic scene, acquiring official status later.

The regime was harsh, but the school was not an unhappy one for most of us, although there were one or two vicious bullies and one or two weaker or odder brethren who were picked on and teased. No school can avoid that, or at least in those days it couldn't. Who could have guessed that Miles Giffard was going to chop up his parents with an axe, put them in a bag, and throw them over a cliff? He might not have been caught if he hadn't washed the axe in hot water, but Scaitcliffe could hardly have taught him to use cold, good as it was as a training ground to teach us to keep out of trouble. Several of my contemporaries have testified when I have met them from time to time that they were happy at the school. We acquired a great deal of useful knowledge, but more importantly we were taught how to go about our work.

If, however, you had no aptitude for languages or ball games, and equally if you were not a conformist, it was another matter. My brother Peter, though an intelligent man and a superb athlete (a brilliant oarsman and a first-class shot) with an enviable gift for making friends, had little aptitude for languages and none for ball games. He was not a conformist. Scaitcliffe did not suit him at all, and indeed it was not until he had been almost three years at Eton, and could find some joy and success in biology and rowing, that he began to flourish.

There was no science whatever at Scaitcliffe. Nothing was done to invite our curiosity about the world around us except through literature. At our little pre-prep school run by two ladies in Windsor we had at least done botany: we had collected wild flowers, pressed them and counted and recorded the number of petals, sepals and stamens. My father taught me about plants and birds, my mother read with me a children's book on astronomy, and took me out at dawn to see mammals. There was nothing of the kind at Scaitcliffe, no biology and no physics let alone chemistry.

Scaitcliffe: A Preparatory School in the 1930s

The teaching within these terms of reference (which were universal in those days) was excellent, almost without exception. Games were well and enthusiastically and sportingly played. There was an good library from which we were encouraged to read whatever we wished, mainly of course fiction like 'Sapper's' Bulldog Drummond stories (based on some very believable inhabitants of Godalming, part of our constituency), R. M. Ballantyne's *Coral Island*, Conan Doyle's Sherlock Holmes and Brigadier Gerard, Percy F. Westerman and Biggles, Arthur Ransome's *Swallows and Amazons*, and above all John Buchan. There were abridged editions of the classics, including Captain Marryat and Charles Dickens There were also occasional evening lectures, most of them more interesting than the Reverend Jocelyn Perkins on Westminster Abbey (an annual and boring event), and in the summer there were Shakespeare plays in the garden, including *Julius Caesar*. There was a weekly art lesson. There was carpentry, and there were Scouts, both of which I much enjoyed. The food was not very palatable, but apart from the fish it was edible, with occasional treats. I am grateful to my father for choosing the school, and to my parents for sending me there.

2
Eton, 1938–43

I went to Eton in September 1938, so my first year there was before the outbreak of the war. Within a few weeks, however, the Munich crisis was afoot, and almost everyone was sent home until it subsided as a result of Neville Chamberlain's attempt to appease Hitler over the Sudetenland, the German part of Czechoslovakia. But I was not sent home, because my father was a master at the school. The time was spent fortifying one room in each house, usually the boys' dining room, against bombing, by piling up sandbags against the windows. This was a more entertaining occupation than doing school work. Eventually the Prime Minister returned from Munich and landed at Heston bearing news of 'Peace in Our Time' and waving a flimsy note signed by Hitler. During the subsequent year a concrete air raid shelter was built for each boys' house.

It is generally accepted now that Chamberlain did the right thing for the wrong reason. He gave Britain an additional year to rearm. A massive naval building programme had been started in 1935, Spitfires and Hurricanes had being flying around whilst I was still at Scaitcliffe, a few tanks were being constructed and conscription had been introduced in 1938. Britain survived the first years of the war by the skin of its teeth, and would not have won the Battle of Britain nor the Battle of the Atlantic if they had been fought a year earlier. Much of my first year at Eton seemed as much like wartime as did the 'phoney war' from September 1939 to the spring of 1940. But Henley and Lord's during my first summer half were experiences never to be repeated. Nothing of the luxury I experienced there was to be seen again, at least until the late 1950s when it just began to re-emerge in a much modified form.

We hankered after that luxury. During the war it was cold and dark and everything was in short supply. There were some noisy and even frightening moments, and there was much unpleasant news. But there were compensations, and in retrospect I am glad that I was at Eton during the war. There was no plutocracy and London society was in a

Eton, 1938–43

state of suspended animation. Money could get you nowhere, because there was nothing to spend it on. We had to make our own amusements, because most of the young masters had gone to war. We had to organise, coach and umpire our own games, which was good for us and made any kind of professional attitude impossible. Some of the old men who were dragged out of retirement to teach us had had interesting and distinguished careers in one field or another, and some of the others who were recruited were eccentric enough to add colour to our lives. There was no motor traffic, so Eton became a country village once again. There were no motor boats on the river, which ran as softly as in Spenser's day.

There were about 1,100 boys in the school, and a staff almost entirely of Oxford and Cambridge graduates, many of them Old Etonians, with the ratio of boys to masters of about eleven to one. The classes (known as divisions) were quite large, about thirty strong in the lower part of the school, because some of the teaching was done by tutors in small groups. The core of the school, a minority of 70 of the 1,100 boys, was College, the original foundation of Henry VI in 1440 (except that he had envisaged poor scholars but it was essential to pay for a preparatory education if your son was to stand a good chance of getting a scholarship). The rest of the school consisted of boys living in the town (Oppidans) in licensed boarding houses, of which there were 25, each about 40 to 45 strong. These houses had become more and more tightly regulated since the 1860s, and they were all run by masters, the last dame having expired in the nineteenth century. The remarkable feature of an Eton education was that every pupil had a room of his own (except in some cases where brothers shared). The room might be very small. Every room was furnished with a folding bed, a desk with bookshelf above and drawers below known as a bureau (pronounced 'burry'), a chair, a table and an ottoman (a small chest which served as a seat). Every boy's room was his castle, though liable to invasion, giving one privacy from the age of twelve or thirteen, encouraging individuality but also making it harder for unsociable boys to make friends and easier for aggressive boys to bully them. Since the houses were comparatively small it was possible for a good housemaster to deal with this problem.

The house was run as to all daily matters of organisation and discipline by a small self-elected (the housemaster could have had a veto) group of senior boys known as the Library, although it would have been unusual to find a book in it. A good housemaster visited most if not all of his boys in their rooms every evening, sometimes just to say goodnight but usually to have a brief chat. He appointed the captain of the house and had thus a daily opportunity to discuss things informally, to consult and to be consulted.

I was in George Tait's 'division' my first half, in upper fourth form. His teaching in that form, which was to continue for years, had already become an institution which few forgot, especially the poetry we were made to declaim. Then in E Block (called Remove) I was 'up to' Denys Wilkinson for more than one half, who had a sharp wit accompanied by quite a subtle form of slapstick comedy and a genius for making Latin, Greek and Divinity entertaining. During my next year, in D block, I was 'up to' Cyril Butterwick and Brian Whitfield. Cyril taught us Horace, which was fiendishly difficult because the word order had been ruthlessly manipulated by the poet in order to make the odes scan. However, there was a certain tunefulness about the verse, and a lightness of touch absent from Caesar and Tacitus, and Cyril was expert at the explanation of Italian wine and other (non-pornographic, of course) pleasures of life in classical times. With Brian we did at least two of the plays of Aristophanes, probably *The Frogs* and *The Clouds*. Most of the jokes seemed to be as childish as we were, although – even more so than with Horace's Latin – some of the Greek of Aristophanes was beyond us. Brian was good at explaining the otherwise unfathomable puns, and the antics of both actors and chorus were lively. By the time we got to C Block, at the age of fifteen, we were attempting Euripides' *Hecuba*, an adult classic if ever there was one about an unfortunate woman who spent the whole of the play slowly going mad. The process was, however, made more bearable by the fact that only half the pages were in Greek, the rest being in English, which enabled us to get to the end of the play by the end of the half.

Our work would have been unsustainable without a 'crib', even though the masters sometimes went through the text with us before setting it as construe. The cribs were slim paperback editions which circulated pretty freely, and which had to be purchased from last year's users. A few rare editions were expensive, but indispensable. There was also a second-hand bookshop in Windsor which sold them. Of course one only needed one copy for each boys' house, as we could get together in the evenings to work through the lines which had been set.

Eton, 1938–43

One difficulty was that our textbooks were bowdlerised editions, but the cribs were not. This was a serious problem if one was hard put to it to understand the language anyway, whether in Greek or English, especially with Aristophanes, where a pun with a pornographic interpretation would have been either modified or excised. The masters must have known that we had cribs, but their difficulty was to prove it, and I remember Brian Whitfield selecting a victim most likely to fall into the trap and who translated a clean joke with the excised dirty words which he had memorised without understanding them. Although everyone did it, and the powers that be knew that we did it, the punishment was very severe, presumably because of the difficulty of detection: one was not punished by the form master or by one's housemaster, but 'put in the Head Master's bill' to await in fear and trembling the sentence of this highest court.

Apart from the authors I have mentioned, we did some Herodotus, Tacitus and Ovid, but mostly in snippets which made them less interesting. We did the whole of two of Virgil's *Georgics*, with his interesting observations on wildlife and the countryside, and then in the two years before we came to School Certificate we read most of the *Aeneid*, one book every half, for this sole purpose legally using a crib, working entirely in our own time, as a part of the curriculum known as an 'extra book'. This in my experience was far the best way of learning the language. In spite of our illegal cribs we spent an inordinate amount of time figuring out the meaning of a difficult classical text as our ordinary daily construe, and we wasted even more time in 'pupil room', of which later, composing Latin sentences with the laborious aid of a grammar and a dictionary. But reading Virgil on our own, with a crib to hand, we could make rapid progress and actually begin to become familiar with the shape of the language in some of its higher reaches.

When we came to the School Certificate, after three years, we had received a classical education in Latin and Greek well beyond the A level standard of modern times. Indeed boys who continued to do classics in the sixth form had read more than the graduates of most universities other than Oxford and Cambridge before they left school. Once a young master came on an exchange year after three years obtaining a B.A. in classics, during which he had learnt no Greek at all, only to find that he had read less Latin than the Eton sixth formers whom he was teaching. Was it worth all the time and effort that was spent on it? I think it was, but the fault lay in the methods which were so rigid, obliging us for the most part to learn the hard – and it was a very hard – way. The subjects were difficult enough without so much of that.

But what else would we have filled our heads with if we had done less classics? The answer, of course, is science, of which we had the option to do none at all after our second year. The classicists had a firm grip on Eton, which they had no intention of relinquishing, and they were a group of men of remarkable ability, all or almost all of them being scholars of high calibre who had also other skills and interests which they pursued with distinction. Many in addition to this were successful athletes. Only in the sixth form had power been wrested from them.

Every form master, or division master in Eton terminology, was automatically a classicist up to the sixth form, who as well as Latin and perhaps Greek taught history and divinity. (There was no English except for those who were not up to doing Greek – about half the school – and no geography at all.) Every boy's tutor who supervised his work was invariably a 'classical tutor' with whom hours were wasted in Pupil Room every day doing individual Latin or Greek composition. This included Latin verses, which however were eventually given up if it became clear that one was struggling. These verses were elegiac couplets, hexameters and pentameters as written by Ovid. One had perhaps learnt the elements at one's preparatory school, namely the permissible combinations of dactyls and spondees with breaks in the middle of each line and elisions when successive words ended and began with vowels. But a more complicated point was not to make a 'false quantity', which was regarded as a cardinal sin. Having understood the rules, probably with some elements of doubt here and there, one had to translate the English into Latin so that it would fit the pattern. In the early stages the English text was manoeuvred to give some hints, for instance by hyphenating several English words which could be rendered as a single word in Latin. One then switched the Latin word order around in the hope of finding an adequate fit, and changed the words if one couldn't.

This was about as far as I got. More gifted boys would be given short passages of genuine English poetry to transform into Latin couplets, and eventually would have to try their hands at the more elusive meters of Horace, but possibly not in hendecasyllabics which must have been testing even for Romans. This was the height of schoolboy achievement in the eyes of those classical masters who themselves possessed the mental and verbal dexterity to do the same thing, whether (in the words of Richard Martineau) they had 'the faintest idea what the classics were about' or merely a good crossword-solving mind.

I suppose that I should try to justify the opinion which I have expressed that on the whole it was probably worth while spending a great amount of time and effort in learning Latin and Greek, and that the alternative would have been to learn more science. Science at schools was not what it is today. Too little thought had been given to the objective, and the method of using experiments to entertain us was defective, whether they were demonstrations by the masters or our own efforts with scalpel or Bunsen burner. This I shall turn to in due course. The positive advantage of teaching small boys the basics of Latin, including many boys who would never get far enough to appreciate the literature, was avowedly first to teach them accuracy in handling a language, and secondly to make them aware of the structure of a language, for both of which purposes Latin was ideal. It had the advantage of being the common root of most of the languages of western Europe, giving us a privileged entry to French, Italian, Spanish and Portuguese, enabling us to read these languages without too much difficulty. Modern languages were thought by classicists to be too indefinite in their structures to serve the purpose, and Latin certainly taught one the difference between the right answer and a wrong one: after all, a Latin verb had to be correct in number, person, tense, mood and voice, and if it was wrong in any of these, it was wrong. To say that any word was 'nearly right' did not make sense. This was an important lesson.

Learning Latin and Greek gave us a key to English as well as continental vocabularies. This helped us to identify precise meanings, and shades of meaning. The fact that English words themselves and their meanings have evolved over the course of centuries, and continue to do so, makes this knowledge even more interesting. It is particularly useful in translating not only into avowedly foreign languages but also into legal, scientific and medical terms. Now that Latin is hardly known, the structure of English is being barbarised. So few people are capable of using a relative clause that even the Liturgy – not exactly (alas) a part of the popular press – no longer uses them, thus dealing a final fatal blow to the rhythms of Tyndale and Cranmer.

Edward Gibbon, one of the masters of the English prose sentence (and paragraph), did not think much of the classical education he had

Eton, 1938–43

received during his two years at Westminster. He pointed out what every schoolmaster should bear in mind, that 'the value of instruction is seldom of much efficacy save in those happy dispositions where it is almost superfluous'. But he did say that his education gave him 'the keys of two valuable chests'. By this he meant Latin and Greek literature. The fact that it also taught him English would not have struck him as worth mentioning, and of course French which as a result of his personal circumstances was his 'first' language.

The Latin and Greek literature we studied at school did mean something to us, and introduced us to the roots of European civilisation – indeed to the roots of Christendom: we 'did' St Matthew's Gospel in Greek not in our Greek course but in our religious instruction (known as divinity) course. It was a striking experience to find that what we knew in English had actually been written in understandable Greek – Greek which was provided with a ready-made and uncensorable crib.

There were more hours of both Latin and Greek than of any other subject, but mathematics, modern languages (primarily French and German) and history all had strong and successful departments with some brilliant teachers (and a few old and exhausted passengers). History, when first introduced as a subject by the appointment of Henry Marten around 1900, had been taught by men with degrees in the subject only in the sixth form, the lower forms being taught by classicists. Presumably because the classicists found it hard work to keep a few pages ahead of their pupils in a subject unfamiliar to them, the historians had made a vital breakthrough and were now employed also to teach the subject in the upper fifth form. This gave them the opportunity to show how different, and how interesting, history could be, in contrast to the dry lists of facts and dates dispensed by the classical masters. Thus the history department coaxed a large number of boys away from Latin and Greek to become history 'specialists' (i.e. sixth formers). And, since every successful institution creates its own momentum, history had continued to flourish at the expense of Latin and Greek.

Science was the Cinderella, although in tune with the political correctness of the time the department was lavishly provided with laboratories and equipment and with a large, indeed monstrous natural history museum, full of stuffed animals and resurrected dinosaurs.

Eton, 1938–43

Geography in those days was a narrow subject, not considered suitable for intelligent (or, at Eton, even unintelligent) pupils. English was not taught to anyone capable of learning Greek because it was supposed (correctly) that anyone who could write Latin or Greek could write English, and English literature could be experienced, or at least tasted, through the elaborate system of tutorials known as 'private business'. This had an interesting and perhaps unplanned result, in that we came to appreciate English literature because it was not forced down our throats in textbooks full of boring footnotes. As far as I was concerned the result was enlightening to say the least.

During the half when we were to take our School Certificate exams, we had to do English literature without any teaching at all. (The same was true of English language, except that we were given a few coaching sessions on the technique of writing a précis.) I found myself having to prepare Chaucer's *Prologue* and *Hamlet* without any help at all. The sensation was similar to that of Keats's 'On First Looking into Chapman's Homer', although I am nor capable of describing it as he did. (This is my favourite sonnet, I think the greatest ever written, and it still amazes me that Keats wrote it one morning before breakast; but *revenons à nos moutons*.)

I had heard of Chaucer and the Canterbury Pilgrims, but I had no idea of the world which would be revealed when I opened the *Prologue*, a world separated from my own by centuries and by the striking difference of language, but full of English people whose characteristics were not described at second hand by the author but by themselves and their contemporaries. I was at once captivated by the quaintness and the vividness and the Middle English simplicity of Chaucer's verse, without of course having to try to understand why I liked it. Even with the help of notes and vocabularies there were words or phrases which I could not decipher, but this didn't matter in the least.

Hamlet equally was a revelation, and as I worked slowly through the text I found it full of magic images which I had never dreamed of, and of course (though it is old hat to say so) full of quotations. I became more and more entranced as I turned the pages. Neither the story nor the characters fundamentally interested me. They didn't strike me as being much more than a vehicle for the language. This of course was a very immature reaction, but I have never grown out of it, nor ever regretted it. I still prefer to read Shakespeare than to see him performed, and I still find him difficult to understand unless I can take my time.

Eton, 1938-43

Others do not seem to encounter this difficulty, which perhaps in me is due to some kind of dyslexia.

Mathematics was taken seriously and the staff of fifteen were superbly qualified, including Bertie Herbert, Harry Babington Smith, William Hope Jones (an eccentric with original and imaginative ideas about teaching) and the famous 'Bloody Bill' (H. K. Marsden) who knew the logarithm tables and most of the British railway timetables by heart and who corrected our work by walking along the front of the desks and reading it and writing his comments upside down. He was quartermaster of the Corps and he used to mark the section and platoon number of each compartment of the railway carriages in which we travelled to camp. He walked along the platform quite rapidly with a piece of chalk in each hand. At the end of camp he dealt with the issue of homebound railway tickets for hundreds of boys. One boy tried to catch him out by familiarising himself with the train times to his home station. H.K.M. duly provided him with a train time which he thought did not exist: but it was the boy who was caught out, because H.K.M. had realised that it was market day with a special timetable. (In the annual *AA Book* the market day and early closing day were given for every town in Britain.)

Another eccentric was the delightful Claude Beasley-Robinson who drove a huge open Vauxhall known as the 'Yellow Peril' and evangelised his classes by standing on his desk and exclaiming 'God is in this room.' He afterwards became a monk.

Science had far fewer masters – eleven as against sixteen – than mathematics (classics had thirty-four), and this staff of eleven taught all the physics, chemistry and biology. There were only thirty-five scientists amongst the 351 boys in what would now be called the sixth form. Science was compulsory during the first two years at Eton and then taken only by choice.

Much thought had been given to making science interesting for the younger boys, by means of practical work and experiments, yet this was not successful, perhaps because too much energy was devoted to showing us what happened and not enough in inviting our curiosity. The whole thing seemed mildly irrelevant to normal life, and was subjected to a great deal of mischief by high-spirited schoolboys. Science, deliberately given an impressively large site to enhance its status, in the event suffered from being tucked away on its own. The problem was compounded by the fact that not only the classical masters but most of those who taught the arts subjects placed little value on a scientific education.

Alington, head master from 1917 to 1933, wrote in *Things Ancient and Modern* that the literary boy should be required to know some arithmetic, and possibly some geometry, but that to demand algebra from him 'is to provoke dangerous reprisals'. He continued: 'When we come to Science I am very anxious that he should be given some knowledge, but very certain that he should be given it in a different way from … his scientific brother. Thousands of boys are … doing experiments in expensive laboratories who know beforehand what to expect in view of the known nature of the materials they are handling and the known quantity of their own incompetence. I doubt whether this is education.' It seems extraordinary to us that he did not set his mind to considering a better way.

Jelly Churchill, a lean retired master who had inherited – as was not uncommon – the nickname of his overweight elder brother, expressed the idea in a more positive way, arguing in favour of revealing to boys 'the practical results that have ensued from the discovery of radium, of anaesthetics and various serums, of rays visible and invisible … the composition of the earth and its relation to the rest of the universe … and the harnessing of electrical forces.' The objective should be 'that his powers of observation should be stimulated' and – here is the sting in the tail – that he 'may recognise his own ignorance and have some idea how to rectify it should the necessity arise'.

Alington had left in 1933 and Churchill had already retired when he wrote in 1937 but the new head master, Claude Elliott, was not exactly a new broom in his attitude to science and he did little or nothing to improve the situation.

Art and music were not badly equipped but the two art masters were still known as 'drawing masters' and they operated in the 'Drawing Schools'. The newly appointed Wilfrid Blunt was a breath of fresh air, a polymath and an aesthete who introduced such diverse activities as pottery and calligraphy and encouraged us to paint in oils.

Henry Ley, the immensely distinguished organist who filled the ancient office of precentor, was listed with the other musicians right at the bottom of the list of masters merely as 'musical instructor'. There was in spite of this lack of standing a lively interest in music in the school, with a very large musical society (in effect a choral society), house choirs and (vocal) quartets and instrumental instruction for quite

Eton, 1938–43

a large number of boys. The school orchestra was much stiffened by teachers and would not stand comparison with today. As to drama, it was not *de rigueur*, being regarded with suspicion by the authorities as a potential hotbed of vice. There were, consequently, no school plays.

Eton, therefore, in spite of its excellence in so many respects and its ability to evolve over the course of time, was an old-fashioned, narrow and to some degree a philistine school. These characteristics were alleviated by the quality of the staff and especially by the width and expertise of their interests. These were disseminated in 'private business' when two or three times a week a tutor could lead his pupils into any subject he chose, and in 'extra studies' – two periods a week for specialists with an ever-widening choice of subjects. There were numerous societies, meeting in the evenings, and expeditions on whole holidays, somewhat curtailed during the war. There was the school of mechanics, where I learnt the rudiments of woodwork, including turning and dovetailing – even secret dovetailing – and made two mahogany tables and a large Bermuda-rigged model yacht which I still look at with pride. Some interests were widely followed by a number of masters, for instance gardening and ornithology. In the former they would collect and propagate rare plants and in the latter I was introduced to the extraordinary variety of birds within five miles of Eton: warblers at Hedgerley, Burnham Beeches, Maidenhead Thicket and in the bird sanctuary near the river, waders at the Slough and Ham Fields sewage farms (less unsavoury than they sound), ducks and geese on the Staines Reservoirs and Virginia Water as well as the many inhabitants of the delightful gardens of Eton and the surrounding fields and meadows.

The school was divided into six blocks or year-groups, A, B, C, D, E and F, each of which was itself divided into three removes, each representing a term's (or in Eton parlance a half's) work. One had to pass in Trials at the end of each term in order to move into the remove above. Right at the bottom, below F, was third form, consisting of only one term's intake of boys, the rump of the ancient Lower School which in the days of old had also had a second form and a first form They, together with the eleven- and twelve-year-olds who had inhabited them, had long ago disappeared, but it was considered advisable to divide those who passed Common Entrance into five layers, namely the bottom remove of E block, the three removes of F block, and the third form. A boy who started in third form thus had to spend five terms reaching the point where his cleverest Oppidan contemporaries had started.

But this was not the end of it. Collegers, the King's Scholars (as opposed to Oppidans), started a whole year above even the boys in E block. This meant that there were eight terms between the scholars and those of their contemporaries who had scraped through Common Entrance. Since it was possible to enter the school at any time between one's twelfth and fourteenth birthdays, a boy who had started in third form at the age of nearly fourteen would be sixteen before he was level, in D block, with Collegers aged twelve. Of course, he would presumably be in the bottom division and they in the top, so they would not be in the same classes, but the system took to its limits the assessment of intellectual ability without regard to maturity. This was selection with a vengeance, but the system had been arrived at pragmatically – it was found to work best – rather than as the result of Educational Theory, whose ugly face had not yet appeared on the Eton scene.

After the reform of the government of the ancient public schools by Act of Parliament in the 1860s there appeared on the Eton scene the towering figure of Edmond Warre who in the last decades of the Victorian era created the organisation which we inherited. Warre was an excellent classical scholar but whether he had any idea of 'what the classics are about' is another matter. He was also, in common with many of his colleagues, a clergyman. As a young master he had been the salient influence in the creation of Eton rowing and in the highly developed system of Eton games, especially cricket, the Field Game and Eton fives. He had also created the battalion of Eton College Rifle Volunteers, revamped before our day as the Officers' Training Corps, now the CCF. He had influenced the organisation of the school's academic work before he became head master, but it was during his reign from 1884 to 1905 that he developed the curriculum system with its blocks and its removes and its divisions and the termly examinations which we inherited, a system which remained virtually intact until the 1970s.

Warre had also codified the School Rules, which, with modifications, were still in force in 1938:

> General Regulations: nine clauses, including references to tobacco, wine, spirits, mineral oil, firearms, catapults, water pistols, inflammable materials, playing cards; cars and motor

bicycles; bicycles (five sub-clauses); golf; and leaving parties (which must not exceed four persons, including the host).

Bounds: nine clauses.

Leave: two clauses in five sections, including attendance at weddings of parent, brother, or sister and uncles, aunts and cousins – and attendance at the barracks at Windsor by written invitation only from the Commanding Officer.

Holidays: five clauses.

College Chapel: five clauses and Lower Chapel (three clauses) and Boys Not on the Chapel List.

Dress: only five clauses, as most of the rules were self-evident. The occasions are specified when a buttoned greatcoat over change with a top hat may be worn as an alternative to full school dress. My brother Peter was put in the bill for riding a horse, which he had rescued from the Kennels area during a flood, down the High Street on a Sunday morning. He pleaded that this was not forbidden in the school rules but he was convicted for not being either in full school dress or wearing a buttoned greatcoat over change. (Top hats were abandoned during the war because of the problem of hanging them in air raid shelters, and were not subsequently revived.)

House Tickets: five clauses, with elaborate sub-clauses. The tickets were dockets which had to be carried around after lock-up, certifying the arrival and departure times at each specified destination by means of a master's signature. One boy who had visited Windsor Castle persuaded the King to sign his house ticket, but it was thrown away by H. K. Marsden as a piece of rubbish like any other house ticket.

Ephemerals: seven clauses. (These were pamphlets or magazines edited and published by boys. They were subject to censorship.)

Book Pound: four clauses. (This was the second-hand bookstore where Cyril Butterwick once purchased a first edition of *Paradise Lost* for a penny. It had evidently been used by a boy from his family's library for holiday work and discarded after use. Cyril did not return it to the family but sold it at a handsome profit.)

School Rules to be Observed on the River: (ten clauses). Boats are required to keep to the side of the river laid down by the

Eton, 1938–43

Captain of the Boats in 1875 and revised by his successors. The use of paddles or of oars, sculls or anything else whatever for the purpose of paddling is forbidden.

Bathing Regulations:(twenty clauses). Rule 5: At Athens boys who are undressed must either get at once into the water or get behind the screens when boats containing ladies come in sight. However: Rule 10: Standard pattern bathing drawers must be worn. Rule 3: Fifth form Nants in middle and lower division may bathe at Ward's Mead. Lower Boys and fifth form Non-Nants may bathe at Cuckoo Weir. Fifth Form Nants are not allowed at Cuckoo Weir.

One of Edmond Warre's most important contributions was the invention of elaborate termly examinations, known as Trials, which lasted a full week at the end of each half and entailed a vast expenditure of energy by boys and masters alike. They ensured that standards were maintained and they gave us such regular practice at examinations that when we came to public examinations they held no fears for us.

The general rules for Trials were elaborate. For example the second part of rule three specified that 'Those who when rising from one block to another fail in Mathematics, Latin, French or Science, are allowed a pass paper on the first day of the following School-time. This privilege is not granted to those who fail in General Total.' The exact number of marks required in each remove is laid down – for instance out of a possible total of 1,200 marks in E block, 920 are required for a Distinction, 810 for a First Class, 620 for a Second Class. A specified number of marks in each remove were required for a Pass in Latin, Mathematics and General Total. Boys who failed in General Total got 'GT-' against their names in the School List and received no promotion. If they were above the maximum age permitted for any block they were superannuated, i.e. obliged to leave. There was no nonsense about awarding a given percentage of candidates a certain grade, regardless of the standard.

These were merely the general rules. There was also a set of regulations printed on the pink sheet of blotting paper placed on every candidate's desk; for instance: 'Write on one side of the paper only, *videlicet* on that which is ruled.' The object of this rule was that once a sheet had been completed it had to be turned face downwards so that it could not be cribbed by a neighbour. It would not have been

Eton, 1938–43

easy to copy somebody else's work because boys sat alternately by Block, for instance with F Block and E Block in alternate places in each school-room. A complete numbered list of places for the whole school was required for this purpose, with all except the more senior masters acting as invigilators. Papers were handed out, and results collected, by these invigilators from the Trials Office, a room set aside for the purpose, which then handed them on to the masters designated to mark them. There was then a frenzy of filling up a card of marks for every boy in every subject, adding them up, handing them to another master for checking, writing them out on a list and, finally, on the last day of the half, 'Reading Over' in School Hall by the Head Master or Lower Master when one agonisingly waited for the moment when ones's name would come up. Then one would report to one's tutor for the card and for appropriate praise or admonition.

This extraordinary system taught us what bureaucracy was like and, more positively, gave us a powerful example of how things should be organised. It familarised us with formal exams.

Our education as specialists, after taking the School Certificate, was radically different. Gone were the old compulsory subjects, the grammar and vocabularies, the daily tests with their one-word answers, all marked and contributing to a fortnightly order, and the mathematical 'extra works' – the Eton term for work done in 'prep'. In their place came Literature and Ideas.

I started as a modern linguist, changing later to history which in essence merely exchanged history for French, German continuing as before. My languages tutor was Peter Spanoghe who read us Bernard Shaw's *Prefaces* and *Plays Unpleasant*, suggesting to us that the world we lived in was not perfect. This was our introduction to radical ideas. Meanwhile Tom Brocklebank introduced us to Voltaire and Rousseau and Montesquieu, which likewise combined brilliant writing (carefully selected, of course, to be digestible) with radical thinking about the world.

In addition to French and German we did four hours of history with two retired men who had been roped in during the war: 'God' Clarke, who had been the chaplain of a Cambridge college, and G. B. Smith who had been headmaster of Sedbergh. Clarke, a calm, gentle, charming man, said that 'after the age of sixty-five there are very few problems which can't be solved with the aid of a knife and fork' and taught us nineteenth-century European history – 'Liberalism and Nationality' – as if he was learning just as we were. His questioning approach to the problems of history was entirely new to us. G. B. Smith, who had an immense range of knowledge and had written many excellent books for pupils of our age, taught us the French Revolution through the eccentric and vivid narrative of Thomas Carlyle, of which Oscar Wilde had said that 'facts are either entirely disregarded or kept in their proper subordinate position'; but it was a wonderful source of comment and criticism, emphasising the parts played by individuals and making the events we were studying even more colourful than a more modern and measured textbook would have suggested. 'G.B.' was my history tutor and he introduced us to the music of Richard Strauss in private business. Even in our house 'library' – a bookless cubby-hole from which the senior boys dispensed organisation and discipline – we had some Mozart on the gramophone, interspersed with jazz and ephemeral popular songs such as 'She had to go and lose it at the Astor'.

In German we did Schiller's *Maria Stuart* (Mary Queen of Scots) with my father C. A. Gladstone, the head of modern languages, and then, with an extraordinary and brilliant wartime master of uncertain but avowedly grand pedigree named Walter Anthony von Simunich Ireland, we translated Macaulay's 'Frederic the Great' into German. This involved long discussions and draftings of our rendering into German of the magnificent English prose. We had to carry on the discussion, or most of it, in German, which surprisingly Ireland made comparatively easy, and at the end of each day we learnt our version by heart. Thus by the end of the term we could declaim in unison the whole of our text. This implanted in our minds the structure and shape of the German language, and the pronunciation, so thoroughly that, however rusty I may be, I have never lost it.

The day began with early school from 7.30 a.m. to 8.20, which had in a previous form lasted from 7.15 to 8.15, and perhaps 'originally' from 7.00 to 8.00, a good example of evolution rather than revolution being the way. An experienced practitioner might get out of bed at 7.25, dress in 3½ minutes, and run to school in the remaining 1½ before the clock struck; or he might know that the master was always a minute or so late. We were not therefore in the best possible shape to play an active part in the learning process. Perhaps, however, we were docile, perhaps our minds were in a state to absorb information. But the great advantage was that by the time it came to boys' dinner at 1.45 p.m. we had done the best part of a day's work.

Breakfast was followed by a short respite for a hurried attempt to remedy the omissions from last evening's preparation, and to avoid a 'rip' or two on the one-word-answer tests which inevitably followed. A 'rip' was, presumably, a genteel way of tearing up our work as being worthless, and it fulfilled the requirement to preserve the evidence without having to undertake a laborious jigsaw-like process of restoration. The paper was simply torn, half way across the top edge, about a couple of inches downwards, and had to be presented to our classical and house tutors for their endorsement. The official name for a 'rip' was a 'tear over', as if the word 'rip' was unacceptable slang. By this system our tutors saw every 'rip' we received, in every subject, and were thus in a position to pronounce sentence; beginning after three or four rips with PS, 'penal servitude', which meant attending every session of Pupil Room, never escaping into the fresh air of leisure and freedom; and ending (rarely) with a flogging from the Lower Master after a variety of interim sanctions had failed to produce the desired improvement.

Then at 9.15 came Chapel, followed by two morning school periods, plus a third on some days. Then, 'after twelve', there was a very long pupil room for Latin composition, taking us through to lunchtime. After that there was a period for games, and two further school periods between 4.10 and 5.45. (In the summer these two periods came first, and the games period later.) Then followed the respite for tea, one of the important occasions of the day, when several boys 'messed' together and ate huge amounts, all provided by private enterprise except for the statutory tea, bread and butter. Tins of baked beans or tomato soup or sweetcorn, boiled eggs if available, packets of cereals and pots of jam were rapidly despatched, together with occasional treats cooked at and collected from the School Stores if anyone had been able to get hold of a brace of pheasants or buy some mallard or teal from the Norfolk wildfowlers, punt gunners who hawked them on the Keate's Lane corner for 1/6d each. Then came a long period preparing work for the next day, between 6.30 and 8.15, when we sat down for supper in the boys' dining room, a light cooked meal, better than nothing. Then there were house prayers – in our case two or three prayers or collects from the Prayer Book, Cranmer's words and cadences which eventually lodged themselves in our memories. Finally there was more preparation time until lights out for lower boys at 9.30 and upper boys at 10.00.

Eton, 1938–43

The luxury of the week's timetable was that Tuesday, Thursday and Saturday were all half holidays (although Sunday was marred by both private business and Sunday Questions (an essay) in addition to the two chapel services). Most schools had only two half holidays, with no school periods in the afternoons, on Wednesdays and Saturdays; but the excuse for having three at Eton was, and perhaps reasonably so, the additional time we spent in preparation, most of it in our own individual rooms and subject to our own timing and organisation. This system was of course far more open to abuse than supervised 'prep' which was the rule at other schools, but idleness was limited by the need to pass numerous short written tests the next day. Eton very much prided itself on the degree of responsibility, whether for themselves or for others, which it left in the hands of the boys; not only in organising their own work, but also in the government of their houses and of the whole school.

Both in the houses and in the school, the system of government by the boys was abused, but in the houses most of the housemasters kept a judicious eye on things malevolent so that autocracy was limited to small matters. Pop, the self-perpetuating body of school prefects, with just four or five ex officio members, was elected by a system of blackballs, by which a small number of members could veto the election of anyone thought to be unacceptable. After a candidate had been proposed and seconded, a box was passed round into which one inserted a marble, secretly, into either the white or the black compartment. Depending on the number of voters, one or two or three blackballs would exclude the candidate. This led to an elaborate system of unhealthy (because negative, and regardless of merit) bargaining, by which it was agreed that if you admit X we will admit Y.

The system was not as bad as it might have been, since there was open discussion of the actual merits and demerits of every candidate who had been excluded at the first round, but it placed temptation in the power of all concerned: temptation to promote one's friends, regardless of merit, and (much worse) temptation to purchase support by whatever means. It taught the lesson (as if there were not enough other ways of learning it) that if you want to succeed you must jump on the bandwagon. Above all, you must ingratiate yourself with those in power. Judiciously used, it produced a much better result than a more democratic system would have done. Abused, it did not. In every circumstance it taught everyone involved that life was not fair, and that

Eton, 1938–43

you could respond to this undoubted fact by whatever available method you thought fit.

1940 was a dramatic year to be at Eton, or indeed anywhere in the English home counties. The first eight months of the war had not suggested to us that anything exciting was likely to happen, but all that changed when Hitler invaded Norway, Belgium and France. Boats from the river at Windsor sailed to Dunkirk and ferried back British soldiers. Churchill became prime minister and at once established an atmosphere of universal defiance. The Local Defence Volunteers, originals of Dad's Army, were soon renamed the Home Guard, a Churchillian touch. Almost all the available men joined, many wearing the medal ribbons of the First World War and knowing only too well what they were about; except those who were already involved as firemen or ARP (Air Raid Precautions) wardens; but at Eton, of course, the boys in the Corps – at least those over sixteen – joined too, which gave the battalion a very different age profile from the normal.

Dogfights between fighter aircraft took place overhead, although not as often as over Kent, Sussex and London. It was a summer of almost unbroken sunshine, so one could see some action in the otherwise clear blue sky. Large flat lorries – the prototypes of the modern 'artics' – were to be seen carrying damaged aircraft back to base. We spent many afternoons digging trenches on the largest playing fields, Agar's and Dutchman's (judiciously avoiding the actual playing areas), and then on the great open fields which still survived in the manor of Eton – North Field, South Meadow and then Dorney Common – to prevent enemy aircraft, including gliders, from landing.

The Battle of Britain being won, the Germans turned their attention to bombing London, starting with the docks where they set some warehouses ablaze, just before the opening of the Michaelmas half. This, by the way, was much nearer Michaelmas, the traditional harvest celebration, than it is now: the summer holidays began in late July and ended in late September, thus including some good cricketing weather in the summer half.

It was not long before the nights started drawing in. The Germans abandoned daylight raids and started coming by night, which was much more alarming. There was a sensation when a German bomber, flying up the Thames valley presumably to evade pursuit from London,

Eton, 1938–43

decided that it would be better off without its bombs and dropped a couple of heavy ones at random.

At that moment (about 7.30 p.m.) I happened to be in m'Tutor's loos performing a routine action, which I suppose should have been achieved after breakfast. These conveniences, known by a shortening of their old monastic name, The Rears, were (as in the Middle Ages, and for the same reason) well ventilated. I heard a tremendous prolonged screech – a whine would be too soft an expression – but no bang. When I emerged, everybody seemed to be in a state of mild excitement, wondering what might be the result of an uncomfortably close explosion.

It turned out that two bombs had been dropped, one on Dr Ley's dining room in Weston's Yard, and the other on the Head Master's room at the end of Upper School. The second one had not exploded, but the first one had, impressively squashing not Daddy Ley but his grand piano, which was visible for all to see, the side of the house having been blown off like a doll's house. Mrs Ley had said to him from the kitchen 'Come though, Henry; dinner's ready.' He had been reading *Punch* in his study, and one of the jokes pleased him. 'You must just come through and look at this,' he said. She did, and both their lives were saved.

The second bomb had dug a deep hole for itself next to School Office, and was pronounced by the bomb disposal squad to be a time bomb. The powers that be, led by Mr Bendell, the School Clerk, took the precaution of removing many bundles of papers from the office, regardless of the danger, and the bomb eventually went off the next evening, destroying the Head Master's room, splintering the panelling which bore the names of every member of sixth form since God knew when and ejecting the bust of Mr Gladstone in Upper School next door from its pedestal. The splinters of the carved panels were painstakingly collected, and restored after the war, and Mr Gladstone was reinstated. Most of the Victorian glass in Chapel was destroyed: only the one ancient window in the west front above the organ mercifully survived. After that Chapel was cold, and we wore greatcoats for the services each winter. Worse might have happened.

There were aeroplanes flying over most nights that winter, and an anti-aircraft gun on the Brocas. The engines of the German aircraft sounded different from the British ones, as they were not synchronised and had an unrhythmical drawl. Occasionally we had to spend a night in the house air raid shelter, which had wooden bunks but was chilly and uncomfortable. One night a special and mysterious and very secret message reached the Head Master from London: a major raid was expected and the whole school had to spend the night in the air raid shelters. Nothing happened to us. But this was the night of the savage raid on Coventry, which killed a lot of people and destroyed the cathedral. It was many years after the war before the facts were revealed about our ability to read and decode the enemy's communications.

Detachments of the Corps in the guise of the Home Guard remained at Eton during the holidays, largely to deal with incendiary bombs, little ones designed to penetrate a roof and set a building on fire. It was discovered that they could be extinguished by a fine spray of water, which was dispensed from a short hose from a bucket with a pump like a bicycle pump, called a stirrup pump. When the Germans got wind of this they added a small dose of explosive to discourage the person with the bucket and pump. The simple answer was to use a dustbin lid as a shield. I was commended for putting out an incendiary bomb which landed on the coal heap in m'Tutor's yard, but I knew it was not dangerous as coal burns slowly.

I remember a landmine which landed on Sixpenny with a tremendous bang and blew out many of the top floor windows of our house. A heavy bomb landed in the garden of Warre House, just where Farrer House now stands, and broke the plate glass in our dining room window, where we were sitting after supper. Everyone except me heard it coming and lay flat on the floor. The odd thing about this one was that all the glass (which might have caused serious injury) fell harmlessly into the garden outside. The blackout was rigidly enforced – no torches were allowed, of course – so outdoor movement after dark was slow until one's eyes became accustomed to the darkness.

M'Tutor, Charles Rowlatt, had been severely wounded in the First World War and had never fully recovered. During my last year he had to take a term off, and Fishy Williams was put in to substitute for him. Boys' houses were run as much as possible by the boys themselves, a good system provided that the Library – the privileged top four or five boys – were reliable. We were reasonably responsible, and were not going to have m'Tutors's spoilt by an incompetent substitute, so we kept everything in good order for Fishy. Only years later did it emerge that the Head Master had doubted Fishy's capacity to run a house and had found the ideal opportunity to try him out. Fishy in due course got his house, thanks to us, but it wasn't a great success. I suppose he had been appointed specifically to teach the slower Latinists, which most of the classical masters hadn't the patience for. His lower lip protruded beyond his upper one, resulting in a spate of sibillants, notably in the model clause which was used to demonstrate a prohibition (the negative of a command) '*Ne psittacum vexaveris*, Don't tease the parrot.'

The Head Master, Claude Elliott, was not an inspiring figure but he had grasped the nettle and ended the system by which every master after two years on probation was entitled to start making a house list, and when he had become a housemaster to remain one for as long as he wished (this was the only way to make some money over and above a paltry salary) without selection and without anyone daring to think what the statistical result might be in a few years' time. Claude had to deprive some would-be masters of this right, and he put a term of fifteen years on a housemaster's tenure, introduced a retiring age for the whole staff at fifty-eight, and persuaded the Governing Body to link masters' salaries to the Administrative Grade of the Civil Service. But for its handsome endowments, this would have made Eton a very expensive school; as it was, its fees were no higher than those of other leading schools although, except during the war, the 'extras' of one kind and another, hyped by the need to 'keep up with the Joneses', were inclined to become excessive.

Claude could be fierce enough to anyone who was 'in the Bill', the official list of defaulters; in which context he taught me one important lesson, although it took me a long time to grasp the implications fully; namely that nobody could or should expect strict personal justice. The context was an ingenious method we had devised for fooling an unfortunate wartime master, a Frenchman who found it difficult to keep order. The old desks in New Schools had inkwells and were fixed to the floor with large screws. We dipped one of these screws in an inkwell and placed it upside down, upright on the desk, and all stared at it. The master came round, took the screw, and put it into his pocket. When he took his hand out it was covered in ink, to his annoyance. He took a few names, as he had been instructed to do by Claude, of which mine was one, and we were duly summoned to the Bill. I pleaded that I was only one of many culprits, and not the ringleader. But I was not a match for Claude. After that the French master found things less difficult, but he left when the war ended and worked for a publisher of modern language school books. He wrote to the Head of Modern Languages at Eton to say that they were publishing a book on German humour. The reply was that it would not be long enough for the school's purposes.

Claude was not an impressive teacher. He had never taught at a school, being a little known Cambridge history don. He had a tentative way of speaking, liberally dotted with 'mm…mm…mm' and enhanced by the theory, which he had conscientiously imbibed, that the best method is not to tell your pupils things but to ask them questions. He chose as his subject for a senior form which he taught twice a week (just to show, so to speak, that he could do it) 'The Growth of English Liberty', not exactly an exciting topic for a lively crowd of frivolous seventeen-year-olds. He compounded the difficulty by asking philosophical questions, starting with 'What is Liberty?' and getting some comical answers as he worked through the ranks. Nor did he realise, when he came to some historical examples of what Liberty is and what it isn't, that we simply did not have the broad sweep of history at our fingertips. Nevertheless I recollected Claude's course on Liberty until I was old enough to think about the question more seriously, so perhaps the proof of the pudding was in the eating. During our last half or two we saw him in less formal circumstances and came to appreciate his dry wit, but he was a shy man known to many boys only for his weekly enunciation of the last prayer at Sunday evening Chapel (he never preached a sermon as far as I recollect): 'God save the King and Queen, Queen Mary and the Realm, and send us Peeeeeeace'.

I have already mentioned a book written by Jelly Churchill in the context of science at Eton. He entitled his book *Changing Eton* and it was interesting to read of the gradual process of reform which had taken place since the Public Schools Commission of the 1860s had abolished the old collegiate institution of Henry VI. The martyred saint had placed the government of the school in the hands of clerical Fellows appointed for life, who in the nineteenth century – and before it – milked the endowments to support their lifestyle and also might hold rich livings either in the gift of the College or of a private patron known to them. They had been replaced by a Governing Body – a newly invented label – on which the Fellows represented worthy institutions including the Royal Society. The Provost of King's College, Cambridge, Eton's sister foundation, was included in order to retain something of the old flavour, and he in my time was the only caricaturable figure amongst distinguished Fellows (mostly Old Etonians) from Academia, Science and the Law, with a sprinkling of cabinet ministers and perhaps a Viceroy of India for good measure.

To Jelly the school had changed markedly since the 1870s, with the regularisation of boarding houses, the introduction of science, modern languages and history, and the highly organised cult of games, which would nowadays be called sports. But now, more aware of the perspective of history, I can see how little the school changed between the 1870s and the 1960s, a long heyday not only for Eton but for the public schools of England. The Eton I joined in 1938 was in most of its essentials the one which had evolved during the mastership and head mastership of Edmond Warre between 1861 and the decline in his powers from about 1894.

This is a snapshot of Eton, not a history. True, the curriculum had changed by 1938 and classics no longer dominated the final years; but the ethos of the school and the activities of its pupils were the ones in which Warre's was still the master hand. Several of his brilliant contemporaries had brought their influence to bear on generations of schoolboys and on the school itself, but the only alternative to Warre's dominant influence might have been that of Oscar Browning, who was sacked in 1875. The two men shared some influential friends and acquaintances, but only Browning himself, a man of outstanding originality, might have created an alternative school – a school in which the appreciation of art played a part, and the cult of games did not.

Warre's imagination and his energy had created a modern school, radically different from the Eton of his own schooldays which still had the characteristics of the eighteenth century. I have described the organisation and the curriculum which were essentially his. Warre, although he was too subtle and too gentle to encourage either tribalism or professionalism, must bear the responsibility for the dominant part which games played in the life of the school during, and for many years after, his tenure. Oscar Browning saw this on the horizon, and hated it.

When Warre arrived as a master, the chapel was being 'gothicised'. This was the term used to describe the installation of elaborate darkened oak stalls, masking the huge spread of the fifteenth-century wall-paintings, and the filling of the windows with Victorian coloured glass (mercifully destroyed during my time at Eton by a German bomb). The pews and the altar were similarly brought to heel. Yet in spite of these externals Eton seems to have escaped the main influence of the Oxford Movement and remained severely protestant, as it had been from the seventeenth and indeed from the sixteenth century. Warre was not a man for frills. Manliness was one of the virtues he wished to encourage. He did not exercise his influence primarily or avowedly through the chapel. There is no evidence of his effectiveness as a preacher. But he did provide the environment for the dutiful Christian gentleman, and the ethos which he encouraged ran so strongly through the school that it continued to produce a type of man distinguished in public life and in the professions well beyond the end of the Second World War. Yet there was a negative side to all this. By the end of Warre's tenure his colleagues said that chapel services were attended with indifference. Art, music and science were brushed aside, or at least kept in their proper subordinate positions. Modern languages nudged out Latin and Greek because they were more useful, and possibly because they were less difficult: two good reasons, but not profound ones. One wonders what Browning might have achieved.

The fact that the amateur spirit and good sportsmanship were encouraged by Warre did much to commend the importance of games. But, by tending to keep them in-house, the amateurism actually increased the force of the cult. House competition and individual success were more important to the wide majority than were the rare occasions of competition against other schools. Association football hardly got a look-in, except among the Old Etonians, who more than once won the FA Cup; nor did rugby. The important game was the Field Game, a survivor of the pre-soccer era, in which passing the ball was not allowed. It was a splendid game for school houses. A full side had eleven players, but you could easily manage with fewer, say eight or nine. It was a cult on its own, with its bully and its rouges and rams and its cornering and sneaking, and the zenith of success was to play for the winning house side. (The Wall Game, even more mysterious, was played only by a small minority of senior boys, because there was only one wall.)

The other popular winter game was fives – Eton fives of course, which had started between the buttresses of chapel and which was already so popular by the 1820s that there was an unseemly rush out of chapel to get a 'wall' (later called a 'court'). A substantial number of courts, faithfully reproducing the best of the chapel courts with its buttress and its dead man's hole, were built in Warre's time; but after

Eton, 1938–43

the First World War covered courts were built, faster but less susceptible to cunning flight and spin than the old ones; and as the years went by, gradually fewer and fewer boys wanted to play in the open courts. Nevertheless, fives was still a splendid game and, although it required some basic ability to hit a moving ball, it could be enjoyed by boys with much skill or with almost none; and handicapping was not difficult, as it is in squash where two unequal players cannot be matched. Given a court, fives needed no equipment beyond a pair of gloves and a ball, and it was easy to get four boys together.

Cricket was superbly equipped and organised in an elaborate hierarchy of Upper Club (which included the XI, the XXII and Strawberry Mess), Middle Club, Lower Club and Upper and Lower Sixpenny. Its climax was at Lord's, the Eton and Harrow match, an ostentatious display of affluence. The huge ground seemed almost empty but the match was said to produce more revenue than any other game except the Test match.

The world of Eton wetbobs was even more elaborate and hierarchical then that of the drybobs, with its Upper and Lower Boats, novices and lower boys, with sculling and pulling and fours at each level, some six or seven hundred sculling boats for hire by the season to individual boys; whiffs and riggers, lock-ups and chances, pairs, dodgers, gigs, tubs, baby fours, bumping fours and house fours, novice and senior eights and, to crown the ceremonies, the Procession of Boats: the ten-oared *Monarch*, full of swells and the cronies of the Captain of Boats, the *Victory* and *Prince of Wales, Britannia, Dreadnought, Thetis, Hibernia, St George, Alexandra* and *Defiance*. There were about eighty-five members of the Boats, but to get there seemed a daunting task to one of the six or seven hundred who did not make the grade, the people who wore the scug caps. Promotion was solely by merit. You had to win races to succeed.

The cost of hiring a sculling boat for the season, which was virtually indispensable, was £7, a huge sum equivalent perhaps to £500 today. There were about eight hundred boats at Rafts, all of them and all the oars and sculls built on the premises, many of them getting old but all lovingly repaired and varnished each winter. The craftsmanship of the boat builders, coupled with the ingenuity of the masters who devised the modifications, was known throughout the rowing world. Careless boys often damaged the delicate timber skins, which were invariably repaired with a wealth of copper nails by the next day. The whole business was run by the imperturbable Alf Claret, sitting at his desk in front of a huge ledger, politely pestered by a stream of boys in his tiny office not much bigger than a telephone booth. In addition to repairs, coaches (whether boys or masters) would ask for alterations in the rig: 'Alf, could you raise the rig of No 2 in CJR's bumping four by half an inch, please?'; 'Alf, I'm afraid I've put my foot through my rigger'; 'What number, sir?'; and so forth. (We were all addressed as 'sir' by all the tradesmen and artisans from the day we arrived at the age of twelve. Consequently we were all expected to be considerate and polite to them.) There was a team of raft hands, aged, loyal and mostly illiterate men, including Charlie, who could not read, and Froggie who been called to the colours (joined the Army) and retired before the Boer War, which impressed us.

Lower boys began by learning not to 'swamp' their whiffs, which entailed rescue by a passing friend or by a waterman, of whom there were several stationed along the bank. All the races were knock-out competitions except the bumping fours and the baby fours, in the latter of which you learnt correct style and watermanship. All the races were long, especially the senior races, the sculling and the pulling involving rowing from rafts right up almost to Boveney Lock, round a ryepeck (a post stuck in the river) and back again, which took about twenty minutes and included the exciting S bend of Lower Hope and Upper Hope on both the upstream and downstream journeys. No wonder that Etonians who could perform this feat in delicate racing boats (steered by themselves facing backwards so to speak) were at an advantage when they reached Oxford or Cambridge: indeed the Eton eight won the Ladies' Plate at Henley more often than any other competitor, happily taking on the best Oxford and Cambridge college crews.

The bumping fours, which were novice fours for those not in the Boats, were the most popular event and provided the most excitement; but the champagne of Eton racing was the house fours, rowing three-abreast downstream from just below Boveney Lock to Rafts, including Upper and Lower Hope. The corners were so sharp that the rudder had to be rigged under the cox's seat and tactics played an important part. Usually fewer than half the houses were good enough to enter a four.

The racing programme occupied thirty-nine days beginning with the School Pulling in the middle of May and ending with the house fours in late July. Masters helped with the coaching, but the entire organisation and discipline, and most of the coaching, was done by boys. The mastermind was the ninth man in the *Monarch*, a senior boy chosen by the captain of the Boats as his chief of staff, since he himself was largely preoccupied with the eight, training for Henley. The ninth man had to be an excellent organiser with a strong personality, producing a list of the day's races with timings and appointing both umpires and harbingers, who rode ahead along the towpath on their bicycles with a megaphone and cleared the course as best they could.

I have said that the house fours were the champagne of Eton racing: The eight did not race at Eton, and it trained in the Olympian remoteness of the Datchet reach, seen by nobody and hardly known about, where there was very little traffic, using the Masters' Boathouse as its base, until it appeared at Henley in all its glory.

The eight set the standard. It was selected, trained and coached with immense care by the master thought to be best qualified for the task – in my day George Tait. Physical strength and fitness were essential, but heavyweights were regarded with suspicion and brute force was not *de rigueur*. The qualities required were first to win races, which selected one from the common ruck of wetbobs, and then to show the balance, agility, quickness and timing which characterised the classic style of English rowing, in which Edmond Warre had been, perhaps, the most seminal figure. None of the modern training methods had been invented: fitness was achieved solely by rowing. Perfection was sought for, achievable only by looseness of muscle and light-handedness. The blade correctly dropped into the water so as to achieve the quick catch which made the boat fly produced a back-splash 'about a foot high and infinitely thin'.

Rowing was recreational as well as competitive. The most enjoyable outing for a wetbob was to scull up to Queen's Eyot, an island just below Bray, on a summer afternoon, where those who had entered their names on a list could answer Absence at 5.45 p.m., and thus be away from Eton from boys' dinner until lock-up at 8 p.m. on a summer half-holiday. The pleasure of sculling as one got better at it, the independence (whether or not one was with a friend or two), the wind in the willows, the gentle swish of the water in the reeds, the hay harvest breeze, the occasional sight of a kingfisher and a sandpiper, the sand martens twittering around their nests in the river bank, the chattering of the sedge warblers, created an idyllic experience. Thoroughly well exercised in the heat of the day, we could buy tea and a pint of beer or

Eton, 1938–43

cider, before slipping homewards downstream in the cool of the evening.

Warre, with his immense skill in work and games, his outstanding scholarship and his unequalled ability as an organiser and administrator, together with his strong sense of vocational Christian duty, his inspiration as a housemaster, his fine presence and his mild manner, created the environment and the ethos for the education of Christian gentlemen. There could have been no finer nursery – although there were a number of schools in the same broad category which were equally admirable – for the men who shaped and ruled the British Empire at its zenith.

Warre was a priest of the Church of England but, as I have mentioned, he did not make any special impact by means of the chapel services. In this respect my contemporaries and I owed what we found to Cyril Alington, head master from 1917 to 1933, whose sermons had the magic touch, a touch we still experienced both in his writings (especially *Fables and Fancies*) and his return to deliver Lent addresses. The chapel services which we attended were his creation, and such enthusiasm (but emphatically not in the technical sense) as they stirred in us were due to him. The witness to his achievement was, indeed, that very enthusiasm, but more profoundly it was in the number of boys who came to the voluntary communion services, especially as they involved early rising. After all, early school began at 7.30 a.m. six days a week, and active adolescent boys of all people might have been tempted to take a long lie on Sundays.

There was chapel every day – compulsory of course – about 9.15 a.m. and lasting about a quarter of an hour to twenty minutes. The main ingredients were Prayer Book prayers from Mattins, a lesson, a psalm and a hymn. The psalms and hymns were sung with gusto, and there was a congregational practice once a week presided over by Daddy Ley (Dr Henry Ley), who could persuade the organ with its sixteen and thirty-two foot pipes to shout and sing as nobody else could, and who familiarised us with Bach fugues, Elgar's 'Nimrod' and Holst's 'Planets' in his voluntaries. The Eton College Hymn Book had just been introduced, a fine collection of three hundred of the best hymns of the sixteenth to the nineteenth centuries (and a few of the twentieth) with both words and music.

The atmosphere was not irreverent but God might have been

forgiven for inquiring whether it was Eton rather than He who was being worshipped. There was quite a scurry by those who had run it fine to be in their seats before a final chime of the bell. Then, as the service began, one boy in each block of seats collected chits listing absentees from the boys at the end of every row who had to fill them in, and handed them to the Masters in Desk who checked them from a seating plan.

The Ram preceded the entry of choir and clergy. This was a procession, a wholly secular ritual, of the sixth form. The sixth form, in Eton parlance, consisted of twenty boys, the senior ten collegers and the senior ten oppidans. It bore no relationship to the sixth form in every other school in Britain, which consisted of everybody who had satisfactorily completed School Certificate, later to be 'O' Level and then the GCSE. Just as the third form was the rump of the old lower school, so the nomenclature of the sixth form had survived the curriculum reforms of Dr Warre. It was, indeed, an elite, the twenty senior boys who had ascended to the rarefied atmosphere above the fifth form, which consisted of the whole of the rest of the Upper School, numbering precisely 797 boys in the Michaelmas half, 1938. The twenty achieved their status by obtaining a good place in the trials order in their last half before School Certificate. That order was maintained ever thereafter throughout their last two years in the school. There was nothing they could do to change it, whether by ability or hard work or any other means. This was the system used in the Navy, and who could expect to improve on that? Once you were a vice admiral, you simply had to wait for those above you to fall off the top rung of the ladder. After all, Nelson was only a vice admiral at Trafalgar. You could obtain any appointment according to your ability, including of course your ability to work the patronage system, but you could not achieve superior rank. The only qualification was to come high in that final trials order at the age of sixteen, but it was vital to be younger than most of your 'remove' when you did so. Oppidans who had taken remove in Common Entrance at the age of twelve stood the best chance of reaching the sixth form, and of the ultimate prize of being Captain of the Oppidans: not a prize as much admired as that of Captain of the Boats, Keeper of the Field, or even Captain of the Eleven, but a prize all the same, carrying with it ex officio membership of Pop.

This elite, in reverse order of seniority, with the Captain of the School and the Captain of the Oppidans entering last (just as in the

Eton, 1938–43

Navy the senior officers are the last to enter a boat, or as the Sovereign is the last to enter St George's Chapel behind the Knights of the Garter), solemnly and slowly processed into chapel on a signal from the verger. Then came the choir, clad of course in the scarlet cassocks of a royal foundation, then the clergy followed by the Head Master, who was the Ordinary. This office ensured that it was he, rather than the conduct, or indeed the Governing Body, who ruled the roost in chapel. Finally came the Vice Provost and the Provost, chairman and vice chairman of the Governing Body.

The sixth form procession was known as the Ram from its similarity to the Ram in the Field Game which converted, or tried to convert, a rouge into a goal. When the procession was over, the service could begin with the conduct chanting appropriately 'O Lord, open Thou our lips'.

We enjoyed singing the psalm and the hymn, but the highlight of the service was the appearance of 'Linky' at the lectern. Lord Hugh Cecil was the Provost, one of the regiment of scholar-statesmen of the House of Hatfield, even if a minor star in that constellation. He had been best man to Winston Churchill and was said to have hurled a prayer book across the floor of the House of Commons, following a long-forgotten precedent, and in opposition to the proposed reforms of the Prayer Book in 1928. Compared in ugliness by his contemporaries to pre-Neanderthal man, the Missing Link, his nickname had stuck, if its origin had been forgotten. He had an admirable facility for making short speeches, especially in thanking a speaker, summing up in a few carefully chosen words, interspersed by pregnant pauses as he searched for the right ones, an address which might have lasted for the best part of an hour. We savoured this quality in his daily introductions to the gospel lessons, touching in a mere minute or so not only the heart of the matter but also incidentals such as the value of a denarius (translated as a 'penny' in the King James Bible) in the time of Our Lord. His performance was enhanced by a tennis eyeshade which he donned with a shaky hand as he reached the lectern, and by his constantly getting lost and fluffing the text as he read it. Whether or not these antics were a deliberate entertainment we shall never know.

Once the service was over, the congregation departed in an orderly rapid gait to face the secular problems of the day.

There were two compulsory services on Sunday, Mattins in the morning and Evensong in the evening, one or other of them with a

Eton, 1938–43

sermon. The evening service included one of a selection of magnificent anthems sung by the choir. The choir school was a part of the Foundation, separate from the School (of which only College was part of the Foundation), the oppidans (about 1,100 of the 1,170 boys) being a tolerated appendage. The tenors and basses of the choir were imported professionals, the leaders known as Rumblebelly and Thunderguts. Their part in the services was an entertainment, often inspiring in its beauty but with a comic element.

Divinity was taught twice a week throughout the school, giving us a thorough grounding in the Gospels and Acts and an opportunity to discuss the Existence of God in the upper forms. Each evening there were house prayers at 9 p.m.

Christian practice was thus integral to our lives, and this by more than its regularity, and it coloured the way we lived and thought. Yet to have called it 'central to our lives' would have seemed to us sanctimonious and even ridiculous because, truth to tell, Christianity in its Anglican form came up with the rations, as Latin and the Field Game did. We took to it, I suppose, rather as we took to them, or disliked it as we disliked them. Understatement was the way of the world, sentimentality was deplorable. As far as chapel was concerned, everyone conformed, but no window into our souls was opened by the Powers that Be. Agnosticism was acceptable. On the whole, atheism was not; but atheists were tolerated, as part of the scene, and were in such a small minority that they were not a threat. But in spite of this, Christianity was a guiding light by which we – often almost subconsciously – formed our standards of behaviour and expected others to do likewise. Countless Etonians served later in life as churchwardens in their parishes.

Christianity may or may not have been central to our lives, but for the majority of us games certainly were. Success in work brought little or no kudos. Success in games brought it in abundance. It was everybody's desire to be awarded some kind of colour, no matter what, in order no longer to have to wear a scug cap.

It was an enviable thing to be a swell – to excel at games and to have a whole collection of caps to hang on the wall of one's room. But this was, inevitably, for the few. Everyone who had not earned a colour had to wear the dreaded and despised scug cap: it was a rigid rule that everybody who was not in school dress had to wear a cap. School dress

Eton, 1938–43

was more or less anonymous, except for a select few who were in Pop or Stick-Ups, namely stick-up collars permitted to the sixth form, captains of houses and the school teams for major games. The status of Stick-Ups was much prized, but since it was available only to a minority of senior boys it did not label the great majority as scugs, as the cap did.

Why did the authorities allow it? The whole school was carried along on the cult of organised games. The system was accepted not because we enjoyed games so much, but rather because we valued success in them so highly. Besides, it is in the nature of a school that most of the pupils are conformists. They accept what they find when they are at the bottom of the pile, and perpetuate it when they reach the top. Many of us had the hope and ambition that by hook or by crook we ourselves might manage to climb on the bandwagon, and anyway the system was too firmly entrenched to make it worth attacking. Many of the masters had gone through this mill, many had themselves been distinguished games players either at Eton or at another school (although some, especially some of the most scholarly, had definitely not), and they would not have returned to Eton to teach if they had not enjoyed their time there. Eton, I suppose, was a classical example of the self-perpetuating English institution.

Eton in those days was an aristocratic and a comprehensive school. That is to say it was neither meritocratic nor selective. I use the term aristocratic with its British flavour. The British aristocracy was never a caste. People fell off the ladder, and others climbed on to it, with every passing generation. Many of Eton's pupils came from what were vaguely considered to be old Eton families, but this is because new families could so quickly integrate with the old ones. Certainly the peerage and the landed gentry were well represented, but so were many families which did not own land, including the families of younger children in a system of primogeniture – which meant both that the big estates were not broken up by shared inheritances, and that the younger children had to fend for themselves. Thus in an 'aristocratic' school many of the boys came from professional or business families which had connections with the landed gentry. However, there were far more families from the 'professional' class than nowadays – a strength; and very few from the entrepreneurial class – a weakness. There were many brilliantly clever boys in the school, but very few of them reflected in their later careers an inventive, technicological or entrepreneurial spirit.

Eton, 1938–43

This is not to say that Etonians lacked imagination, initiative or originality. Far from it. It would be interesting to collect evidence of the plethora of original, enterprising ideas backed by the British genius for improvisation which Etonians contributed to the Second World War. After the war they showed that they didn't lack the spirit of adventure. They could be found all over the world discovering and responding to extraordinary challenges. Yet, on the whole, they took the world as they found it and did what they could with the material to hand. Their contribution to politics continued to be so pervasive and so distinguished that one could not explain it solely as the consequence of money and social connection. Many were ambitious, and most of them approached their careers with style.

The seventy scholarships, free to those who could not pay, provided an intellectual elite, but they were all accommodated in a single hothouse correctly known as College, so their influence (except on each other, which was important) did not filter through the school, where it would have been even more valuable. The academic make-up of the oppidan houses was more or less in the lap of the gods, because boys had to be entered at birth to get in and there was no reliable way of knowing how clever each one would be. Most houses had the benefit of some clever boys, but some were unlucky.

There was a Common Entrance examination, just as there is now, and the standard was higher than it was in less famous schools. Common Entrance excluded the stupidest boys, but its main value was to place those who passed in layers of merit. The oppidans who were placed in remove or upper fourth were of very different calibre from those placed in third form. As I have explained, the latter started three or four terms below the former. The difference in age between the cleverest and the least clever boys as they moved up the school would be regarded as extraordinary nowadays – and was quite striking more than half a century ago.

About half the boys were not considered clever enough to learn Greek, and *per contra* it was thought necessary to teach them English. They were known as 'kappa boys' because each of them had against his name in the school list a small Greek letter 'k'. The choice of this symbol had apparently depended on the fact that there was, for some unknown reason, a surfeit of kappas in the relevant font in the school's own printing press – known from its ancientness as the Caxton Press. Thus, just as every boy who had not won a colour at games was identified by compulsorily wearing a scug cap, so every boy not clever enough to learn Greek was marked as a 'kappa boy'.

It could be said (and often was) that at least the lower reaches of kappa boys were incapable of benefiting from the kind of education which Eton, and all the other leading public schools and grammar schools, offered, but the system did benefit the late developer who would have been excluded by a tougher entrance test (like the later much-vilified 11 plus) and it enabled the school to demonstrate (to those who were willing to accept the fact) that there are many different kinds of cleverness.

The Renaissance, with its instruments the universities and schools, had widened the literate elite beyond the ranks of the clergy. In the sixteenth and seventeenth centuries literacy became the passport to power and success, and the classical languages were the passport to an education which would provide it. The habits of a Renaissance education were under attack throughout the twentieth century, but in a conservative institution with a self-perpetuating constitution the attack took the form of a century-long siege. The kappa boys, however, leavened the lump. The Eton system, although it was confined by a code of assumptions, did encourage freedom of thought, and also freedom of opinion which is not quite the same thing; and it built individual self-confidence. The strait-jacket of public examinations did not in those days squeeze out individual ideas by the desperate requirement for knowledge. We were encouraged to criticise all kinds of writing, rather than being taught what to write in our exams.

The kappa boys made a valuable contribution to Eton's education. They did provide their ample share of philistinism, but this was not their monopoly. It was entrenched in the attitudes of many of the masters – a point which I have already made in relation to much of the teaching of the classics, the shallowness of artistic appreciation, and the cult of games: characteristics which were to be found in our leading universities as well as our leading schools. As far as the wider world was concerned, many Eton boys were lost without trace from the moment they left the school until the time of their demise. But they included clever boys as well as those whom the academic system generally regarded as dim-witted.

A notable but gradual change in the composition of the British ruling class during the second half of the twentieth century has been the virtual disappearance of truly 'thick' offspring, as the result of a striking change in genetic make-up. In spite of the transformation of society wrought by the First World War, the class which dominated the political and social life of Britain survived. It was, as it always had been, numerically very small. It was often referred to (more by outsiders than insiders) as the 'Upper Ten', meaning that a true upper class consisted of a mere ten thousand or so people, a tribal group much prone to intermarriage. The most obvious instrument of this system was the 'Season' in which eligible girls (debutantes) were presented at Court each year. That did not by any means cover the whole of the Upper Ten, but outside this small vicious (or should one say charmed?) circle it was still 'not done' to marry somebody who was not 'out of the top drawer'.

At the top of the social pile, therefore, there was almost universal inbreeding, and a strong tendency for the handsomest, not the cleverest, girls to be selected by aristocratic husbands, many of whom the system itself over the course of several generations had rendered somewhat wanting in grey matter. The tallest mothers had the stupidest sons, and you could measure the standard of Common Entrance at a public school (at Eton more than any other) by the size of the boys' shoes. The smaller the shoes, the more new blood had been brought in, and with the blood the brains.

Of course this is not the whole story. The rich were bigger than the poor, and they lived longer, because they were nurtured on a balanced diet of a kind which working class families could not afford. By 1910 the Eton Corps was able to provide a guard of honour for the Coronation consisting of a hundred boys all more than six foot tall – something which even the King's Company of a Guards regiment could not aspire to. By the 1940s there were about four hundred boys taller than six foot, many of them much taller. Inbreeding was not the sole cause; but it helped.

During the second half of the twentieth century this phenomenon sank without trace, partly because the chance of being big was open to all: there was hardly an indigenous group of people of any class throughout Britain which did not include many who had moved from other districts. The railways began it, and the Second World War contributed. The increase in size previously available only to cattle and sheep, the result of scientific cross-breeding, was now available to the human race as well.

The 'Upper Ten' no longer exists, and the upper middle class in general produce offspring whose IQs are above and not below the national average. This is one reason why the upper middle class are so difficult to dislodge from the best schools, and even more controversially from the best universities. This is why they get so many of the top jobs in a range of careers wider than their predecessors would have deigned to honour with their presence. Paradoxically, those components of the old 'Establishment' strong enough to resist and survive the social revolution of the 1960s, which finally destroyed the Establishment as such, rose phoenix-like from the ashes, the old monster in new form. The new meritocracy has replaced the old aristocracy. That is progress.

3
The Navy, 1943–45

HMS *Collingwood* was a shore station at Fareham in Hampshire, near Portsmouth, designed like other similar establishments in Suffolk and Lincolnshire and elsewhere to train raw recruits as rapidly as possible so that they could go to sea as ordinary seamen and learn the ropes on the job. A large number of my squad were boys from the Gorbals, the Glasgow slums notorious for their razor-slashing gangs, and on the first night in the hut there was violence which led to a charge of attempted murder – with what result I never found out. Fortunately it was at the other end of the hut.

Five hundred men joined *Collingwood* each week: a squad of a hundred each weekday. They stayed for twelve weeks, the total number thus being six thousand. Each morning the six thousand together with their instructors paraded for Divisions on the extensive parade ground. They were led by a matelots' band with a small repertoire of traditional marches. The professional bands in the Navy were those of the Royal Marines in their white helmets. Every battleship and large shore establishment normally had one, and of course the musicians, although professionals, also did other jobs in their ships, mostly as gun crews. But a Royal Marines band could not be spared for *Collingwood*, so we had a band made up of ordinary sailors, who performed the task with zest, combining it with other duties. If you could volunteer as a competent musician, you had a good chance of a job ashore.

Our squad was given a number, and two corrugated iron huts with fifty men in each, with twenty-five double bunks, twelve or thirteen on each side, with lockers between them. The huts were heated by a couple of coke-burning stoves.

I was ready for the lack of privacy and the confinement of one's territory to a bunk and a locker. What I had not anticipated was the overwhelming sensation of isolation from the outside world, almost mysteriously preserved by the Navy from the days of the 'Wooden World', when the crew of a warship might not step ashore for months or even years. Quite apart from the oddness of the uniform (our civilian clothes were packed up in a parcel and posted home), we were pitched into a new language; and, as with the clothing so with the words, there was a total and calculated lack of introduction or explanation. We were not allowed 'ashore' for two or three weeks, by which time it was normal civilian life which seemed peculiar. There were, unsurprisingly, no available telephones. Obviously we had no choice but to comply, and we were pressed more firmly into the mould by fear of ridicule.

On the first day we were issued with the clothing which filled our lockers: two suits (number 1 for Sundays and leave ashore) with bell bottom trousers, jumper and jersey, collars and silks, vests and pants, socks, boots and gaiters, soap (measured by the inch) and a large tin of pipe or cigarette tobacco; together with a wooden stamp with our surnames and initials about half an inch high which we dipped in white paint and stamped on each article of clothing. Woe betide the recruit who stamped his collar on the wrong side. No advice or information was given. We just had to find out.

The men issuing the kit were mostly three-badge able seamen, wearing three chevrons on their arms like sergeants in the army, which signified that they had completed nine years' service out of the twelve they had signed on for (not that there was any release for them during the war, even if they had completed their twelve). Some of them had been recalled as reservists, and some had signed on for the further ten years which would lead to the end of a naval rating's career at the age of forty. These veterans, most of them aged between thirty and thirty-five, many of whom were thought to have earned a job ashore, knew all the tricks of the trade, and kept out of harm's way.

Jumpers and trousers were stowed in our lockers inside out, not only to keep them clean but because this was the only way you could put them on: the uniform was tight-fitting and had evolved so as not to get caught in anything, but also to enable one to roll up the trousers easily on the command 'Off boots and socks, scrub deck'. The trousers had to be ironed in seven horizontal folds, all the same width. The only decoration on the uniform was the triple white stripe on the collar, designed to keep the grease from one's pigtail off the jumper; and the silk, designed as a sweat rag to tie round the brow. The stripes on the dark blue indigo-dyed jean collar commemorated Nelson's three great victories. The collar was the object of persistent scrubbing to lighten the colour and demonstrate, however unconvincingly, that we were not raw recruits. The silk (never now worn round the brow) was worn loosely round the neck, folded and ironed so that its lower end could be tied by tapes on the jumper. Wearing your silk too long, like wearing your cap flat-a'back, was a sign of conceit not acceptable to the powers that be.

My mates were not all Glaswegians, and were mostly good to know, although many of their names have gone now: a delightful man from Slough; a cockney missing his mum's steak and kidney pie; a large clumsy slow farm hand called Tooley; Bill Houston, older than us, in his upper twenties, who had volunteered from South America, and another South American who was torpedoed and dead within six months. Then there was Perkins, aged about thirty, who had joined the police in order to avoid being called up, and used to repeat 'What on earth's the point of joining the police if you're called up by the Navy?' – a good question. The only man who had a real baby-face and looked about fourteen was called Poppett.

Our training was in the hands of a petty officer, who cajoled us and herded us around and taught us seamanship and drill with – all considered – a good deal of humour, and of course a wealth of terminology which would have been incomprehensible as well as shocking to a landsman. We hardly saw – or at least we certainly didn't speak to – an officer for the whole twelve weeks, although a lieutenant was in command of the squad and gave the orders on the parade ground at Sunday Divisions.

Finding our way around required familiarity with the new language. Thus we learned what everything was, what it was for and, in an elementary way, how it worked. Forrard and aft, the focsle and the quarterdeck, the main top and the foretop, the bow and the beam and the quarter and the stern, port and starboard, inboard and outboard; the deck and the bulkhead and the deckhead with its channel plating; cleats and bollards, bends and hitches, flags and pendants, messdecks and tables and stools, ladders and guardrails and booms, scuttles and deadlights, cutters and whalers; anchors and cables. These words had been devised and retained not for reasons of tradition but because precise labelling was vital for efficiency and above all for safety. They were still being added to as the hazards of using a term which might have two possible meanings continued to become apparent; as, for instance, in a destroyer going slowly astern, when the captain ordered 'Let go' referring to the anchor, and the officer on the quarterdeck fired the depth charges.

The Navy, 1943-45

There was equipment near the parade ground for teaching us the elements of seamanship, which culminated with the rigging of sheerlegs: two large poles lashed together near the top to form a crane for shifting heavy weights, together with all necessary stays, blocks and tackles. This was quite a complicated 'evolution' (a naval term) and required strength, quickness and teamwork.

Towards the end of our time in *Collingwood* we made a start on gun-drill. Old guns were used but the modern medium-sized gun, between four and six inches (measured by the diameter of the barrel), required a similar crew of seven or eight men, each performing much the same, simple, operations although some tasks required more aptitude and practice than others. As with seamanship, the intention was not simply to teach us to perform essential jobs, but to train each of us to do all the eight jobs of the crew, and at the same time to be alert, moving time and again on the command 'Change rounds'.

Foot drill on the parade ground was used to teach us to do exactly what we were told and to do it quickly and precisely, all together. The rigging of sheerlegs and the duties of a gun's crew took us to the next stage, 'changing rounds', when each man performed a different task essential to the whole. This was the essence of naval training, leading towards the confidence that in the end we could – or at least we would – do anything, go anywhere.

Physical training played an important part. There was a massive net near the parade ground something like a giant goalpost but not quite vertical, known simply as 'the rigging'. Often enough we had to go over it, and quickly. It was a real help in giving us a head for heights. There were six huge gyms, one for each division of a thousand men, and the schedule was such that we all spent a session in the gym each day; but the emphasis was not on physical strength – it was on alertness and quickness of movement. There was bending and stretching and jumping galore but for much of the time we would simply rush around the place, up and down the bars and beams and ropes, port, starboard and midships, all at the double, chased and chivvied by the instructors.

The genius behind this physical training was Captain Garnier, Royal Marines, who had devoted his adult life to the welfare of what would nowadays be called 'deprived' boys in the East End of London. He had come to the conclusion that most of their problems were due to constipation, and had set up several gyms to remedy the situation, with startling success. Listless urchins had been transformed into alert and energetic youths. Garnier was persuaded to transfer his efforts to *Collingwood*, was given a commission and a rank senior enough for the task, and he brought along his volunteer instructors, who were metamorphosed into petty officers in the Navy. He was given carte blanche to build the six huge gyms, and his methods worked wonders with young sailors, as they had with cockney children. By the time we left *Collingwood* we were quite fit. We were always hungry, though the food was edible. In three months I had put on a stone and gained an inch in height.

The idea was that after twelve weeks we would be fit to join ships as ordinary seamen and then to learn on the job. In due course those who had the potential to become officers would be transferred to an appropriate training establishment. However, by 1943 it had been realised that this method was wasteful because some potential officers were thousands of miles away and their ships might not return to a home port for more than a year. There was a desperate need for officers, as many as possible and as soon as possible. Therefore a more efficient sausage machine known as the 'Y' scheme was invented, by which people with an adequate educational qualification could be picked out early and sent to sea in a dedicated ship for a specified period. Instead of merely working as one of the crew, they were also given some training. The ships chosen for this purpose were two old light cruisers of the D class based on Rosyth in the Firth of Forth, and I can remember to this day the crammed and crawling train journey from Portsmouth to Inverkeithing to join HMS *Dauntless*.

These ships had minimal regular crews, and as many trainees as could be crammed in, teenagers with five passes in School Certificate who had survived a selection test (which included an early version of an 'intelligence test', precursor of the dreaded eleven-plus) and three months in HMS *Collingwood*. We experienced a higher level of discomfort than in *Collingwood* for that reason. Every sailor had, as well as his kitbag, a hammock, an unwieldy sausage some five feet long lashed up with a rope like a parcel. But nobody slept in a hammock unless they had to. Messdeck tables and stools were comfortable enough when one got used to them, and hugely more convenient. A stool, by the way, is a bench, probably six to eight feet long and about a foot wide. Sailors quickly adapted to sleeping on them, never falling off however much the ship rolled. The seamen's messdecks, as in all warships, were two or three large spaces, usually near the bows, from which fixed furniture was entirely absent except possibly for some lockers. The tables and stools were folded up against the bulkheads or the deckheads. Some lockers were on the messdecks, but others were fitted in wherever there were a few feet of available space all round the ship. Space also had to be found to stow the hammocks – 'netting' as it was called. In the old days the hammock netting had performed a useful purpose by being placed along the sides of the ship, protecting the crew from splinters. Now most of it was an encumbrance, taking valuable space.

Hammocks were slung from a hook attached to the bulkhead at both ends. The total length taken up varied, since the ropes at each end could be lashed at varying lengths, but it had to be remarkably long, perhaps ten feet in all. The deckhead was unlikely to be more than about seven feet above the deck, especially as it was covered with channel plating, consisting of perforated metal strips to which all the numerous wires and pipes and ducts were fixed. Hammocks had to be two or even three deep in some places, which certainly did not make for comfort. When the petty officer of the watch came round with his shrill bosun's call, shouting 'Wakey, wakey, lash up and stow' he meant just that. Lashing your hammock with eight marlin hitches was a difficult job given plenty of space, and with no space at all it might be described as a challenge, especially as it had to be performed quickly. It was of course essential because nothing could be left loose on a mess deck – or anywhere else – in case it should float around and block pipes and pumps in the event of an emergency.

The trainees were a different mixture from that of the *Collingwood*. Most were from grammar schools (more or less the only state education beyond the age of fourteen), the remainder from public schools. The great majority of those who were gradually weeded out during the next five months or so were 'dipped' not on academic or intellectual grounds but for being unsuitable officer material in other ways. A few could not manage the navigation or the signalling, but most of the failures were on the grounds of inadequate character and personality. The judgement of the Powers That Be was almost unfailingly correct, partly because the weeding was a very gradual process, a few falling out of the race every fortnight as their weaknesses became more apparent. The object of the exercise was not to select good officers, let alone the best possible officers, but to reject those who would not make adequate officers. The acid test was whether or not they possessed 'OLQ': officer-like qualities. Did they possess the qualities to make decisions quickly in every conceivable circumstance, and to announce those decisions in a manner which would ensure instant obedience? Everybody wore an identifying armband, so he could be spotted from a distance.

Such was the shortage of officers – a result not nearly as much of casualties as of the extraordinary rate of expansion of the Service – that those who made the grade were quite likely to be confronted with mind-boggling responsibility before they reached the age perhaps of nineteen, certainly of twenty. Ignorant and immature, they had to be able to make the best of things in a difficulty and to act with a degree of authority which would make them credible to the men whose situation depended on them. There might be – in an ideal world there would be – an experienced petty officer to hold their hands. But there might not. There was just as severe a shortage of petty officers as there was of officers, for the same reasons. And it took much longer to create a petty officer than a junior officer who could be put through the sausage machine in nine months.

The production of officers in the Navy was, of course, different from that in the Army and the Air Force. The subaltern who could command a platoon in the Army had to be more evidently courageous under fire than a young officer in the Navy. He had a much more direct responsibility for the lives of some thirty men, and much more direct support from a tolerably competent and experienced platoon sergeant. In the Air Force courage and skill were indispensable, but the officer depended on the men, not the other way round. In the Navy a young officer, even as a member of an experienced team, might have actions to perform and decisions to make in which failure could cost many lives and unimaginably costly equipment. What was drummed into us was the need to act quickly and decisively. The objective was to select people in whom others could have confidence. The awful thing was that throughout the process one could often spot the people who would be dipped at the next fortnightly review.

Experience at sea, and on the lower deck, was essential. The objective in the *Dauntless* was to achieve this, and at the same time to make the most of opportunities for training. The two did not mix very happily, because the routine work of the ordinary seaman, or for that matter the able seaman, was extremely boring. This was a problem for the peacetime Navy. Every day some time was passed by 'working part

The Navy, 1943-45

of ship'. Part of ship in this context was simply a convenient way of dividing the ship's company into sections, just indeed as had been done even in the *Collingwood*. In the days of sail there had of necessity been many sections, so that every seaman knew exactly which sail, which ropes and which gun he was concerned with. The system still made some sense in a battleship with its numerous turrets of main and secondary guns. But in a smaller ship it was simply a convenience. Each division would have one or more officers and one or more petty officers to command it, and each mess (perhaps about fifteen hands) would have a leading seaman to supervise such organisation as was required. The petty officers supervised the time given to 'working part of ship', which simply meant doing the unskilled maintenance in a certain area.

The messdecks had to be kept spotless anyway, by the members of the mess. Captain's rounds took place once a week, usually on a Friday. The captain came round and looked into every corner, put his finger along every surface and peered into every nook and cranny which could carry dust or dirt, and he inspected the men themselves and their kit. If he found one speck of dust there was trouble, not only for the leading seaman (or 'leading hand') in charge of the mess, but for everybody. The remainder of the ship was in theory kept clean by 'working part of ship', but there was much more manpower than there was dirt. Most of the decks were 'iron' (i.e. steel) although cruisers and battleships still had teak surfaces on the focsle and the quarterdeck, which needed scrubbing to keep them clean. Indeed sailors still had to kneel down in rows and 'ho'ystone' the deck, scrubbing it with a 'holystone' of pumice. But the iron deck merely needed washing down. This was achieved by rows of men, boots and socks removed, trousers rolled up, scrubbing away with long-handled brushes, using just water.

The water, of course, was sea water. It would have been ridiculous to waste fresh water. Indeed in the smaller and older destroyers there was (as in old houses) only one fresh water tap, and woe betide anyone who used it other than for drinking. Clothes had to be washed ('dhobied', borrowed from India) in a bucket of cold salt water. In *Dauntless* we had enough fresh water for dhobiing, as well as washing our bodies, and indeed we had the luxury of a few washbasins ('ablutions'). But scrubbing deck consisted of washing it down with sea water, as if it didn't get enough of that anyway. Once we had all 'scrubbed forward' we had to turn about and 'scrub aft', a process which would continue until the time allocated for it was up.

The Navy, 1943–45

Paint was essential to prevent ships rusting away. The task of painting ships was endless. It was said that some of the older battleships were held together by paint, and statistics (tempered, as most statistics are, by fertile imaginations) were current as to how many tons had been scraped off *Ramillies* or *Rodney* when she was in dock for a refit. Judging by the amount of time spent by the average sailor applying paint, these statistics were not incredible.

It would have been impossible to scrape the ships' sides. Each coat of paint had to go over its predecessors; but as to the smaller equipment on deck, especially moving parts (capstans and ammunition lockers for instance and all the guns), it was necessary to scrape off a good deal of old paint before applying new. This was a godsend to a petty officer with too little work for too many men.

The peacetime Navy had invented many ingenious ways of creating work, and enlivened them by making every ship in a squadron or flotilla compete, the first ship to complete a task hoisting the appropriate signal at the mainmast and bringing credit to the captain. These tasks were known as evolutions. They included operations such as mooring ship which involved fixing a swivel-piece between the two bow anchor cables. This was a complicated process during which a mistake could lead to the loss of an anchor and all its cable, requiring an embarrassing recovery of the lost equipment in full view of all the ships.

Evolutions had been discontinued during the war, when there were better things to do. A few survived in *Dauntless* as a training ship, including the rigging of sheerlegs which I have already mentioned in *Collingwood*. There was also a lot of boatwork. Hoisting seaboats, whalers and cutters, had a real zip to it, and made a pleasant change after a session scraping paint. Moreover, these particular evolutions were ideal methods of teaching us to handle equipment, extensions of what we had started to learn at *Collingwood* under the heading of seamanship. There was also a good deal of more formal training, including gunnery, navigation and signals.

The gunnery consisted of a more advanced approach to gun drill. We still had to rush around doing the seven or eight tasks – seven or eight or indeed more, depending on the number of ratings who could be spared to handle the ammunition. The *Dauntless* was armed with single 6-inch guns each riveted to the iron deck, with a steel shield to protect the crew but no form of turret. It was rotated left or right by the trainer, and elevated or depressed by the layer (the most difficult job, though requiring a knack rather than a skill, counteracting the movement of the ship, tricky but vital in a heavy sea); both winding large brass handles.

The 6-inch gun was the largest for which a man could handle a shell, and this needed the strongest men available. The propellant, the low explosive which propelled the shell up the gun barrel, had to be loaded separately. Then the breech was closed and the detonator fired electrically, either by the 'captain of the gun' (a leading seaman) or by remote control. This detonator was, of course, a high explosive, a small device which had to be tested at the beginning of each gun drill, and which, should it fail, was the subject of the unforgettable instruction: 'This should not be possible but it may 'appen due to backlash in the system or errors crep' in', which we first heard from Polly Perkins, our petty officer in the *Dauntless*. Polly was a wartime petty officer who would probably not have risen above leading hand in peacetime, and many of his interpretations of King's Regulations and Admiralty Instructions and the Manual of Seamanship had a delightful touch of originality: reports , for instance, were to be written with an 'indelegible pencil'.

We learnt elementary navigation, or chartwork, taking bearings of objects on shore with a compass, often in the Firth of Forth. In order to get a good 'fix' of the ship's position one needed the bearings of three landmarks, which then had to be converted from Magnetic to True North before they were entered on the chart; and before one could make that adjustment one had to account for deviation, namely the error in the magnetic compass induced by metal objects and electrical fields around it, although these had been minimised by placing Flinders bars in the pelorus, the compass housing. The only essential was to remember whether to allow for the deviation or the variation first. If one was taking a bearing off the chart and then reading it from the compass, it had to be done the opposite way round. 'CDMVT' did the trick, whether read forwards or backwards. Gyro compasses were fitted as standard in all warships by that time, but required an electrical supply which would not have been available in a small boat, or with a power failure. So we had to learn how to cope without them.

The signals we learnt were the Morse Code, semaphore and flags. We could have more or less done without semaphore, in which two hand-held flags were held in a different position for each letter and number. This had been derived from the pre-electric telegraph systems by which messages were conveyed from one high point to another on

The Navy, 1943–45

large signal arms. Semaphore was only used for ship-to-ship messages, and it was remarkable to us how fast an experienced signalman could spell out the words, almost at dictation speed, rather as text messages are used with abbreviations nowadays.

Flag signals depended on the Signal Book, and we were only expected to learn the basic vocabulary. The signal book, as in Nelson's Trafalgar signal, had a large choice of words and phrases each signified by two flags, and the combination of a knowledgeable captain (or officer of the watch) and a probably even more knowledgeable yeoman of signals almost always avoided the necessity of spelling out a complete word. Each ship was identified by its pendants (pronounced 'pennants') consisting of a letter and two numerals. The flags were kept in lockers on the signal platform just below the bridge, and bent onto the halyards with extraordinary dexterity by the use of Inglefield clips (many little devices like this bore the names of the admirals who had invented them, including the Battenburg course indicator). The speed at which a signal could be hoisted and acknowledged was a matter of pride.

By far the most useful system was the Morse Code, both audible and visible (or 'audio' and 'video' in modern Latin). It simply had a combination of dots and dashes for each letter, and experienced telegraphists could use it as fast as they could write. It was more difficult visually, conveyed by a signal lamp, than it was by audible dots and dashes: it is harder to convert seen signals than heard signals into the letters they represent – in fact, as I later discovered, Indians couldn't do it at all. However, it was very useful for simple signals from ship to ship, not least because it could not be heard by anyone to whom it was not addressed. With daily practice we gradually became accustomed to these methods.

Shore leave was mostly spent in the North British Hotel in Edinburgh (now a very different modern 'Caledonian') where one could purchase a hot bath and a substantial meal. This was a huge railway hotel, built before the days of running water, as the bathrooms and lavatories had been converted from large bedrooms, and had much more room inside them for a queue than outside. This was a mere matter of curiosity with the loos, but useful in the bathrooms so that several ratings could share a bath, topping up the hot water as required.

The third and final stage of training for an officer was in HMS *King Alfred*, a shore station in the new swimming pool and bowling alley on

The Navy, 1943–45

the sea front at Hove, next door to the Sussex Division of the Royal Naval Volunteer Reserve, with two outstations, one at Mowden School and the other at Lancing College. The first fortnight was spent at Mowden, a prep school, when we were boarded out in the lodging houses of Brighton and Hove, very numerous and complete with their landladies, but not in use for their proper purpose during the war. It cost sixpence to have a bath. The only useful lesson I learned from them was to boil a clock if it wouldn't go.

Then we spent five weeks at Lancing, ideally equipped with classrooms and dormitories and ample playing fields for drill and for manoeuvres for which, imaginatively, ice-cream tricycles were used. Ice creams were mostly sold during the Thirties (a penny for a water ice, 2d for a vanilla bar and 3d for a choc-bar) from these vehicles under the slogan 'Stop Me and Buy One'. They were ideal on the cricket field for manoeuvring in line ahead or abreast and learning the rule of the road, and in particular to maintain 'manoeuvring distance' between ships and to know what to do if another ship was on a steady bearing, preparing us for the time, now not so far away, when we would be junior watchkeeping officers on the bridge: lessons which Admiral Sir George Tryon, Commander-in-Chief of the Mediterranean Fleet in the 1880s, had never mastered, leading to the collision of the *Victoria* and the *Camperdown* by which more than 800 lives were lost, the most costly of all naval peacetime balls-ups.

In the *King Alfred* there were four officers for each division. In command was a lieutenant-commander being rested after a gruelling period at sea, probably in command of a small ship; and there was a lieutenant, an instructor-lieutenant and a senior RNVR sub-lieutenant who dealt with the drill. The instructor-lieutenants were men with degrees in mathematics or some comparable skill, more than competent to teach us navigation but without the patience of ordinary teachers: I got into severe trouble for denying that the moon rose in the east, and rapidly unlearnt the education which had encouraged me to question not merely what I knew to be untrue but what I thought might be.

Lancing Chapel was open but empty, a vast, soaring gothic church undarkened by stained glass and uncluttered by – well, by anything, except two grand pianos which some of my contemporaries could play. It was a good place to spend time in, oblivious to the goings-on outside.

Finally we spent a few weeks at Hove, where we slept in bunks in the underground car park (one of the first of its kind) and where the

The Navy, 1943–45

boarded-over swimming pool was the dining hall. At last we had reached the end of the weeding process. We were the survivors accepted as suitable midshipmen, and were measured for our uniforms by all the smart London tailors (and some not quite so smart) who had set up shop in the town, from whom we could choose without any variation of price: Gieves being the mark of good taste in the Navy.

At the end we had a chance to choose a short specialised course, and I was astonished to find how much one could learn in a week with a first-class instructor and a lot of hard work. I learnt the whole basics of astro-navigation, which involved a working understanding of the Nautical Almanac and a great deal of spherical trigonometry and arithmetic. We even started to practise with a sextant, trying to take a sunsight from the terrace overlooking the Channel at noon each day, although we didn't get much further than realising how difficult it was.

As fledgling officers our reward was a fortnight's course at the Royal Naval College at Greenwich, living as gentlemen with our meals served by stewards in the superb Painted Hall, where we could pick up a smattering of the Navy's style. The effect was slightly spoilt by V2s, the rockets which were starting to replace the flying bombs known as V1s or, in more homely language, doodle bugs. One could hear the V1s coming, and then the engine cut out some seconds before they exploded; but the first one knew of a V2 was a very big bang – at which we were all commanded to get under the table, although this had an element of shutting the stable door after the horse had gone.

The Royal Navy during the Second World War was an institution far beyond this author's descriptive capacity, even in snapshot form. Whether we see the Navy as evolving from the time of King Alfred or of King Henry VIII, it has been over the course of centuries a major player both in the history and the folklore of our country. On the Navy depended Britain's exploration and exploitation of the trade routes of the world, and Britain's contribution to the process was called by historians the expansion of Europe. It enabled Britain to become the first world power in history and to preside over the Empire on which the sun never set.

The tradition which began with the heroic deeds of Drake and Raleigh and the defeat of the Spanish Armada achieved its most notable triumph at Trafalgar, with the defeat of the combined French and

The Navy, 1943–45

Spanish fleets that contributed to the foundation of the nineteenth-century Pax Britannica. In the First World War the Royal Navy was still by far the largest navy in the world, and Welsh steam coal filled the depots at every strategic oceanic link around the globe. After 1918 there was disarmament and then the 'cuts' (yes, history repeats itself) with many officers 'axed' in mid-career, and Britain fell into second place behind the United States. But a massive building programme beginning in 1935 inaugurated the Navy's second twentieth-century heyday.

The 1935 programme restored the same kind of naval power as the arms race of the Dreadnoughts had provided in 1914, the stupendous climax of the ironclad battle fleet, capable of containing Germany and dominating the Mediterranean. But by 1939 it was already too late to ensure command of the air and, like the battle fleet of 1914, the Navy had not the resources to win the submarine war and stave off Britain's starvation. Only by frantically building hundreds of smaller ships, destroyers, frigates, sloops, corvettes and minesweepers, could that be achieved – and it was a close-run thing. The importance of air power had not been fully grasped, but in many other respects the advance of the Navy's technology had been remarkable, especially in submarine detection. This saved us from defeat.

The Navy which I entered was thus a huge organisation. And since everything was shrouded in secrecy it was beyond imagination for the tiny cogs like us to get much measure of the whole machine. How the small professional regular Navy of the interwar years contrived to stretch itself into this Leviathan has received too little attention. Spread very thin, stretched constantly to breaking point, these few unsung heroes saved the nation from defeat. We remember 'The Few', the pilots of the Royal Air Force, who deservedly gripped the country's imagination during the Battle of Britain in 1940. Yet there was also this other group of naval men without whose services Britain could not have won the war.

By 1942 the smallest ships were manned almost exclusively by wartime officers and ratings, and even the smaller destroyers had only a small minority of professionals. Only the big ships, battleships, aircraft carriers and cruisers, still required a majority of regular officers and key ratings to work their elaborately technical weapons.

In these circumstances it was both the role and the objective of most RNVR officers to be in small ships, rather than large ones in which they

The Navy, 1943–45

would be small fry in a big shoal. Regular, RN, officers, wore straight gold braid rings on their sleeves to mark their rank. Wartime officers were known as Royal Naval Volunteer Reserve officers (although most of them would have been called up anyway and were only volunteers in that they had volunteered to be officers) and were regarded, by themselves and everyone else, as amateurs, which indeed is exactly what the true (pre-war) RNVR officers were: patriotic yachtsmen. They wore wavy braid rings and were vulgarly known as the Wavy Navy. (The only other brand, RNR officers, with cross-diagonal rings, were former Merchant Navy officers who had been trained and commissioned in the Royal Navy. They were rare birds, because almost every available Merchant Navy officer was employed in a merchant ship.)

The distinction was a valid and valued one. Apart from their lengthy initial training, RN officers had mostly qualified after long courses as lieutenants in one speciality or another – say gunnery or signals or navigation – and it required their expertise to work a large ship. They also had long experience which set them apart from their wartime colleagues and, as a result of the distinction which was immediately evident from the uniform, everybody knew what was to be expected.

There was also a strong distinction between executive or 'seaman' officers and specialists, the latter wearing coloured ribbon between the gold rings: purple for engineers, white for paymasters, blue for instructors and red for doctors. The executive officers regarded themselves as the aristocrats of the Navy: engineers were still sometimes referred to as 'plumbers' and visualised in overalls holding an oily rag (strictly speaking, a bunch of cotton waste), but gradually the prejudice against specialists was being eroded, and during the war the paymasters were rebranded as the Supply and Secretariat Branch. The formerly rare birds known as 'electrical gentlemen', vital in large numbers with the advent of radar, were now in uniform with green ribbon. The transformation of the Navy from seamanship towards technology, started by the advent of steam, continued inexorably, although it was not until perhaps the 1970s or the 1980s that it became evident that the Navy was dominated by technology and the old concept of a 'seaman' had at last become irrelevant.

A snapshot of the Navy during the Second World War would have to include descriptions of many types of ship, and is clearly beyond the scope of this volume. I shall confine myself (more or less) to a description of life in a fleet destroyer, because that was what I experienced. This class of ship was the most typical of naval life, lying half way between the big ships and the little ones. What interested me was the organic nature of a group of a couple of hundred adult males drawn from every, or almost every, variety of background performing a large number of essential technical tasks in an organised way, as well as coping with the common necessities of life such as eating and sleeping and going to the heads.

Destroyers were first built to destroy torpedo boats, small craft which could approach large ships and discharge their deadly weapons. The destroyer had to be faster than its quarry, but needed nothing more than a small gun, perhaps a 12-pounder, to work its execution. In the course of time the torpedo boat and its hunter were combined as one type, and the name 'destroyer' stuck. It then became apparent that destroyers were needed to defend the battle fleet, in which case they needed to be as fast or faster than the battleships (the Dreadnoughts, super-Dreadnoughts and their successors) and, in particular, the battle cruisers which were even faster (because more lightly armoured) versions. Hence the fleet destroyer, larger than its forebears because, as well as being speedy, it had to have a fair range and it had to be able to keep up with the battle fleet in a high sea. Then it was realised that instead of carrying only two torpedo tubes it could carry as many as six, and eventually eight, all of which could be fired at an opposing battle fleet in a single salvo.

The fleet destroyer then followed the trend with which we have become familiar in the age of motor cars: each model is slightly bigger and better than its predecessor. In spite of the torpedo, the gun remained the key to naval weaponry; for the torpedo could not travel at more than 40 knots (about 45 miles an hour) nor was its range more than about two miles. The gun had been perfected as a weapon by 1914. A big one could hurl a shell weighing about a ton very accurately for an optimum range of about nine miles, or an extreme range of about fifteen. Filled with high explosive and when necessary engineered to pierce armour like a sort of self-propelled screwdriver, with its long trajectory taking it hundreds of yards into the air it landed on the enemy's deck at a steep angle. A single direct hit, as first shown at Jutland (1916) and finally with the sinking of the *Hood* by the *Bismarck* in 1942, could sink a massive capital ship.

The Navy, 1943-45

Thus, if destroyers were to be large enough to escort the fleet they needed guns as well as torpedoes. The single 12-pounder became a 3-inch, then a 4-inch, then one became two, then four, eventually 4.7-inch guns. Why 4.7? This was the largest shell, with explosive and propellant combined, that a man could handle. A tenth of an inch all round makes quite a difference in weight, as is demonstrated by a salmon for anyone who is baffled by mathematics but knows how to catch fish. The best-equipped fleet destroyers, the gallant Tribal class built just before the Second World War and almost all lost in it, had eight guns in four double mountings, but four was found the most effective compromise for the 'Emergency Programme' fleet destroyers which formed the common ruck: for it was not the number of guns but the ability to direct them accurately to their target which became the priority.

I joined HMS *Relentless* in Colombo in Ceylon, now Sri Lanka, and I got there aboard HMS *King George V*, bound from Britain for the British Pacific Fleet which was being assembled for the assault on Japan. She refuelled in Colombo before continuing her long voyage. Thus I had a taste of what life in a big ship was like before joining a small one. The *King George V* carried about fifteen to twenty RN midshipmen, who lived in the gunroom under their sub-lieutenant and had a miserable time. The hierarchy of the Navy was traditional and complicated. Midshipmen were officers, but not yet commissioned officers, and in a big ship they lived in a separate mess, the gunroom, inferior to the wardroom. Although they had proper jobs to do they were still under some degree of formal training. They had no cabins and no furniture but a chest, and each had to keep a journal (some of which were admirable compilations, full of every sort of description and illustration). Their origin was in the boys, often the sons of friends, whom captains had taken to sea and set on the road to a commission in the eighteenth century.

There only were two of us, RNVR midshipmen, with them, and they envied us the general and in their eyes unrestricted freedom of the education which we had enjoyed, and the fact that although we were mere amateurs we were going to smaller ships in which we would be less insignificant than, in spite of all their training, they were. They had mostly joined the Navy as cadets at Dartmouth aged thirteen, for the eighteen-year old entry was only just starting to creep in, and they had gone to sea at sixteen. For two or more years they were the dogsbodies, just at a time of life when everybody wants to move on, and most of them were disillusioned with their lot. Some of them left the Navy after a few years, only the more ambitious doing their best to scramble up the ladder of promotion. On the other hand, it was the training they had gone through which produced men of the stamp of our own captain in *Relentless*, of whom later. These midshipmen at the age of sixteen or seventeen had absorbed an unequalled understanding of the Navy and its ways, and an ability to handle situations which would have been far beyond most of their contemporaries in any other walk of life. A midshipman, for instance, was in charge of a battleship's launch, a very large open motorboat capable of carrying about a hundred men, and to see a midshipman bringing a launch up to a jetty in a choppy sea to take on board a hundred liberty men (most of whom had enjoyed too much alcohol on their trip ashore) was quite a revelation. His crew would be a leading seaman, an able seaman in the bows and a stoker to look after the engine. Everything depended on his own firm but quiet authority, which had already become almost instinctive.

King George V had a complement (or crew) of 1,650 and, with each deck divided into many compartments so that damage caused by flooding could be controlled, it took a long time to find one's way about. The largest gun turrets, descending into the bowels of the ship for access to ammunition, with many doors and airlocks to prevent the spread of fire, each had four fourteen-inch guns, a crew of 120 and a weight of about 2,000 tons (as much as a fleet destroyer).

We stopped at Gibraltar and then at Malta, which by now was out of range of enemy air attacks. The harbour full of large warships, and the 'gut' or main street of Valletta heaving with sailors bent on having a good time ashore, were memorable sights. We then spent some time at Alexandria (where the squalor was an eye-opener), because we were required to bombard the island of Milos, still occupied by the Germans. The Suez Canal had only recently been reopened and had not been dredged during the long period when ships had had to go round by the Cape of Good Hope, and on our passage through it we frequently touched bottom and swerved around alarmingly. In the salt lakes lay the surrendered Italian battleships, magnificent examples of modern engineering and a fine sight, but in such a chaotic state that it was said that it would have taken a year to bring them into service.

At Colombo I had my first taste of the Raj. Even a humble midshipman was assigned a boy servant who called him 'Master' and insisted

The Navy, 1943-45

on putting the toothpaste on to his brush for him. We then travelled to Trincomalee, where I joined HMS *Relentless*.

Relentless was one of the flotilla of eight 'R' class fleet destroyers of the emergency war programme. In most respects they had the latest updated equipment. The flotilla leader, *Rotherham*, had slightly more space for officers, but all eight were similar, though not identical in detail. They had been built at several different yards to the same Admiralty specification, but there were minor differences in layout, which increased at every refit when small modifications were made, sometimes at the captain's personal suggestion. They were a just over 100 metres in length and 10 metres in width (beam), drew about three metres of water and weighed about 2,000 tons. Their complements were about 220 men.

Massive battle fleets with several squadrons of battleships and battle cruisers did not survive after the First World War. If more than one battleship or aircraft carrier was at sea in the same war zone they might be hundreds of miles apart, and each required a screening escort of destroyers. This required, in theory at least, that they should be able to steam as fast as a battleship, which in the most modern class had reached about 30 knots. Aircraft carriers, being more lightly armoured, could manage a few more knots, but in calm weather they still had to turn into the wind to launch their planes.

The engines and propellers of destroyers and capital ships were almost identical, except that the destroyers had two, each producing 20,000 horsepower, battleships four and aircraft carriers five. In a destroyer, weighing 2,000 tons, 40,000 horse power would produce 34 knots in theory, about 30 or 31 in practice. In an aircraft carrier, weighing more than 30,000 tons, 120,000 horse power would produce just about the same speed. Battleships, with heavy armoured plate, were a little slower than carriers. In other words, you could multiply the weight by about 15 and the horsepower by 2½, and get the same result.

The quest for speed meant that the whole middle section of a destroyer was taken up by its two boiler rooms and two engine rooms, everything else below decks (including of course the crew's quarters) being in the bows or the stern. Putting the boiler rooms together, ahead of the engine rooms, enabled a simpler arrangement of funnels, or piping of the steam into just one funnel, than arranging them in series, but made it more likely that a single shell or torpedo would completely deprive the ship of motive power by taking out both boilers or both engines. It was satisfying to visit the engine rooms when the ship was manoeuvring, and to hold 20,000 horsepower in one's hands as one turned the throttle wheel

These ships had astonishing acceleration, but at full speed they drank fuel greedily, so for the most part we travelled at not much more than 15 knots, 'economical speed', covering about 400 nautical miles in a day. In the Indian Ocean we quite often refuelled at sea, either from a battleship or aircraft carrier, or a tanker. It is not surprising that we carried an engineer officer to look after this massive machinery, although most of the work could be done by one of the ERAs or engine room artificers, who had undergone a full engineering apprenticeship and were rated as petty officers. They could make almost anything – as indeed was essential, since it would have been impossible to carry a full range of spare parts. The men in charge of the boiler rooms, still known as stokers although oil had replaced coal between the wars, were good mechanics but without the same level of skill. As well as maintaining the pressure of steam in the most economical way, they had to ensure that the ship did not make smoke, except when required to create a smokescreen.

Destroyers were plated with steel a mere quarter-inch thick, except along the central waterline where it was half-inch. The plates were riveted together, although welding was just starting to come in for jobs of this size. The ships had a good deal of flexibility, quite alarming to the uninitiated in a heavy sea, but this prevented them from breaking up when battered by waves. Welded ships, being more rigid, were not yet as satisfactory in this respect. The underwater parts were painted with red lead, which was fairly effective in discouraging weed growth. In a really heavy sea a destroyer could not safely manage more than about 12 knots, although they were magnificently seaworthy and could roll more than 90 degrees before they capsized, or so we were assured. The upper deck was awash in a heavy sea, with a handline rigged to hold on to as one went fore and aft, which was often necessary because the whole of the midship below the upper deck was full of machinery.

The main armament consisted of four single 4.7-inch guns, two forward and two aft, protected by steel shields at the front and sides. With crews of about eight – an extra hand or two was always useful for humping ammunition – they were still worked manually by the gunlayer and trainer turning brass wheels, but centrally controlled by an officer in the tower above the bridge. The guns might have been moved electrically, as some of the smaller guns were, notably Bofors anti-aircraft guns, but electrical mountings were still temperamental even on a lighter gun. Mechanised or semi-mechanised systems of loading were just starting to come in, but they would have required far more weight and space than was available because all the guns were required to swivel through a very wide angle of about 270 degrees.

Well-protected below decks was the transmission station, a small compartment full of men winding handles, with a wonderfully ingenious box full of clockwork designed to calculate the range and, most essentially, the 'rate' of a moving target. The 'rate' was the rate of movement to right or left, depending on the estimates of its course and speed made by the gunnery officer in his control tower using either binoculars or radar.

One of the three radar sets in the ship was a direction-finding one in the gun-control tower. It was efficient at estimating the range and bearing of the target, but the rate had to be calculated using this information. It was also unable to spot anything as small as the splash as the shells fell, which was essential in order to correct the aim and, in particular, the range. Radar was vitally useful by night or in fog, but we still carried starshell and a searchlight to illuminate a target in darkness, and binoculars and optical rangefinders were still essential equipment.

Firing starshell required a different technique from high explosive, as the shell had to explode beyond and above the target, where it would burn brightly, descending slowly by parachute. However, the aim would be to detect the target by radar and fire the first salvo before resorting to starshell, surprising the enemy – as was famously achieved by the *Duke of York* when it sank the *Scharnhorst* off North Cape. We were smaller fry, and never approached perfection, to say the least. When we used the searchlight, it had a nasty habit of lighting up on a reciprocal bearing, that is to say exactly the opposite of the one intended, to the acute embarrassment of those responsible.

You started by firing a 'ladder' in which each shell landed 200 yards beyond its predecessor. This enabled the gunnery officer to get the range, provided that he could spot which side of the target the splash was. After that, once the target had been straddled, the idea was to fire all four guns at once (euphemistically called a broadside) with a good chance, provided that the rate was correct, that one might achieve a direct hit.

The Navy, 1943–45

From time to time destroyers were used for bombarding enemy shore installations, in our case on the Andaman or Nicobar Islands, which had some slight strategic importance in relation to the Burma campaign. Although subject to retaliation, this was by its nature a more academic exercise, as the elevation of the target had to be taken into account, and even if the target was stationary it was thought best for us to keep moving. Sometimes we took on board a Royal Artillery officer to help with the spotting. These operations must have been useful to the people who requested them, but to us the result did not always seem to justify the effort.

Anti-aircraft fire was a much more difficult matter: in fact a distant target rapidly moving in three dimensions was more than one could hope to hit from a moving platform, especially when the ship was pitching and rolling. Short of an unusual stroke of luck, the best one could hope for was a near miss with a lethally explosive shell. Since there was only a slim chance of actually hitting an aircraft, these shells had to be exploded by a time-fuse, and the fuse had to be set before each shell was fired, indeed before it had even been loaded. For this purpose there was an ingenious fuse keeping clock, but having calculated what the range of the target would be when the shell eventually arrived in its vicinity, one had to place the shell on a tray and twist the fuse in its cap to the right position, insert it in the gun, fire it and then wait endless seconds for it to reach the target.

Quick-firing smaller guns were far more effective against aircraft, although their range was much shorter. (This truth had to be rediscovered in the Falklands war forty years later, when some of the targets were not aircraft but Exocet missiles.) We had a quadruple two-pounder 'pom-pom' behind the funnel which was effective in spite of its low muzzle velocity, and made an impressive display when firing tracer, lighting up the shells, which was a help in anti-aircraft shooting. These pom-poms were being replaced by Swedish Bofors guns with a higher velocity as each ship came in for a refit.

There were a couple of twin Oerlikons, very heavy machine guns, one each side of the bridge. Their effectiveness depended on the skill of the operator, who had to swing the guns to follow the target: it was a knack, which one member of the crew possessed to a high degree. I remember him well, because he was a nuisance in every other respect – dirty, late, idle and offhand and always in a scrape. But he might have saved a lot of lives in a nasty moment. These Oerlikon guns had gyroscopic sights, which calculated the lead which was required, depending on how fast the gun was swinging; so the operator only had to aim at the target, not to calculate the lead. Clay pigeon shooting was used for training – a little light relief for some people who would, and some who wouldn't, ever get to fire an Oerlikon in anger.

The main armament of guns in a destroyer would hardly have scratched a battleship, but the torpedoes were a different matter altogether. We carried two sets of quadruple 21-inch torpedo tubes in the waist of the ship, above the engine rooms. A single torpedo could cripple a large warship, and might even sink it. Two or three hits would almost certainly put it out of action. (The torpedoes carried by aircraft were smaller – 18-inch – ones, but even they were most effective.) In a classic torpedo attack a destroyer would fire all eight torpedoes at intervals of a few seconds, the ship meantime turning very slightly away from the target so that they fanned out and did not all run at the same angle. The snag about torpedoes was their comparatively short range (up to about a couple of miles) and, in particular, their slow speed. They travelled at only 40 knots, about 45 m.p.h., and if the tracks could be spotted, which was not difficult from the crow's nest, there was often time to turn parallel to them and avoid them. They were lethal at close range, but in good visibility a battleship or cruiser could expect to blow a destroyer to bits before it could get close enough to fire its torpedoes.

These 'tin fish' cost £1,000 each, which is about £35,000 in today's money, and their delicate mechanism including various depth settings (to keep them running straight they were driven by two propellers moving in opposite directions) required something like the skill of a watchmaker. But the tubes from which they were fired by a blast of compressed air were simple. Torpedoes could be fired for practice without explosive in the warhead, and would come to the surface at the end of their run and be recovered for further use – unless they had been wrongly set: an expensive mistake, leading to a court of inquiry.

Apart from its guns and torpedoes, the destroyer had a heavy anti-submarine arm in the form of depth charges. These were steel cylinders a good deal larger than a standard 5-gallon oil-drum filled with high explosive. In the centre of each charge was a detonator which was fired by water pressure when the charge had sunk to a given depth. This was a simple but effective system. There were two throwers on either side of the ship near the stern, and two sets of rails over the stern itself. Four charges (two, then two more) were fired from the throwers, to a range

The Navy, 1943–45

of about 30 metres, and four were dropped, in pairs, from the stern rails. This 'pattern' of eight charges created a hefty combination of underwater explosions which would damage or sink a submarine if it was near enough.

A submerged submarine could be detected by ASDIC, which together with radar was the most important technical development of the inter-war years. A fish-shaped 'dome' was lowered beneath the keel, quartz crystals being used to transmit a narrow beam which made a 'ping' sound through the water. The beam was moved a few degrees through the points of the compass each time it was transmitted, and if it contacted a solid object it made a second 'ping'. The interval between the two 'pings' gave the distance, and if the object was moving towards one the second 'ping' was at a higher pitch than the first, and vice versa. The operator had to be musical enough to estimate this 'Doppler' effect, which is evident in ordinary life when any noisy object approaches or departs rapidly, most obviously when a high-speed train passes through a station. The operator would report 'Echo high' or 'Marked high' or 'Echo low' and so forth, immediately giving the captain some idea of the foreign body's position and course. (A whale could only be identified by its size, but a shoal of fish would give a muffled 'ping'.) An accurate result depended on the quick plotting of a series of contacts by an officer in the chart room just below the bridge, the position of each 'ping' being marked in relation to our own position on a large-scale diagram.

In the centre of the paper, lit from below through a glass sheet, was a point of light denoting the ship's position, and responding automatically to any changes in our course and speed. All one had to do, therefore, was to mark the bearing and the distance of each 'ping' from our own position shown by this point of light. The approximate course and speed of the target and its direction soon became apparent, but one had to be quick at mental arithmetic to provide accurate information. Given a stopwatch and a pair of parallel rulers this was not as difficult as it might seem because in six minutes a target moved one-tenth of its speed in knots, in three minutes one twentieth, and so on. In practice this often came down to measuring the distance over three minutes, and multiplying the result by twenty to give the speed in knots. However, one had to work by a dim red lamp with often a good deal of noise and rather damp conditions, and the ship rolling and pitching like nobody's business. Not being a mathematical genius I devised a simple set of

The Navy, 1943-45

rulers which enabled me to read the speed of the target immediately, after any number of minutes, or even half minutes, without having to do the sums. It surprised me that nobody had thought of this, and I felt that I must have missed something that was obvious to everybody else. However, I submitted it to the Admiralty, who paid me £5 for it, nearly £200 in today's money. It struck me as impressive that this hefty establishment, so governed by traditional ideas, was open to any little suggestion that anyone, however junior, might submit. Actually, this system was the origin of countless useful gadgets, and had been so for generations.

Given the enemy's course and speed, the captain had to calculate how long it would take us to run over the target and then drop our depth charges astern and allow the exact time for them to sink before they exploded; but the difficulty was that the ASDIC contacts ceased owing to the narrowness of the beam (essential for accuracy) when the target was still some distance away There was therefore a dead period which had to be calculated between the moment when the beam was lost and the moment at which the pattern of depth charges could be fired, and even if the course and speed of the submarine had been estimated accurately it had an interval in which to take evasive action. This problem was remedied in due course several ways: first of all by ships working in pairs, the idea of Captain Walker, the hero of the Atlantic battle, and later by developing projectiles ('squids' and then 'hedgehogs') which could be fired ahead of the ship instead of the depth charges which were dropped astern.

We had three radar sets on board: the gunnery one in the director tower above the bridge, an aircraft warning one and a surface warning one. 'Video display units' were just coming in, illuminating the contacts made by radar on the circular screen of a cathode ray tube and thus giving a map of the situation with one's own position in the centre, a pre-Copernican arrangement one might think. These displays gave a snapshot of the situation moment by moment – of a coastline or any ships in the area, an entirely new phenomenon. The radar gave one a previously unobtainable instant map by night. We also had HF/DF (high frequency direction finding) which pinpointed radio signals by other ships within visual distance, about thirty miles. During a refit we were equipped with LORAN, the first long-range radio navigation system, which however depended on eventually fitting beacons all over the world. It did not always work, but in theory, by getting the bearing of two or three beacons, we could fix our position without recourse to the laborious business of taking sun- or star-sights with a sextant. The use of sextants depended on an accurate chronometer: one second of time was equivalent to a mile's difference in our position, and although we could check the chronometer daily from the Greenwich time signal we had to know how many seconds (if any) it was gaining or losing in the interim. Our most difficult navigational problem was to make an accurate landfall on a low-lying coast, particularly where the coast consisted of a widely dispersed group of islands. Fortunately this was the captain's sole responsibility.

The whole of the three armaments – guns, torpedoes and depth charges – had to be carried on the upper deck, as did the anchors and the seaboats and much else besides. If we go aboard the ship when she is tied up in harbour, by a gangway just aft of the funnel on the port side, we shall see how narrow the ship is, a little over 30 feet in the measurements of the day. We turn left towards the bows and thread our way between the funnel and the motor boat, which is hoisted on davits high enough to be clear of all but the largest waves. These davits or cranes are swung out over the sea when the boat is to be lowered. We pass the galley (the kitchen), then climb a ladder up the 'step in the focsle' (forecastle), walk past a couple of Carley floats, life rafts able to support a good number of men either inside them or hanging on to the ropes. On our right is the wardroom, the officers' mess. Above are the sponsons (platforms) for the Oerlikon guns and signal lamps. We pass 'B' gun on the deck above us and come to the focsle with 'A' gun and its 'ready use' ammunition lockers (most of the ammunition is stored in the magazine low down in the ship), the anchors and cables and the steam-powered capstan.

There are two anchors, one each side in hawse pipes, secured by a hefty steel clip which can be knocked off with a sledgehammer; then, if the capstan brake is off, the cable will run out 'going like the clappers' from the cable locker below. To anchor the ship, cable (i.e. chain) is required at least three times the depth of the water: it is the cable, much more than the anchor, which holds the ship. If we moor to a buoy, the anchor has to be detached and a man jumps down on to the buoy and secures the cable to it. If we are tied up to the dock wall, this will be done with the flexible steel wire ropes, which are coiled down on the focsle at several points.

The Navy, 1943-45

From the sharply pointed bow (the eyes of the ship, with the jackstaff for the Union Flag) we turn to go aft along the other (starboard) side, and as we descend from the focsle we see the other boat, a whaler, a sturdy timber boat pointed at each end and either rowed by a crew of five or sailed with a mainsail and a little mizzen sail at the stern (the rig is that of a yawl).

There is no capstan for lowering or hoisting the two boats. They are secured to the davits by ropes with pulleys (called tackles pronounced with a long 'a') and when they are to be hoisted the command is given on the tannoy to 'clear lower deck' which means that every man who is not on duty must turn out at the double. They man the ropes like a huge tug-of-war team. A petty officer givers the commands: 'Take the strain – marry' (and the two ropes are brought together) '– hoist away.' It is a good feeling as a hundred or more men stamp it out along the deck and up comes the boat.

There is plenty of equipment on the upper deck without adding two steam capstans to hoist the boats, but it is probably done manually as a deliberate peacetime 'evolution' to give the hands a bit of exercise and preserve something of the ropework of the days of sail.

Forward and aft of the two sets of torpedo tubes are two small deckhouses, one of them with the pom-pom gun and the other the searchlight mounted on it; a small mast taking the radio aerials from the mainmast, the HF/DF aerial and the surface warning radar aerial. There is also a torpedo davit, a small crane for hoisting torpedoes on board; then there is a larger deckhouse, on which 'X' gun is mounted, and alongside it a set of depth-charge throwers and racks of spare depth charges. Then, right astern, is 'Y' gun and the depth charge racks from which the charges roll over the stern; a small (sheet) anchor, the wire ropes for tying up to a jetty and the fairleads and bollards for rigging and securing them.

Below the upper deck, the sternmost compartment holds the steering gear, including the servo-motor which moves the rudder when the wheel in the charthouse (just under the bridge) is turned. Then comes the spirit room in which the rum is stored. Each day when 'Up Spirits' is piped at noon the leading hand of each mess will appear to draw the grog, meted out in copper jugs by a chief petty officer, and witnessed by the officer of the watch, who will sign the spirit book. Each seaman receives his tot of rum, with two parts of water added so that it will not keep and cannot be saved up for a drunken party, the idea of 'Grog' Vernon, admiral in

The Navy, 1943-45

the West Indies in the eighteenth century. 'Cuppers' or 'sippers' are bad enough on a man's birthday, when he has a gulp or a sip from each of his messmates. The petty officers, however, have the privilege of drawing their rum neat. Special occasions are celebrated by the signal 'Splice the main brace', which means a double tot for the whole crew.

Then, forward of the spirit room, is a petty officers' mess and two double cabins for officers. Early in the war there were cases when almost every officer and petty officer had been put out of action by a single direct hit to the forward part of the ship, so now some of each were accommodated aft. The whole space below deck between this and the step in the focsle was taken up by the engines and boiler rooms, with up to about 400 tons of oil fuel in tanks in the ship's bottom.

Forward of the step in the focsle, most of the enclosed space on lower deck consists of the messdecks, or crew's quarters, which are no more and no less than spaces for the crew, almost devoid of equipment except for the mess tables and stools, which are folded away when the ship is at Action Stations, and some lockers. There is no space for bunks. That did not appear in British warships until long after the war. Below the captain's cabin and the wardroom are two officers' double-bunked cabins and a petty officers' mess, as are the ablutions, simple but adequate for everyone to keep clean. The captain customarily eats alone, isolated from idle conversation and gossip, and he will give notice when he wishes to eat in the wardroom.

Right in the narrow confines of the bows are the heads (the crew's loos, kept clean and tidy under the supervision of a leading seaman, the captain of the heads); and the paint locker and the cable locker.

Ladders lead to all the spaces above (and for that matter below) the upper deck; namely the bridge and the various spaces and compartments appended to it. The bridges of all British warships were open, with a narrow shelter under the windscreen at the front, where a chart and currently needed information could be kept more or less dry together with a tiny space for the ASDIC operator whose running commentary could thus be heard directly by the officers on duty. It would not have been practical to have an enclosed bridge and to rely on radar to give an all-round view of the situation, especially in the air. In the centre next to the compass was the captain's chair: the other officers on watch, perhaps two and sometimes three, would not expect to sit down, constantly occupied by their duties and, apart from all else, always on the lookout.

The Navy, 1943–45

Just behind the bridge was the signal platform with the flag lockers and the halyards for hoisting the flags, and on either side were sponsons (platforms) for the lookouts with their binoculars, for the signal lamps and for the Oerlikon guns. Immediately forward and below the bridge was the wheelhouse, manned by the coxswain himself in action or where accuracy and experience were essential; and the engine room telegraphs, ringing down to the engine rooms the number of revolutions (of the screws, per minute) required on each main engine, forward or astern. All the orders for the wheel and the telegraphs were given by an officer on the bridge, calling down a voice pipe, i.e. just a pipe. Immediately below the bridge was the chartroom where one of the officers who was navigating the ship at any moment would do his work, and the captain's sea cabin – a mere bunk, where he could take a nap in a quiet moment, if any.

High above the bridge and astern of it was the gunnery control tower, with just room for the officer and a petty officer, equipped with an optical rangefinder as well as radar. The mainmast carried the crow's nest for a lookout, the signal halyards, radio aerials and identification lights. These latter made a pattern of coloured lights on the yardarms which had to be changed daily in accordance with a code book. It was a heavy responsibility to ensure that they were correctly set, and a subject of prayer not only that they were indeed correct, but also that any ship we sighted, especially merchant ships which tended to regard the whole system with unwarranted scepticism, had also got them right.

Who were the 220-odd white adult males who occupied this sleek 2,000-ton box of quarter-inch-thick steel? They were arranged in a rigid hierarchy, in which, however, every grade included men from different backgrounds. The upper crust were the officers, about a dozen of them, studiously set apart from all others. There is and was a subsidiary grade known as 'non-commissioned officers', but that is a different matter: every aristocratic layer must have its reliable, experienced, subordinates, set above the common ruck. The most rigid division is still the division between the officers and everybody else. In Britain, ever since the emergence of the gentry as a political class in the sixteenth century, there has been a flexible if not indeed a scarcely detectable boundary between the gentry and the nobility – much more so than in other Western European nation states. There has been no concept of caste in the aristocracy, and in spite of the high wall between

The Navy, 1943–45

the aristocracy (including the gentry) and everybody else, it has always been possible for a person of the humblest origins to climb to the peerage; and the passage in the opposite direction has always been wide open too.

During the reign of Queen Victoria the concept of 'an officer and a gentleman' took root, but that merely meant that officers ought to behave in a given way, even if some of them manifestly failed to do so. Field Marshal Lord Roberts referred to the British soldiery as 'heroes on the battlefield and gentlemen at all other times', a far cry from the Duke of Wellington's 'scum of the Earth'. But the rigid division remained. The Navy in 1914 was still an aristocratic service. The names and titles of peers and the sons of peers are dotted generously throughout the Navy List, from admirals to midshipmen. Gradually the lump was leavened, and the officers of the Second World War were selected without much reference to social background – except that educational qualifications were required, for which in most cases money was a help if not essential. But the rigid barrier between officers and men remained intact. It remained intact in the Red Army, although the aristocracy and the gentry had been consigned to the rubbish bin of history, and it remains intact in the US Army although its officers are selected on merit alone. It is the rule in all the organised and disciplined armies of the world.

The Navy did, however, have a time-honoured system, going back at least to seventeenth century, by which the common seaman, the 'tarpaulin', could become an officer. The British Army had no such custom, although a non-commissioned officer was occasionally, in wartime, commissioned for merit or for gallantry in the field. The route in the Navy was the long steep climb through the ratings from ordinary, able and leading seaman to petty officer and then to warrant officer; thence to commissioned warrant officer, and thence for a very few to lieutenant. After the normal eight years as a lieutenant, if he had not retired, he would become a lieutenant commander, the equivalent of a major in the Army. It is true that in the Army a man could follow a similar route and be commissioned as a lieutenant as quartermaster; but in the Navy the route was open to a much larger number, and any role was open to a lieutenant. A lieutenant commander was quite likely to get a seagoing command, at least in wartime. A second route had been established shortly before the war, in order to pick out the ablest ratings without obliging them to go through the mill of fifteen or twenty years of service before they even became warrant officers: they were known (from the old aristocracy of the lower deck) as upper yardsmen.

The criteria for manning the ship – deciding its 'complement' – were to consider precisely what expertise was required to work the whole ship at action stations, including of course the maintenance and repair of equipment, and then to add a modest margin to allow for accidents; and to take into account that it had to be possible to operate the ship, although not at action stations, in two watches, because the crew could not be expected to carry on indefinitely working twenty-four hours a day. 'Two watches' meant that there was one crew on duty and another off duty, but it did not involve duplicating every skilled role.

The twenty-four hour day was measured in watches of four hours each, except that the dog watches, between 4 p.m. and 8 p.m., lasted only two hours each, which enabled the time on duty to be alternated each day. The middle watch was from midnight to 4 a.m., followed by the morning (4 to 8), forenoon (8 to 12), afternoon (12 to 4), then the dog watches and the first watch from 8 p.m. until midnight. Each watch was subdivided into half hours, still known by the number of bells which marked them: thus seven bells in the forenoon watch was 11.30 a.m. The ship's bell was still used to mark them in harbour, and the routine orders which accompanied them were conveyed by bugle calls. The 'Tannoy' – the 'public address system' as it would be described nowadays – still relayed the bugle calls in big ships, but not everybody could identify them.

The twelve-hour working day on watch, which working in two watches entailed, was a hard one, because routine work had to be fitted in as well. The art, quickly acquired, was to sleep soundly for at least three hours out of four when not on watch or involved in routine work; and on top of that to cat-nap for ten minutes whenever an opportunity occurred. The captain had no such leisure: he had a bunk in a cubby hole below the bridge, known as the captain's sea cabin, and would give orders to the officer on watch to wake him if any ship was sighted or if any event occurred. Captains became extraordinarily adept at waking in a second or two, taking in the situation, giving orders and then, if there was no immediate problem, at once going to sleep again. Another remarkable quality which had been acquired by practice by regular officers was their acute eyesight which enabled them to see distant objects in a poor light before anybody else could, and also to see detail such as a ship's name or pendants before others could do so. This was a matter

The Navy, 1943-45

of effort and practice and almost anyone could improve their ability over the course of time. In the same way we soon got used to being on duty for the middle watch one night and the morning watch the next, with the day split into four-hour slices.

A new ship was commissioned with a complete crew at either Devonport or Portsmouth or Chatham, all of which had large barracks in their dockyards, and a peacetime commission would normally last for about three years. The ship then returned to its home port flying the 'paying-off pendant', a slim streamer of bunting theoretically and traditionally one-and-a-half times the length of the ship. The crew were paid off and the ship was refitted and modified, ready for its next commission with a new captain and a new crew. Even in peacetime the length of a commission depended on the 'exigencies of the Service', and in wartime there was no question of sticking to a fixed period: in fact re-commissioning more or less went by the board. A slow turnover in the crew therefore went on all the time: for instance, skilled men might be required to fill gaps in other ships, and when anyone was promoted they would move to a new berth. Ships required a boiler-clean taking three or four days every few months, and would need to enter a well-equipped dockyard for an overhaul and a refit from time to time, perhaps once a year or eighteen months. A prime need was to fit the latest modifications in weaponry: it seems extraordinary in the twenty-first century when new weapons take years and indeed decades to build, that improvements were coming in week after week during the war: new radar sets, for instance, or new gun-mountings and control systems. A refit might take several weeks, a good chance for shore leave and an obvious opportunity for making changes in the crew. As it happened I joined *Relentless* more than a year after she had been commissioned and there had already been many changes in the original crew: the captain, Lieutenant Commander George Barstow, RN, being amongst them. He had been 'rested' from a sea-going appointment by becoming a divisional officer at the *King Alfred*, and he was kind enough to offer to take me with him as a midshipman when he returned to sea as the captain of a fleet destroyer.

Thus, paying off had ceased to mean very much, but when the war came to an end the ships which had been longest in commission in distant parts of the globe tended to be sent home first, with the result that I found myself back in Britain a few months after VJ Day, fresh from the dry heat of the East Indian Fleet (we had happened to be the first Allied warship to enter Singapore after the Japanese surrender), steaming gingerly into Chatham on a foggy November evening worthy of Charles Dickens.

Second in command was the first lieutenant, an experienced officer responsible for much of the day-to-day running of the ship, and then there were perhaps three or four other executive officers, lieutenants or sub-lieutenants who had achieved a watch-keeping certificate (granted at a captain's discretion) and were thus qualified to take charge on the bridge of the ship at sea. At least one other officer, and preferably two, had to be on watch to assist the officer of the watch, whether lieutenants, sub-lieutenants, warrant officers or midshipmen, which means that in total about nine or ten executive officers were needed. Depending on various circumstances, the guns or the torpedoes might be under the supervision of a warrant officer (the gunner or the torpedo gunner) or of a chief petty officer (the gunner's mate or the torpedo gunner's mate). There was always an engineer officer (a lieutenant or a warrant engineer) and the mixture of sub-lieutenants and midshipmen varied from ship to ship. Each flotilla of eight ships or, if it was operating separately, each half-flotilla, would have a doctor, a surgeon-lieutenant, who would serve in any ship which had room for him, and each flotilla would also have a chaplain. Unlike the Army, the Navy did not confer a rank on a chaplain. He was an officer, and that was that.

Apart from the captain's cabin there would normally be three double cabins forrard, or two doubles with a single for the first lieutenant; and two double cabins aft. Occasionally there might not be room in a cabin for a midshipman, in which case he would have to find a space in the officers' quarters to sling his hammock; in harbour he could enjoy the luxury of the bunk in the captain's sea cabin.

The wardroom was the officers' dining and sitting room but you had to be careful what you said there: it was drummed into us to 'remember the wardroom hatch' through which any injudicious remark would be relayed around the ship by a steward. There was strictly no alcohol drunk at sea, but rather more than was reasonable when the ship was in harbour. Only the wardroom had alcohol: except for the daily tot of rum, neat for the petty officers but diluted as grog for the lower ratings.

The main work of an officer at sea was watch-keeping: four hours

The Navy, 1943-45

on the bridge and four hours off in two watches and, when things were quiet, four hours on and eight hours off in three watches; but there were also a host of other jobs which had to be shared – or, rather, allocated by the captain. The officer of the watch would normally have two other officers to share the duties on the bridge as he thought best. They took turns to control the ship, giving orders to the helmsman and the engine room, playing a part with the navigation (there was a charthouse just below the bridge), keeping bearings and distances of ships in company, giving orders for signals, supervising the lookouts and the ASDIC operator and above all keeping a lookout themselves with binoculars. When keeping station by night there was a very strictly enforced blackout, for even a cigarette could be seen a mile away, and all ships followed a zig-zag course to make them difficult targets for torpedoes.

Orders were given by the senior ship to follow one pattern from a book of zig-zag diagrams, entailing alterations of course of perhaps twenty or thirty degrees every few minutes. Apart from anything else, an accurate stop-watch was essential. Naval binoculars were of superb quality and one hoped to be able to detect the actual moment at which the ship we were escorting – perhaps an aircraft carrier or a troopship – put on its helm, mainly by watching its bow-wave and wake. Adding or subtracting a few revolutions on the engines, or adjusting our course until were on exactly the right bearing before the next turn was due, were quite wearing tasks, and a subject of prayer in a heavy sea with poor visibility.

The crew were divided into 'parts of ship', a traditional but artificial system (probably four in a destroyer: focsle, quarterdeck, foretop and maintop) mainly in order that every member of the crew could have a divisional officer who had a rather mixed bunch of responsibilities. The most visible were his appearance in command of his division at the Sunday parade when in harbour which was actually known as 'Divisions', and as the representative of any rating who might appear at Defaulters, the captain's court at which miscreants were paraded one by one in front of him and meted out standard penalties for all the common offences, mostly consisting of loss of pay and loss of leave. The coxswain stood at the captain's side whilst each defaulter removed his headdress and, if the offence was not denied, was 'scaled', losing a specified amount of pay and leave for each hour he had been 'adrift' in returning to duty (the watch not on duty always had a night ashore in harbour, having to be back on board at 8 a.m.). Disciplinary offences were dealt with by 'Jankers' which stopped leave and imposed extra work of as unpleasant a nature as could be devised, plus doubling around carrying a rifle above one's head under the command of a petty officer. More seriously, a man might be given a few days in cells, which for small ships were on shore, but the worst offences were handed up to a higher authority and tried with full procedures, a rare event. Divisional officers were also expected to help with compassionate problems and in general to try to help ratings in awkward situations to deal with them.

The executive officers also had to act as navigation, signals, gunnery and torpedo officer and to supervise other departments for which various degrees of expert knowledge, experience and responsibility were required. In most cases petty officers could be relied on for the necessary technical knowledge, and of course for their experience and good judgement. There had to be a focsle officer responsible for the working of the anchors and cables and for the sometimes alarming handling of the coils of flexible steel wire rope. If the captain went alongside a jetty in too jaunty a fashion it was the focsle officer's fault if the ship's side was dunched, but it was also his fault if the wire snapped, which could cause serious injury. The quarterdeck officer had a similar but much less exacting role.

There was a writer to administer the ship's office, but he had to be supervised by the captain's secretary, who was merely an officer considered to be at least semi-literate and told off to do the job. The main task was paying the ship's company, once a week in harbour but inevitably less regularly when we were at sea; 220 men paraded in front of this officer at his desk waiting for their names to be called by the coxswain, each removing his hat for a wodge of rupee notes to be placed in it, which he acknowledged loudly with the one word 'Sir'. There seemed to be almost as many rates of pay and allowances as there were ratings, but with repeated checking not many mistakes were made. Each man's conduct sheet (printed on linen, designed to last his full time in the Service) also had to be kept. When he left the ship, in ninety-nine out of a hundred cases, his report consisted simply of the two magic symbols assessing his conduct and performance: 'VG. Sat'.

One of the most tiresome minor jobs was to be confidential book officer, responsible for two weighted sacksful of secret books ready to throw overboard, kept in a hefty safe, one of the sacks containing the

The Navy, 1943–45

code books. The ordinary codes for routine signals from the Admiralty depended on a new page every day to decode simple messages giving information, for instance, about all the ships known to be in the area. The more secret codes depended on a similar system with an additional hurdle consisting of a plastic board with slots in it through which only some of the numbers on a paper sheet inserted into it were visible, and a third hurdle varying the position of the paper sheet. This took some minutes to set up. The telegraphist on duty took down the Morse code and an officer translated it into plain language. It was a tedious job, done by any officer not otherwise employed, and by the time you had finished all you got was a list of ships' call signs, which themselves then had to be looked up, with their latitude and longitude at a given time, and possibly their destination. The telegraphists became extraordinarily adept, many of them being able to read a book whilst writing down the translation of the Morse code heard through their earphones, so it was essential not to use a fountain pen which might run out of ink. They could identify the sender in many cases by his style, that is to say his individual rhythm of dots and dashes, as one can identify individuals' handwriting.

Various confidential books would be needed by officers fairly regularly and had to be signed for, but trying to keep track of them was a chore one could have done without in the face of spectral courts of inquiry about missing books.

The officers in *Relentless* were as mixed a bunch as you could hope to see, especially in a small ship. George Barstow, the captain, was the model of a 'Pusser' officer, Dartmouth-trained from the age of thirteen, who had done two or three years as a midshipman in a big ship, a year or two as a sub-lieutenant and then the statutory eight years as a lieutenant, the last four in small ships during the war, before promotion to a 'two-and-a-half' with the chance of a command. He never made a bad decision and, knowing more about his job than anybody else, he was respected by all.

The first lieutenant when I joined was an RNR officer, a rare bird, who had learnt his trade in the Merchant Navy: another true professional, and a man of sound judgement. He was replaced by a South African lieutenant when we refitted at Simonstown, the Royal Navy's base near Cape Town, where there was precisely space for two fleet destroyers alongside one another in one of the two dry docks which had been built each to take a ship of the line, a battleship of the Nelson era. This South African was a nice enough fellow and an adequate officer of the watch, but he had poor judgement and was not up to the job of first lieutenant. We also picked up a South African sub-lieutenant there, a vulgar repulsive man who was not fit to be an officer at all. Although there were many admirable British settlers in South Africa, nearly all of them farmers, the lifestyle tended to attract the kind of British rating who wanted to kick the natives around, but hadn't a hope of kicking anyone around – rather the other way about – in Britain. The policy of apartheid was not spelt out until many years later when the Boers got a majority in the South African Parliament, but it was already in place in Cape Town with separate park benches and buses for whites and non-whites and, although the negroes on farms were well treated, the non-whites in cities were mostly 'coloureds', many of whose predecessors had been Indian indentured labourers, and people of mixed race who lived in grim shanty towns, some of them within the city. I swore I would never go back to South Africa, and I never have.

Another lieutenant was a pleasant and reliable Englishman called Lockwood, but he and I and the warrant engineer were the only British executive officers. The Engineer was one of those venerable men probably nearly forty years of age who had come up the hard way, well qualified and respected, who knew how to get the best of life. Three sub-lieutenants were an Australian regular, a splendid New Zealand RNVR officer in Laurie Smith, who became a doctor after the war and with whom I have kept in touch spasmodically ever since; and Oliver Burd who was Canadian, but being an orphan came to Britain and joined the RN. He was my closest friend and we spent many hours putting the world to rights. He was a radical and something of a loner and sadly he was burnt to death a few years after the war in a hut at an Antarctic base, where he was a member of an expedition. The doctor was an agreeable junior doctor who had had the usual short training course in the Navy to help him in his role of having to deal with every kind of medical problem in four destroyers, including surgery when necessary. When he left for another job the sick bay attendant, with a nurse's training, was in charge. A chaplain replaced him, Charles Richardson, doing a difficult job in a small ship as well as could be expected, and I was sometimes the sole member of his congregation at his Communion service. Many years later when he was a vicar in Yorkshire he asked me to become his son's godfather. The warrant engineer was replaced by Lieutenant (E) Kevin Walton, an ingenious and

The Navy, 1943–45

companionable wartime officer who had been awarded the DSC for controlling and extinguishing the fires in HMS *Onslow* when she was severely damaged, and who was to receive the very rare Albert Medal (later exchanged for the George Cross) after the war when he (like Oliver Burd) was in the Antarctic and carried out a remarkable rescue of a companion trapped in a crevasse. I kept up with him sporadically until he died in his late eighties, still inventing a gadget on his deathbed.

The coxswain was the senior chief petty officer, responsible in a general way for discipline rather like the regimental sergeant major in the Army (big ships had a master at arms specifically in charge of discipline). The other chief petty officers were the gunner's mate, the torpedo gunner's mate, and the chief engine room artificer (there might be two of them). There might be a stoker CPO, but more probably a petty officer was in charge of that small department responsible for the boilers, and there was a yeoman of signals (the signals petty officer) and a cook. They had their own messes (one forrard, one aft) but all the other ratings lived on the messdecks.

The leading hands included specialists – gunners, torpedomen, electricians, telegraphists, signalmen, stewards, cooks, the writer and the sick bay attendant, stokers (the stokers had their own mess – just a table and two 'stools' with pots and pans like every other mess); but some of the leading hands were just seamen who could turn their hands to many jobs – four of them would be captains of guns, for instance. The remainder of the crew were able seamen (with perhaps the odd ordinary seaman, still learning the ropes). They could be expected to turn their hands to all the simple jobs, manning the guns and the depth charges, acting as lookouts, making up boats' crews, and so forth.

Spare time was 'piped' (all orders were preceded by the sound of the bosun's call) as 'Hands to make and mend clothes' and most of the hands could indeed manage a needle and thread for repairs, but there was almost always somebody who was handy with a sewing machine; and someone who could cut hair, even if with unsophisticated results. The cooks in the galley prepared the basic food (with a predominance of stews, whatever their title) and baked the bread, but other food was doled out raw and many seamen were good at making the best of it, especially in making a dough, pronounced 'duff', which meant any kind of pudding that could be devised from the ingredients, although almost every 'duff' in practice tended towards raisins encapsulated in

The Navy, 1943–45

pastry. The spice of life in a destroyer lay in the mixture of skills, aptitudes, backgrounds and personalities, assumptions, attitudes and accents, English, Welsh, Scottish and Irish, Australian, New Zealander, Canadian, South African, which made it an organic institution. The Navy knew, by long experience, how to mould them into a unit with a single objective. Even nicknames were standardised in the Navy.

4
Post-War Oxford

After the First World War the armed services released all those who wished to re-enter civilian life immediately after the armistice, resulting in high unemployment. The lesson was learnt, and after the Second War the system was first in, first out: everybody had a class number according to their length of service, and I remained in the Navy until October 1946 when I was given a place at Oxford on the basis of my school results in the then equivalent of A Levels plus a letter from my housemaster. This enabled me to get a slightly accelerated release and to become a commoner of Christ Church, Oxford for the Michaelmas term to read Modern History.

The universities were willing to expand immediately in order to cope with six years of backlog. A few people had done a shortened wartime course of two terms, arranged as being better than nothing (which just about sums them up), and a few school leavers unfit for military service had embarked on normal degree courses, but most people had joined the forces straight from school. They now descended on the universities, including those who had begun but not completed their degrees before the war. I thus joined a college with undergraduates aged between about twenty-six and eighteen, but the latter were still only those unfit for service because conscription was still in force and most eighteen-year-olds had to join the armed services for two years. Thus almost all the undergraduates had some experience of war service, and one or two of the older ones had been lieutenant colonels (and one or two of the dons, unsuited to a military role, had been mere privates or corporals). The colleges deserved great credit for their flexibility, and managed to fit people in by the sharing of rooms and by a higher than usual proportion living out of college in 'digs'.

The comparative maturity of the undergraduates and the kind of experience they had acquired made this a uniquely interesting time to be at Oxford, for which I am grateful. Some people seemed to be able to take up their academic work where they had left off, and allowances were made for others who found it hard to re-establish themselves.

Personally I found that the art of writing essays had deserted me, and I used to unfold and read the essays I had written at school with something like despair. I now suppose that I was suffering from some form of writer's block: it was an odd sensation but it had to be put up with. My facility started to return gradually two or three years after I had left Oxford: it came back as inexplicably as it began, but lots of people had worse problems to cope with and everybody was accustomed to making the best of things.

Most of us worked quite hard, and it was an odd sensation to be in the company of approximately the top two or three per cent academically, although there were a few who had crept in with very modest credentials for one reason or another. The majority were from public schools but there were plenty from grammar schools because, as well as being able to compete for the open scholarships which were part of the endowments of every college, everybody was now supported with government money to pay the college's fees. This money did not fund any other expenses but there were state scholarships to fill the gap. The lack of things for money to buy was a useful leveller. One of two rich undergraduates had contrived to buy a Jaguar or a Bristol (the first Bristols appeared in 1946), but they were a very small race apart, even in a smart college like Christ Church.

Christ Church was indeed the grandest of the Oxford colleges, or so we believed, with few dissenters. Founded by Cardinal Wolsey, it had been taken on by Henry VIII after Wolsey's execution, and included the cathedral of the new diocese of Oxford as its college chapel, the head of the college being the Dean. The canons were dons, mostly professors, only a handful of them rather than the hundred originally envisaged. The Governing Body (every college was required to have one of these new-fangled institutions as a result of the reforms of the 1860s, masterminded by Gladstone, himself a Christ Church man, and by Lord John Russell) consisted of the Dean and canons (the Chapter) and all the established dons, who were, and still are, oddly called Students. It would be difficult to imagine a more complacent and amateurish group of people to manage the college, much of their energy being expended on petty internal disputes and miniature empire-building. Meanwhile they were happy to let the Government pay, using the vast college endowments to maintain the buildings and the style of a permanent grand country house-party. Thus over the post-war years the independence of the universities slipped away, for he who pays the piper calls the tune. It was not until the time of Margaret Thatcher that this comfortable world was shaken. Ironically, she discovered exactly the problems which Gladstone (one of the few other prime ministers with a family background in trade) had been set to solve. All or almost all the members of the Governing Bodies of all the colleges, including most of the dons and many of the professors, were irremovable regardless of their competence; and although it is fair to add that they were without exception appointed on merit and not by patronage, they could if so inclined contrive – especially as they became senior – to get away with doing very little.

The Christ Church dons, in spite of this extraordinary complacency, were clever, congenial, interesting to meet and in many cases excellent company. Their teaching was conscientious, often stimulating and sometimes brilliant, but on the other hand it was amateurish. It was handed down in a rather offhand kind of way, with little thought or understanding about the needs of their pupils. There were a few exceptions – in the History department only Steven Watson approached his teaching professionally – but there were also a few eccentrics whose contribution to learning – their own and anyone else's – was wayward to put it mildly.

Oxford's most important quality was its liberalism: the almost universal toleration of every point of view, opinion, theory and belief. Toleration if it is the rule rather than the exception carries with it respect; not exactly respect for views opposite to one's own, but respect for the right of people to hold those views without being hounded or ridiculed. Oxford was a hotbed of argument, and there are few more effective weapons of argument than ridicule or indeed than satire, that more delicate but sharper knife; both of which were freely called upon, but seldom viciously. It was this tolerance which liberated, and indeed transformed, many undergraduates, for schools are not on the whole liberal institutions. The better schools tolerate eccentricity, and in purely academic work in sixth forms there is a degree of liberalism; but people who hold minority views and in many cases simply independent views, or who express their views in unusual ways, are not on the whole looked upon kindly, either by the regime or by their contemporaries. As to the armed forces, they are the least tolerant institutions one can imagine. I remember a petty officer who was challenged when instructing a class responding to an interruption: 'Give the correct answer, right or wrong.'

Post-War Oxford

The downside of this liberal atmosphere was the tendency for life to be a bit too easy-going. There were a few rules about dining in Hall a given number of evenings and not being out of college after a certain hour; and no doubt one was expected to turn up for one's tutorials, and if this was not officially stated the reason was presumably because common sense dictated it; and no doubt, too, allowances were made for the maturity of the undergraduates. But what was missing was the 'zip' which was such an important part of school life and of life in the Navy. There was virtually no routine. I suppose the reasons were that there was almost no hierarchy and no competition, and that the college as a whole had only the vaguest objectives, which nobody would have dreamed of enunciating. Whatever the reasons, I found this lack of structure rather debilitating, whereas I suppose others found the opposite.

The social life, in the broad as well as the narrower sense, was lively and stimulating. The point of a university is that all kinds of subjects can be and are debated, and whilst the contribution of the teachers is important, what matters most is that the undergraduates educate each other. The (almost) unique advantage of Oxford and Cambridge is their collegiate system in which several hundred students live together in institutions uncommonly like the monasteries which preceded them – even if uncommonly unlike them in certain important respects. Nobody has improved, except in matters of detail, on the architectural layout of the monastery, above all on the quadrangle in which people circulate freely. The splendid rooms in Peckwater Quad were more akin to Chatsworth or Blenheim than they were to a monastic cell, and the only reminder of Tom Quad's original purpose as the living quarters for one hundred canons was the residual framework of the cloister which was never built. Nevertheless there was nothing easier than to wander round these superb student hostels to meet and chat to one's fellow undergraduates. Over the course of three years one could learn about and experience almost any branch of culture which interested one. For example, I liked classical music, but it had nothing to do with my subject of study, nor was my interest in it academic. Within the college there were dozens of people who liked music, with every imaginable degree of taste and expertise. The long-playing record was replacing the old '78' and sound reproduction was improving rapidly. Like most of my friends, my taste tended towards the centre ground, but by the time I went down I had quite a good knowledge of European (especially, I

Post-War Oxford

admit, German) orchestral (mainly) music of the seventeenth to the nineteenth centuries, with at least some appreciation also of medieval and Renaissance composers. Jazz was an important cult, but there was no pop music in the modern sense until the Sixties.

Every kind of subject was discussed and conclusions – or opinions – unsustained by logic or evidence were soon demolished; although prejudice was regarded as a respectable feature of a free society and views which would be regarded as outrageous nowadays, including many which cannot legally be stated in public, were accepted as the price of freedom. Libraries were magnificent and it was not too difficult to get access to some which might have been held as sacred – for instance the Codrington, the library of the rarefied and generally inaccessible All Souls College which had (and has) no undergraduates. In spite of its huge number of volumes the library was spacious and, with its marble floor, even echoing. As Dr Johnson said, 'If a man would prance as he reads, let him read at the Codrington.'

One could attend as many, or as few, lectures as one chose, and listen to dons whose current research had not yet been published, but most people chose the star turns of scintillating speakers well stocked with wit and satire and paradox – for instance A. J. P. Taylor of Magdalen on modern German history. Hugh Trevor-Roper on the seventeenth century and Keith Feiling on the eighteenth were others who attracted large audiences. Canon Jenkins had an audience of one for a course on theology, and on the only occasion when that one faithful student turned up late he found Jenkins unabashed lecturing to an empty room.

We were fortunate at Christ Church in having a trio of wonderfully stimulating Modern History dons in Hugh Trevor-Roper, Charles Stuart and Steven Watson. Steven was married and lived out of college, and his approach as I have already mentioned was much more professional than that of the others. He was a prolific editor of published constitutional documents and towards the end of his Oxford career he took up the formidable task – from which several predecessors had chickened out – of writing the volume of the Oxford History of England on the Reign of George III. Charles Stuart, a specialist on that period, published almost nothing throughout his long tenure as a typical rather old-fashioned sort of college don – attentive and conscientious over his pupils, much liked and respected by them, the very image of timidity until he opened his mouth.

Hugh Trevor-Roper was a brilliant but mischievous man already notorious for the delight he took in making ruthless attacks on colleagues. Admittedly Oxford was a rough sea for those who risked publishing careless work, and obviously university life depended on unsustainable conclusions being criticised and challenged. But the trouble with Trevor-Roper was that he did it for fun, and he did it ruthlessly with the objective of destroying those who were unfortunate enough to be picked upon. He was, in the shorthand of the day, a full-time professional shit. He never grew up (or at least not until he was old enough to be harmless) and there were a lot of wounded waiting in the wings for him to make a fool of himself – which he notoriously did by pronouncing the forged Hitler diaries to be genuine. The whole story of a plane crash and a single, or at least a single literate, survivor; and a huge pile of the Führer's diaries lying for decades hidden in a hay barn: it was all just so wildly unlikely that it is incredible that Hugh pronounced them genuine, one of his main reasons being that there were so many volumes that they were unlikely to have been forged, exactly the opposite of a more sensible approach. Admittedly he soon started to suffer from doubts. But he had made an idiotic mistake and there were people who did not intend to let him forget it. Then as he neared retirement he accepted the Mastership of Peterhouse, Cambridge, without taking the slightest trouble to find out what it entailed, with resulting years of discontent for himself and (perhaps more importantly) for the college.

Hugh used to run campaigns to get people selected for this or that, whether or not his victims wished to enlist his support. His most successful was to get himself appointed as Regius Professor of Modern History, one of the absolutely top plum jobs in the academic world. Being strait-laced, I was surprised, and deplored his success, but I admit with hindsight that it was a good appointment in view of Hugh's scholarship and his style, and also, even if in a rather selective field, his reforming zeal. He was later made a life peer by Margaret Thatcher: it dismayed me that such an irresponsible man could be so elevated. His campaign to get the Regius Professorship is well documented, but nobody has admitted knowing why he was made a peer. The answer I am sure must be that he was recommended by Robert Blake, who had been made a peer a few years earlier as the historian of Conservatism. He was the biographer of Disraeli, although as he proceeded with his task he became increasingly critical of his subject and more and more an admirer of Gladstone. Indeed he chaired the committee which oversaw the editing of the Gladstone Diaries for the Oxford University

Press, found Colin Matthew to do the job and persuaded Christ Church to take Colin on and give him Gladstone's rooms in the College, in Canterbury Quad, as his office.

Robert became a pillar of the Establishment, Master of Queen's College, scholarly, orthodox, urbane, charming and far from politically naïve. But in my day he was a young don at Christ Church, a historian although actually a member of the PPE (Politics, Philosophy and Economics) rather than the History faculty, teaching nineteenth-century history. He was a close friend of Hugh Trevor-Roper, but he seemed to be a steadying and indeed a restraining influence. That does not now appear to have been the case. It is clear from Hugh's biography by Adam Sisman that Robert was very much one of the mischievous gang of three together with Charles Stuart.

The other side of Hugh Trevor-Roper was very different. He was an outstandingly gifted historian and an inspiring tutor. He was witty, charming and excellent company for undergraduates, and above all he was generous in his judgements and never cruel or malicious. We did live in awe of his intellect, but he took us to pieces in a civilised way and he made the study of history an exciting field of discovery. He exuded originality and enthusiasm without being pompous or domineering and there are generations of his pupils who still value his friendship and the trouble he took to help them, without apparently forming the same harsh judgements of his personality as I have done. He gave some one-to-one or at least one-to-two tutorials and listened patiently to inadequate attempts at essays, making his comments gently and economically but with such vivid clarity that I remember them with gratitude to this day. Most of his teaching in college was in small seminars of about four undergraduates, and they worked well. More than anyone else he was the life and soul of the college, already famous for his life of Archbishop Laud written almost when still an undergraduate and, topically, for his best-selling *The Last Days of Hitler*, which established conclusively that the Führer was dead. He was rather childish in a harmless way in leaving his Bentley, purchased with the profits, parked in the college for all to admire, and his jurisdiction as Senior Censor was summary, severe and sometimes unjust, but nobody minded this because they were accustomed to worse.

Hugh never wrote another long book, for which as his life went on he was often criticised. But his reputation as one of the master historians of his day, with strong claims to be the supremo, continue to grow as the years roll by, his forte being the long essay. His unfinished work (one of his worst shortcomings was turning to new enthusiasms before the task in hand was complete) is now being published, edited by disciples. There is a wonderful volume of essays under the title *History and the Enlightenment* (he became more and more a historiographer) and the fascinating scholarly *The Invention of Scotland*. The title is apt enough but I do not think he would actually have used it, because this is not, as one might expect, a mischievously destructive book but a thorough investigation of the myths and forgeries, and in some cases the pure invention, of much that has passed as history in the Kingdom of North Britain for which Hugh had much respect and affection. The reason why Hugh did not publish it, though not admitted either by his biographer or by the editor of the book itself, is simple enough: it deals at enormous length with the forgery of Ossian, regarded by many Scots as the cornerstone of their ancient culture. This is a long and interesting story of failure to spot a forgery. How could Hugh, who had failed to spot the forgery of the Hitler diaries, publish such a book without inviting ridicule? He had made plenty of enemies who would have been only too delighted to join in the fun.

Those of us who read History at Christ Church were fortunate indeed to learn from Hugh, from Charles Stuart, from Steven Watson and from Robert Blake. There were stimulating dons in other subjects, and there were scholarly men seldom if ever seen, perhaps glimpsed skittering across the quad after emerging from behind their oaks, the massive doors of every room enforcing privacy when it was desired. There were eccentric lazy men like the one who taught law, and men so shy that even if sociable they never expected to speak; and a couple of duds in Canon Jenkins and in a repulsive ancient classicist called Dundas who regarded himself as a sort of father figure to help the undergraduates. There were two sorts of Classics dons, the Mods dons who taught the first year of linguistic study, known as Classical Moderations, and the others who taught the philosophy and the ancient history which came afterwards and led to the Final Examination. Dundas, one of the former type, although unwholesomely fascinated by the beauty of the male human figure (preferably nude), had little idea beyond this of what the Classics are about. He was one of the last of that odd Victorian type, half cultivated intellectual and half philistine, who regarded the Greek and Latin languages as the playthings of a puzzle-solving mind (often called a crossword-puzzle mind during the nineteenth and twentieth centuries). An element of this philistinism was often a desire to excel at games (now called sport) and it was this aspect which invented the English amateur, seeking perfection but within the bounds of gentlemanly behaviour, and above all not for money. There were some Oxford and Cambridge dons with this characteristic, including J. C. Masterman, who played tennis with the grandest of the grand, and left Christ Church after my first year to become Provost of Worcester College, the fixer, the kingmaker, half culture, half not. But they were more numerous as masters in the public schools, perfecting cricket and lawn tennis and soccer and rowing and fishing the dry fly, and the use of the 12-bore shotgun. Wonderful athletes, full of ingenuity, craftsmen and indeed artists at their recreations, the inventors of sportsmanship and fair play and of what is and what isn't cricket. They can be traced right back to the mid-Victorian era and the best account of them is in Noel Annan's book, *The Dons*.

The Modern History syllabus was formidable, as was no doubt the case with other subjects. It covered the whole of English history from the beginning (which was the Romans) to the present day and a good deal of modern European history; English constitutional documents, the *Politics* of Aristotle, a special subject which involved the use of original sources (i.e. documents rather than textbooks), and translation from Latin. The technique for coping with the vast field of English history was to decide which periods interested one and to read very carefully selected textbooks to cover the periods which could not be studied in detail. We never had any guidance on this or any other technique from our tutors. Whether others found the same I'm not sure. Perhaps it was just part of an Oxford mentality (or philosophy) of sink or swim.

On most days of the week, except when trying to complete an essay, the serious work was over by teatime, and the college had all the appropriate clubs to enable us to take some physical exercise in a more or less competitive framework if we wished to do so. My father had surprised me by saying I should very likely make many of my friends in the Boat Club if I chose to row, which for me was a natural choice following my enjoyment of the sport at school. I had not reckoned on the fact that all the members of the Boat Club, and every similar organisation, were highly intelligent, and that they had a wide range of interests. The benefits of taking part in sport were therefore wider than they had been at school, and at the same time provided fresh air and exercise and the competitive atmosphere which was otherwise lacking, and which suited me well. Admittedly there was a certain amount of heartiness too (particularly in the rugger club) but it was confined to appropriate occasions and was not oppressive.

At the other end of the scale was the Warrigals' Club, devoted to playing village cricket. Village cricket is no longer known in England, its successor being club cricket even if sometimes not very skilfully played. Village cricket was different, with daisies and dandelions on the pitch controlling the spin of the ball, and an unmown outfield. Since a ball would not reach the boundary along the ground, any ambitious shot had to be airborne, and it was not done to play defensively. These were the days of gamesmanship but there was no gamesmanship about village cricket, and probably only two or three players owned pads, most batsmen having to make do with one pad, surreptitiously borrowed in the changing room – in which of course there were no showers. The yokel, the blacksmith and the cobbler played alongside the doctor, the parson and the squire. All repaired to the pub for a pint of beer after the game. Television put an end to village cricket, because it made it possible for those who had no access to coaching (partly because cricket is such a difficult game that competent coaches have always been in short supply); or to watch matches at their county ground to see how an off drive, or even a late cut, could be played. The television set became the cricket coach, and as it happened the value of the farmer's grass declined after the post-war years, and lawn mowers, powered by petrol engines large enough for a 1930s car, enabled the outfield to be shorn.

We took our rowing seriously and aimed to improve our performance in a sophisticated way, although a few college crews were made up with a minimum of training to enjoy themselves during Eights Week. There were bumping races in the Lent and summer terms, and university competitions between colleges for coxless fours (the champagne of rowing) and pairs and single sculls. Any coaches we could get hold of were amateurs, but their efforts were bolstered by George Harris the Boatman, a master boatbuilder with his own business on the Isis and a skilful professional sculler. Christ Church had its own boathouse because the college owned the Meadow which included the river bank. Some other colleges had shared boathouses but the majority still relied on barges, picturesque but inconvenient. The University Boathouse was on the opposite bank, but in fact most of the university rowing happened elsewhere.

Vincent's Club was a sort of semi-official forum for university sport. Its members were those who had been awarded Blues, with a limited supporting cast from the second rank of athletic prowess. The premises were quite poky, and it was said that the whole of Vincent's would have fitted into the lavatories at the Pitt, the club's opposite number at Cambridge. In a typically English anomalous way, however, it was actually Hawkes at Cambridge and not the Pitt which performed the same function at the 'other university' in relation to sport. The people who played cricket and rugby for the university included an undue proportion of Rhodes Scholars from Canada, Australia, New Zealand and South Africa. Together with the native players, mostly public school boys, some of them would get international caps or at least play first-class cricket for their counties as amateurs, still sharply divided from professionals. Athletics were in good shape, with Roger Bannister achieving the world's first four-minute mile on the Iffley ground and Christopher Chataway not far behind him. But for the great majority games were strictly recreational and, on the whole, pursued in Oxford's easy-going manner. Christ Church and Trinity had their own packs of beagles. Rural Oxfordshire in those days was still a brown country during the autumn and winter months, displaying a wonderfully rich range of colour rather than the endless dull greens of modern agriculture, giving a now vanished delight to an occasional afternoon following the beagles – at a respectful distance and without expending undue effort crossing the numerous ploughed fields.

The main activities of the evenings were drinking and conversation, the standard of the latter varying inversely as the volume of the former, for Oxford was a man's world with only a handful of women's colleges. Besides, entry to the latter was so highly competitive that the lump of single-minded scholarly ladies was unleavened by the broader spectrum of humankind in the men's colleges. A few of the older undergraduates were married, and lived out of college. But female company for the majority was largely confined to weekends when visitors would be invited perhaps for lunch at Iffley or Woodstock or men would go up to London or elsewhere to meet a friend and indulge in whatever form of recreation the wider world provided. Relationships between the sexes were much more formal than nowadays, and as nowadays many people abstained, or set themselves to do so. This is not to say that casual sex was uncommon, but on the whole it was tactfully concealed. If it resulted in pregnancy, then either marriage followed or the father was obliged to pay maintenance for the child to the mother, but the unmarried mother was still not well regarded in society and often left her home ground to bear her offspring. Extra-marital sex tended to be either premarital sex or, at the other end of the spectrum, in a brothel. Married men had affairs and mistresses as they presumably always have done, but the concept of 'partners' living together virtually as in marriage but without the commitment was almost unknown. The divorce rate had grown rapidly, and many marriages between young people, especially wartime marriages or marriages which had been ruined by the circumstances of the war, ended that way.

The clubs or societies which met in the evenings were exclusively male affairs. One of the most congenial was the Twenty Club, in which the subjects for debate were unconventional, for instance 'That Work is the Curse of the Drinking Classes'. One or two dons were always invited, and contributed to the discussions. An increasing number of dons were getting married and they lived outside the colleges. Consequently, they played a lesser part in college life, but some were invited to most of the club dinners. There was one Christ Church dining club of the kind regarded by itself as very select and by everybody else (even if they were too polite to say so) as pompous and snobbish, Loder's Club, which had its own silver and enforced some daunting initiation rites. The Chatham preserved the residue of an original serious purpose. Others were devoted to special intellectual or academic subjects.

Christ Church Hall was an impressive place to dine, with long refectory tables and backless benches, and waiters or waitresses serving the food. Indeed, undergraduates were gentlemen addressed as 'Sir' by the college servants, of whom the backbone were the scouts, each looking after a staircase of about six rooms, and doubling up as porters or waiters in Hall. The food was adequate and came within one's termly bill ('battels') anyway, so no economy was effected by finding a cheap meal elsewhere. There was also an endless round of parties varying from a few friends drinking in a room in college to elaborate club dinners, at all of which a great deal of alcohol was consumed. English cooking was totally unsophisticated, and no luxury foods of any kind were imported. For instance the only cheese you could buy was 'cheese': that is to say what passes for 'Cheddar' (in a variety of guises, as it still is); because nothing like Stilton or Cheshire cheese had been produced

Post-War Oxford

during the war and the old local cheeses were not revived until the Sixties or Seventies. English fruits and vegetables of the commonest sorts were plentiful, and oranges and bananas were imported, but the choice of ingredients and the methods of cooking were entirely different from those of the modern world. Everybody was used to this, and the company in Hall was of course congenial. One could have a drink in, or standing outside, the Buttery beforehand. Conversation was the main activity of the evenings.

Draught beer, either mild-and-bitter or bitter, was the commonest drink, drawn of course from wooden barrels kept in the cellar below at about 52 degrees Fahrenheit not by any artificial process but simply by constructing the cellar in the right place and in the right way. It was important to tap a new barrel correctly and to let it settle for the right length of time. The reputation and success of pubs in Oxford as in any other old English town depended on the brewing of the beer, often locally, and the way it was looked after, and the Buttery at Christ Church had the expertise to produce the same results. Draught lager or brown ale or Guinness or bottled beers were sometimes options but were not common. Hardly anybody drank spirits owing to the cost, mostly as the result of the duty charged by the Government. Wine, except sherry and port, was only drunk on special occasions, again because of the duty before the existence of the Common Market. Most of the wine available was French. There were no 'new world' wines from Australia, New Zealand or North or South America, and although excellent wine had been grown by the Dutch in South Africa since the eighteenth century, not much of it was exported. Cheap wine (*vin de pays*) was never exported because the duty was on strength and volume, not quality, and it would have been disgusting anyway because it did not travel nor did it keep. There were a few quirky exceptions such as Algerian red or Jugoslav 'Riesling', but most of the wine available – from wine merchants, not grocers – was an expensive luxury item. That was why it was so highly taxed: the Victorians thought that if you could afford to drink wine you could afford to pay tax on it. Fortified wines, sherry and port, were relatively much cheaper, a bottle of sherry costing £1 and of port £2 (£1 in 1947 would be £35 today), but somehow we managed to consume an impressive quantity. There were a few popular restaurants in Oxford, and they were not expensive. It had been illegal during the war to charge more than five shillings for a meal, and it took a long time to get people accustomed to paying more. Without exception only traditional English fare was on the menu. A few outlying pubs like the Bear at Woodstock or the Rose Revived or the Trout were patronised on Sundays, but only a small minority of undergraduates had cars.

The three terms lasted only eight weeks each. A very few people attended the Long Vac Term, so nearly everybody disappeared towards the end of June and did not come back until early October. This pattern, perhaps surprisingly, does not seem to have changed much today. Of course the purpose of a university is the pursuit of learning and although the undergraduates disappeared they had ample time to read undisturbed by the diversions of Oxford life. As for the dons, they had the opportunity, if so inclined, to get on with their research uninterrupted by the chore of teaching. Very few undergraduates did any paid work, and many travelled abroad, but without air travel they were mostly confined to Europe, and with a limit of £25 foreign currency (for a year) some ingenuity was required. Hotel rooms on the Continent were not expensive and as far as I am concerned we got more benefit from using local buses or hiring bicycles than we would have done by using cars. War service had taken people to far-flung parts of the world, so not everybody was keen to repeat the experience.

I was fortunate to be at Christ Church in all its magnificence, but post-war conditions acted as a great leveller between the fashionable colleges and the others. The main reason was, I think, that all or almost all of the colleges, previously so varied in size, contrived to take about 400 to 500 undergraduates, the Government subsidising both the colleges and their students. In the colleges with smaller premises, a higher proportion of undergraduates lived in 'digs', but by some means which I have never fathomed the smaller ones managed to teach almost as many undergraduates as the large ones. Perhaps this was partly due to the decline of the old college culture in which it was customary for all the dons, many of them unmarried, to live on the premises. When this obligation gradually declined, college life lost much of its old character, probably to the disadvantage of the undergraduates. The result was particularly evident in the immediate post-war years, but has surely in the longer term been beneficial to the university as a whole. Incidentally, the difference in size between the large and the small colleges was never as pronounced at Oxford as at Cambridge.

5
Eton Again

I have written at some length about Eton in the late 1930s and the early war years. I also spent the whole of the 1950s there, teaching history. The Fifties seem to be generally regarded as a time dominated by post-war problems when there was not much joy in life, yet there was much to be thankful for; and although much that was perceived as 'out-of-date' was to be swept away in the Sixties, I look back on the Fifties as one of the most stable in British history, a law-abiding period of which we have never since seen the like, and a period of full employment without much social and economic discontent. At Eton the decade was one of gentle, not radical, reform.

It was not necessary to lock one's front door, or the door of one's car if one had one. Throughout Britain alcoholism and alcohol abuse in general reached an all-time low. There was not much money about nor much prospect of making a fortune, and consequently almost no fraud, almost no greed and no sense that society had become too materialistic. There was still a much more rigid class structure than there is today, but the war had had a powerful levelling effect and much of the tribalism and ritual of the old regime had been softened or had disappeared altogether. Certainly there was poverty in comparison with the economic growth of the next half-century, and minorities like single mothers and homosexuals were not regarded with much sympathy, but they were not quite the victims of the strict and narrow conventions of earlier times and there was almost universal sympathy for the underprivileged and the disadvantaged.

The end of the war was greeted everywhere with relief and a longing to get back to normal. The national aim of a 'return to normalcy' was nothing like as dominating as it had been in the years after 1918; nor, *per contra*, was the expectation of a Brave New World. There was, however, much more of an acceptance than in 1918 that things had changed and were going to continue to change. The Conservatives were rejected in 1945 because the huge number of people who had been in the armed services, almost all of them aged under about thirty-five,

Eton Again

were fed up with the artificially hierarchical life which they had tolerated for the last six years. The 1945 election was a sort of tidal wave of opinion, very different from the tidal wave of demobilisation which flooded the labour market after 1918. The idea was a massive attack on 'capitalism' (i.e. private ownership) by the nationalisation of the railways and the coalmines by the first post-war Government. Surprisingly, state capitalism in industry was soon found not to be much of an improvement. The advent of a National Health Service and an enhanced Welfare State were approved by almost everyone, greeted with almost universal approbation. People were already used to such high taxation in wartime that the cost of these benefits did not seem unaffordable. To that degree, there was a sense that a fairer and juster society was being created, and there was a feeling, perhaps mild or even muted, that a better world was emerging.

When I joined the staff at Eton in January 1951, 43 of the 89 masters had joined or rejoined the staff since the end of the war. Of the 43, 14 had been on the staff before the war. So it can be said that half the staff had changed in six years, and those who returned brought with them experiences very different from the usual ones of schoolmasters. Nevertheless, the Eton of the 1950s was not much different from Eton before the war. The head master, Robert Birley, was, however, a very different person from his predecessor Claude Elliott.

It was a common quip that nobody had ever discovered why Claude Elliott had been appointed. Uninspiring and unenthusiastic, tentative in manner and personality, he had a good academic record and proven administrative competence to recommend him: he had been awarded the OBE during the First World War for his efficiency as a civil servant (he was too deaf for the armed forces). But Robert Birley was a real schoolmaster. He had even been considered for the head mastership at the age of twenty-six, but Elliott was better qualified to enforce essential reforms of the staffing system, most notably limited tenure for housemasters and its concomitant an early retirement age, at fifty-seven.

Birley was a liberal of traditional stamp, who reverenced British institutions with a historian's mind but wanted to reform them. He came with a reputation conferred on him by the antediluvians of the Old Etonian establishment as 'Red Robert'. It was totally unjustified. Nobody of less revolutionary bent could be imagined. Birley was not a great administrator: he was carried away by his enthusiasms and his interest in individuals. Elliott never enthused or inspired a single master or a single pupil. Birley was a brilliant teacher and an inspiration to many boys and many members of his staff. Elliott's scholarship was on the record, but stone dead. Birley's recreation was to work in College Library into the small hours, always on a voyage of discovery. And he wrote long letters to individual masters, taking up suggestions they had made and discussing them as if they mattered – as indeed, even if at the expense of more important things, some of them did. His teaching, his occasional lectures and his sermons were, directly or indirectly, his response to what he had discovered. Rather than damping down the intellectual life of the school as Elliott had done, he woke it up. He wanted to appoint masters, especially in the Cinderella subjects, who would do for those subjects what he was doing for history. The result was not always productive: eccentric appointees came and went; but at least he tried, and added colour; and after all, if his appointments were failures they disappeared.

Tim Card in his history of Eton in modern times judged Elliott to have been a more effective head master than Birley, a judgement justified only by the criteria of the tombstone. It is a mistake – an all too common mistake – to judge a head master by what he did rather than by what he was.

This is a snapshot – a subjective snapshot maybe – of Eton as I saw it in the 1950s, not a history. Birley's inspiring and creative personality and his intellectual clout cannot be judged by statistics. He was a leading light and he kept the soul of Eton alive in the last decade of the *ancien régime*, before it was subjected, by slow attrition, to the whims of the neophiliacs and the straitjacket of public examinations.

Peace had returned to Britain, but not prosperity. There was a shortage of all material goods. Since there was no affluence, and professional men were still able to afford the fees, there was only one class of Etonian. Towards the end of the decade a few shiny new cars, the property of stockbrokers, began to find their way to Eton on the Fourth of June or St Andrew's Day. But for the most part there was no money to throw about for the purpose of showing off or buying friends.

History was queen. More than 40% of all specialists (i.e. in modern parlance the sixth form) were history specialists. The alternatives to history were classics, modern languages, mathematics and science, and all of these had to do four hours of history each week as the main contribution to their 'general education'. The beauty of the system was that the history specialists also had to do a modern language, French or German, and to do it properly in company with the language specialists.

This, then, was the heyday of history as the central feature of an education in the Arts, and a valuable appendage to a scientific education, too. It was also in its heyday as a university study for undergraduates. It was regarded by the enthusiasts who taught it as a way of answering most of the questions which arise about the nature of society and the evolution of human affairs. It taught people to think and to write: to develop logical arguments and to commit them to paper. It gloried in the diversity of the cultures which it studied.

Education was still linguistically based, as it had been since the Renaissance. Too much time was spent on Latin and Greek, insofar as the same results could have been achieved, and achieved with much less pain, in much less time. Nevertheless the classics taught the foundation of the Western European languages, implanting the understanding of English and making it easier to learn French and German. (Italian and Spanish were not yet mainstream languages in schools; Russian was ahead of them, but not far.) I am still enthusiastic about history and at least one modern language as the ideal sixth-form education in the Arts.

There was no systematic study of English literature, but this was compensated for by the fact that modern languages were still studied in a literary way. French literature, and even German literature (not a rich seam to mine, but more than enough for schoolboys), perhaps did almost everything educationally that English literature could have done, with the added advantages of not spoiling English literature by turning it into a schoolroom chore, and of introducing pupils to the way in which people from a different cultural background told their stories and expressed their thoughts – a huge bonus of cultural riches. Some English literature was studied in 'private business' with one's tutor, or as an option in two hours a week which were rather eccentrically set aside as 'extra studies'; perhaps more for the benefit of masters who wanted to teach their own pet enthusiasms than for the pupils who could choose to study them.

Modern history was, thus, studied by the whole of the sixth form, for eight hours a week by the specialists and four hours by everybody else. No English was formally taught, and no geography, let alone economics, which was sensibly left to the universities. History, of course, was a useful, and I think well chosen, depository for boys who could not digest a full dose of foreign languages, who were not by any stretch mathematicians and who were not interested in science; but it also had more than its share of the brightest stars, an increasing share as the decade passed and more and more clever boys chose to escape from classics.

The only exception to this system was one tried for a few years for boys who were considered not even clever enough for history. The Common Entrance standard was not at all exacting. Only about half the school learnt Greek, and it could fairly be said that the other half were hardly worth teaching Latin either, although after three years (following on four at their prep schools) most of them passed School Certificate in the subject, and some got credits. So a special syllabus was designed for the also-rans. They were called 'E' specialists (there were about a dozen of them) but nobody was allowed to discuss what 'E' might stand for. Their syllabus was a concoction of English, geography and current affairs; but it quietly disappeared after a few years. Its subjects were, after all, no easier than history, and were discovered not to be any more interesting.

Modern history had a good pedigree at Eton. It had been started by Henry Marten whose strongest suit was perhaps to make it interesting to boys of all academic levels. He wrote a full series of textbooks at two levels for boys below the sixth form. These were still the best-known history textbooks in British schools as a whole, written either by Warner and Marten or by Marten and Carter. There were copious footnotes illustrating important points by entertaining and memorable (if trivial) anecdotes. By my time it was already becoming fashionable to mock Marten's books on the grounds that the only thing anyone remembered of them was the footnotes. There was some truth in this, but the same boys who remembered only the footnotes would not otherwise have remembered anything.

Marten built up a good department, with luminaries such as Tuppy Headlam, and although in terms of hours the greatest contribution to teaching history was still in the 1950s by classical masters in the lower reaches of the school, they were using his textbooks. As well as being classical experts, they were jacks of all trades, trying to keep a chapter ahead of their pupils, and thus at a distinct disadvantage to the 'proper' history beaks, who were better equipped to make the subject

Eton Again

interesting. Both Elliott and Birley, head masters from the 1930s until the 1960, were historians, and appointments had been made with a good deal of care. Elliott regarded history as a subject fit for scholars, but thought that anyone could teach modern languages. Birley inspired the younger history masters by his example.

The department during the course of the time I knew it included some brilliant colleagues, including Alan Barker, Brian Rees and Giles St Aubyn. This produced much cross-fertilisation of ideas and fruitful conversation and argument. The two senior men were steadying influences, Dick Routh and David Graham-Campbell. Routh was head of the department, conservative, thorough and by now ponderous. He did not like being hurried, and was teased by his younger and less responsible colleagues. He insisted that the teaching be shared out, so that everybody taught a clever 'division' one half and a less clever one the next. This made us all workmanlike and it gave us all opportunities. Routh also insisted that we should all teach the whole syllabus and all the periods it included. This was very hard work, but it kept us learning and gave us a wide range of knowledge. Two masters, who had taught at Dartmouth and came to Eton when Dartmouth ceased to recruit cadets of sixth form age, were horrified at the ground which they were expected to cover. We were equally surprised at the narrowness of what had been expected of them in their previous job.

Admittedly, very little medieval history was taught. On the whole it was and perhaps still is a more appropriate subject for undergraduates than for schoolboys, because thoughts and actions become harder to understand the further away they are. In common with almost every school in Britain, we started with the Tudors. We taught both English and European history from 1485 to 1914, and in addition American and British imperial history, two favourites of Routh's which I think were valuable. Very few schools did American history, but our pupils got at least a concept of the development of the United States. We had the chance to get an idea of the Constitution, the Civil War and the westward expansion. Who could forget the chapter heading 'Manifest Destiny Lays a Golden Egg'? As to the British Empire, one of the subjects we concentrated on was the development of dominion status, particularly in relation to Canada.

David Graham-Campbell succeeded Routh as head of the department, and later became Warden of Glenalmond, the Rolls-Royce of

Scottish schools. One of his interests was in the writing of English, primarily as to lucidity but also as to rhythm and cadence, on which he produced an admirable textbook.

The slant of most of what we taught was broadly speaking political, within which the religious disputes of the sixteenth and seventeenth centuries were rather dry to schoolboys. They could cope pretty well with transubstantiation as against commemoration but I am not sure that they understood about justification by faith or by works, or comprehended the arguments for predestination, much more than the average clergyman, or for that matter the average schoolmaster. However, they could grasp the broad sweep of ideas and were not afraid to express their own opinions. On the whole the teaching was good enough to bring alive the people who had contested those opinions in their own times.

For English history we relied largely on *The Oxford History of England*, which had started to appear in 1934 and of which most of the volumes had appeared by the early 1950s, the main exceptions being some of the late medieval ones where source material was in short supply. Several of the volumes were works of real distinction, and although they were primarily political narrative they included learned summaries of social and cultural developments and industrial and economic 'progress'. Eton had a magnificent history 'pound', and by using the books over and over again it was possible to loan every history specialist a copy of the relevant volume at modest expense. The series stood the test of time well: only four volumes of its successor series had appeared by the year 2000.

European history of the later eighteenth and the nineteenth centuries was relevant to the twentieth-century world: roughly from the French Revolution through to 1939. The instability and apparently endless political revolutions of the Continent made a good introduction to modern political ideas and ideals. It was said (perhaps by himself) that Giles St Aubyn started every period of history (whether English or European) with Napoleon. Certainly the revolutions of 1848 provided digestible food for thought about liberalism, as well as some acute and readable commentary on the development of Marx's thinking. In the early twenty-first century it has already become difficult to recollect how influential were Marxist ideas on the whole of the twentieth century, or at least up to about 1985. The Italian Risorgimento was another of our favourites, full of colourful characters and of radical

Eton Again

ideas pitted against *anciens régimes* – in fact three of us even wrote a textbook on it.

Boys entering the school had a 'classical' tutor chosen by their housemaster to supervise all their schoolwork, but when boys graduated as specialists, into what is now called the sixth form, they were able to select a tutor whose teaching had interested them, or at least a person they could get on with, or perhaps who was recommended by a friend. Each boy had at least four regular sessions with his tutor each week: one session individually, going through an essay he had written; two sessions of private business during weekday evenings; and one on Sunday.

Most of the classroom teaching was by lecturing, although a good deal of it consisted of explanation and analysis on the blackboard. A lot of time was spent taking notes. Making carbon copies – more than one or two on a typewriter – was very laborious, involving cutting a stencil as a mastercopy and then turning the handle of a temperamental machine. The results (in purple ink) were usually blurred, or faint, or both. The first photocopiers (Giles St Aubyn had one) involved an inflated pad and coatings of chemicals and took a long time to produce enough copies for a whole class. Nowadays note-taking is hardly necessary, which is a merciful release of time, although the act of taking notes from a lecture is a most valuable skill in itself in any administrative or executive professional career, obliging one to attend closely and to make a précis as one goes along. It also helps a lecture to sink in. However, from the teacher's point of view, lecturing several times a day is extremely hard work. Many practitioners indeed would consider it simply impossible. But it was relieved by much asking of questions – which often received discursive answers, leading to further questions – and there were many successful attempts to produce red herrings. For the most part these contributed to the process of learning because they engaged the pupils in what was being said, and led to discussion. Most of us gave more attention to the great literary historians – notably Clarendon and Macaulay – than their prejudices made academically respectable, but if something of their style rubbed off this was a good investment of time.

Afternoon school ended at 5.45 p.m., so a master got home around 6 o'clock for a cup of tea after an exhausting day – which had often included coaching or umpiring a game during the afternoon –– only to

Eton Again

have to be the life and soul of the party to a group of pupils who arrived for private business at 6.30. This was much more relaxed than a school period, but it involved a good deal of mental effort even if one was listening to classical music on gramophone records with those boys who were interested or wanted to learn. It involved preparation. One could read, or get them to read, one's favourite authors: I was keen on Thackeray's sharp sardonic wit, and also on Ibsen's less obscure plays, which were domestic in scale and in style yet brilliantly constructed to reveal the truth, past and present, about each character by what others said about them. There was inevitably an element, even if only for a minority of those present, of forced feeding. After two sessions of private business from 6.30 to 8 p.m. one felt ready for a supper break before making a start on correcting essays and preparing the next day's lectures. This did not happen every day, but it did not leave quite enough time for recreation, and Sundays gave no real respite because of the session with one's pupils called Sunday 'private': a good idea for putting the Day of Rest to a some useful purpose, and more so for keeping boys out of mischief for an hour or so, but very wearing for a tutor who needed his recreation more than his victims did.

Rugger and soccer were still banished to the shorter Lent half, when the weather was at its least suitable for any outdoor game, especially soccer. The Field Game was universally played during the Michaelmas half. It still seemed an ideal game for a boarding school consisting of a large number of fairly small (of say 45 to 50 boys) houses. As far as any game could, it embodied the combined merits of both soccer and rugger, though not at the most refined levels. It is fair to say that the development of soccer owed more to the Eton Field Game than to any other variety of primitive football, the Old Etonians winning the FA Cup on several occasions in the late nineteenth century and Lord Kinnaird in particular being a seminal figure in the development of the Association's code. The Field Game and soccer had common roots: the one having developed so as to prevent the passing of the ball (which rugger allows, provided that the pass is not forward) and the other to facilitate it (restricted only by the offside rule). In other words, the Field Game had as respectable a pedigree as soccer did, but had evolved differently, specifically in order to make it an ideal school game, whereas soccer was designed to make the most of talent.

The cult of games was almost as powerful in the Eton of the 1950s as

Eton Again

in the 1930s, but the games themselves, like the Field Game, were appropriate school recreations of great imagination and ingenuity, the unadulterated products of English amateur gentlemen. The most ingenious and refined was Eton fives, now in decline and played by only a fraction of the number involved in the inter-war period. Cricket at Eton was governed by the pursuit of excellence, the coaching being undertaken by men who had won blues, or had even played for their counties, in this most difficult of games – a game allowing of no second chance in the attempt to hit a fast and eccentrically moving ball. Not much allowance was made for the less skilful boys who would have been happier on the village green than on Agar's Plough or Lord's. It was considered by the cricket establishment that it was better to get out playing a correct shot than to hit a six with a cowshot. The game was also very time-consuming, and fewer than three hundred boys played it with much enthusiasm.

Rowing, on the other hand, was enjoying a heyday: there were about 750 wetbobs. It cannot be claimed that they all enjoyed it; but there was more on offer for the unskilled than was the case with cricket. There were races for all, there was quite a pleasant form of exercise available in half an hour, and there was the delight of sculling up the Thames on a lovely summer's day. Moreover, there was a highly refined, difficult and demanding challenge for the elite.

Eton contributed more than any other institution to the development of English rowing, especially in its extraordinary success in the Ladies' Plate at Henley, where school crews were still expected to take on the best of the Oxford and Cambridge colleges, and in the influence of Old Etonians at these two universities. As in so much else, the 1950s were the last decade of the *ancien régime*, in which lightweight schoolboy crews could challenge almost the best. How was it done? The last coaches in a long and distinguished line were one Cambridge Etonian, and one Oxford, Tom Brocklebank and Bobby Bourne, coaches of the eight in the later 1940s and the 1950s, who not only knew the secrets of making a boat fly uncannily through the water, but were able to teach boys how to do it.

Eton produced four outstanding rowing coaches between 1860 and 1960: Warre, de Havilland, Brocklebank and Bourne: two of whom practised their art in the these final decades. Some of the others who coached the eight were brilliant oarsmen or competent coaches, but only these four could produce the magic. Another of them, Archie

Eton Again

Nicholson, cooperated with Peter Haig-Thomas, a successful Cambridge coach, to write a book on *The English Style of Rowing*, a valuable depository of what would soon be a lost art. The rowlock consisting of the 'fixed pin', timber-lined within a square metal frame, was the icon of this classical style, with the ingeniously shaped leather 'button' on the oar gently pressed against it, not only to stabilise the boat's trim but automatically turning the blade off the feather, to enable the oarsman with light hands and relaxed muscles to drop it into the water.

For decades the modern swivel rowlock had been challenging the fixed pin. Eton, almost alone, held out. When eventually Bobby Bourne, the last distinguished advocate of this primitive but ingenious device, decided to retire, the deluge of modern times swept away the remnants of the classical style which, in common with all centenarians, had few contemporaries to mourn its demise. So the old English style of rowing faded away mourned only by a few veterans and leaving English rowing no less successful.

The numerous boat sheds were full of boats built by craftsmen on the spot. How many sculling boats there were is unrecorded: certainly more than five hundred. For lower boys they were whiffs, clinker built with three strakes and very sturdy; but the majority were riggers, veneer-thin mahogany skin-built sculling boats, not of course as light as championship boats but masterpieces of craftsmanship nevertheless, some of them as much as forty or even fifty years old. Each winter they were rubbed down and lovingly revarnished by a team of raft-hands and boatbuilders. But they could not last for ever, and after the gap of the war years and the post-war shortage of both materials and craftsmen we decided to try to build a fibre-glass boat. There had been one or two attempts to build fibre-glass fours at Oxford and on the tideway, but the first models were not as fast as boats made of the traditional mahogany skin, nor had they the flexibility that gives a racing boat life. We, however, wanted a strongly built boat, even if it was not quite of championship lightness and speed.

The doctrine was that sculling was the basis of all Eton rowing. Boys learnt from the start to balance, propel and navigate their own individual boats. When they stepped into a four or an eight, they did not rely on others to balance it, but instinctively contributed their own skill to that of the crew. And the theory is that if you make a man paddle his own canoe, he soon learns the most economical way to do so. This is

Eton Again

still accepted doctrine, although no club can accomplish it on anything like the scale of the old Eton College Boat House.

The beauty of the plastic boat was that it would be made in a mould, and could be repeated over and over again with far less skill and in far less time than a timber one. The skin would be harder and easier to repair than timber. We would still use a timber frame, but it could be simpler than the traditional pattern.

As 'river master' responsible to the head master for safety and good behaviour and the general functioning of the Boat House (but with no input into rowing or coaching policy) the possibility of building fibreglass boats seemed to me to offer the only way of renewing our stock of sculling – and perhaps later other – boats. Frank Claret, Alf's son, was a master boatbuilder, and enthusiastic, but the technique was experimental. We roped in John Herbert (known as 'Bertie'), a retired housemaster and Cambridge blue, a mathematician known, from his wartime invention of a floating airfield known as Lily, to have a flair for original ideas in engineering. We expected that we should have to build several prototypes before we got it right, and we wanted to make the first one very strong and then fine down the subsequent marks. The question was how thick the skin would have to be. We enlisted the leading expert from a pioneering plastics firm, who assured us that his material was stronger than wood – indeed, he said, it was even stronger than steel. 'So is wood in some circumstances,' said Bertie. 'How are you measuring the strength?' The expert was not ready for questions from mere schoolmasters, and prevaricated. 'Well,' said Bertie, 'there are only two ways: tensile strength or elastic limit. Which are you using?' This brought the expert to heel. He had to admit that he did not know, so our prototype was, indeed, experimental. By a remarkable stroke of luck, we got it exactly right first time. It was fractionally heavier and stiffer than the old mahogany boats, but only fractionally. It still had enough flexibility to give it life when it was being sculled. I think it was the first plastic sculling boat ever to be built.

As with every other sport, rowing has developed in technique over the course of many years, and I have no doubt that the pleasure of rowing in a good crew is undiminished. However, the relentless application of scientific methods has left no room for the old amateur approach, and in the competition to produce speed and endurance the value of sculling, although still recognised, has been cut down to size. Dedication to mileage in all weathers has robbed the sport of its idyllic character, and its appeal is confined to fewer boys who are willing to make sacrifices of time and effort all the year round. The fairness of a course is more important than the luck of the draw, when the best hope for the loser of the toss was to get ahead and take the enemy's water round a corner or in shelter from the wind. Eton rowing, however, is still in the forefront of the modern sport, and has been so since the post-war period, a magnificent triumph for those involved.

Many of the features of Eton life were self-perpetuating, notably the classical teaching and the cult of games. As far as games were concerned, Pop, the self-electing body of school prefects, with all its influence in a world of schoolboys, was what kept the cult going. Pop was one of several Eton institutions sorely in need of reform. Two others were the Corps, little changed since before 1914, and the Eton Mission, still a vehicle of nineteenth-century evangelism for the benefit of the lower classes. It had been challenged once, but was firmly buttressed by the Establishment.

Pop was a corrupt institution in the eighteenth-century sense. Membership was governed by the personal whim of the existing members, although in many cases good judgement was shown in making choices. Blatant lobbying did not succeed, but subtle lobbying and favouritism did. The institution was riddled with minor abuses of power, but it had immense prestige amongst the boys and could only have been reformed at the cost of limiting their right of self-government. Besides, people who suffer from injustice quickly learn how undesirable it is. There had always been a strong element of self-government at Eton, giving senior boys a great deal of responsibility and allowing them to discuss and decide the best course of action in all sorts of circumstances. This played a big hand in producing the individuality and ingenuity and perhaps indeed the aptitude for politics for which its old boys were (and still are, though in much smaller numbers) renowned. The problem was that nearly all the members of Pop had been elected because of their prowess at games.

Partly, perhaps largely, because of the responsibility given to boys, and in spite of injustice here and there, or at best 'justice tempered by prejudice', there was also in the school a high degree of tolerance and liberty. Inevitably amongst teen-aged boys there was teasing, amounting sometimes to persecution and bullying, but it was far from rampant and the degree of responsibilty given to boys resulted often in its being sooner and more sensitively detected and controlled than it would have been by a more remote authority. Eccentricity was not only tolerated, it was admired. Such reforms of Pop as took place under Robert Birley's regime were subtle and gradual.

The Corps was a different matter. Nobody loved it. It had been virtually compulsory for many years – at least for half a century, since 1914. It was theoretically voluntary but it required determination to escape it, and very few did. Since 1938 – the advent of conscription in the face of the threat of war – it had given boys at least some inkling of military discipline and military ways. The general perception was that it was a useful introduction to National Service, but it was no more than a sausage machine, as much disliked as National Service itself.

National Service was held to have some benefits, both for the individual and for the nation. It taught people discipline and it taught them to put up with things. But it was a huge waste of time and an opportunity missed, for Britain was such an unmilitary nation (it still is) that it would have been thought quite wrong to use compulsory military service as a deliberate means of imparting training in citizenship. There was a sigh of relief when it was announced in 1957 that it was to be phased out. Britain in the future would have to manage with a professional or Regular Army and its Territorial battalions of volunteers.

Nobody had thought what in these circumstances should happen to the Corps. The general perception was that if it was not compulsory (as it was at all public schools) it would simply cease to exist. This would have been welcome to some, but it would have been strongly resisted by many. Eton had a strong and deeply rooted tradition of sending a large number of boys into the Army, some merely for a few years and others for a full professional career. Still, there was no hurry for a decision. The best thing to do, perhaps indeed the only thing to do, was to wait and see.

The Corps was virtually compulsory for the masters who officered it, as much as it was for the boys. The masters who had served right through the war, or for the major part of it, had earned a rest, but most of the younger masters had done some war service or, at least, National Service after 1945. If dragooned by the head master, as inevitably most of them were, they took on the task with a sense of duty, realising that it had to be done and hoping to escape after a few years. I found myself in 1957 in precisely this position but was thwarted by circumstances and dragooned by the head master into taking command.

Eton Again

With a gust of youthful optimism, I said that I would take it on if it could be voluntary – and he agreed. He did not think it would work, but he had the courage to let me try: I say courage because he knew that he would face a barrage of criticism not only from Old Etonians but from the armed services themselves: if Eton went voluntary, they feared, others would follow suit.

It struck me that a voluntary Corps could make a contribution to the training of boys aged say sixteen to eighteen in ways which would be valuable not only if they joined the armed services but also if they did not, and moreover that the nation had to get over the 'National Service syndrome' and reawaken the voluntary spirit which had contributed so much to Britain's survival in the early years of the war, indeed in both world wars, though in rather different ways. Many men of the generation older than my own had seen the threat of war and had joined the Territorial Army in the 1930s. But since 1938 – a space of twenty years – there had been no volunteering, and the very notion of serving in the Army was viewed by the majority with distaste.

I had been much impressed by Field Marshal Slim's book on the war in Burma – *Defeat into Victory* – in which he described the qualities he required and the methods he had used to train young officers. In his final chapter he warned that these lessons should not be forgotten: 'they may be needed again'.

I suggested to Birley that we should confine the Corps to 'specialists' (the sixth form) getting rid of the fourteen-year-olds who were hardly taller than their rifles and who could not cope with physically demanding training. We agreed that the maximum number should be limited to 180, the essential for success being that there must be more candidates than we had room for; even if only one more candidate than there were vacancies. If the Corps was select, people would join it. This later caused us trouble with parents who wanted their boys to join – for one reason or another – but whose sons, after interview, were refused; and we did expand the numbers up to 250, which we were able to do without quite satisfying the demand.

A huge advantage was that we could select the very best officers. We only needed a few, and were thus able to accept the resignations of all who wanted to leave (and one or two who didn't). We had many discussions about how to approach the task. The main problem was that the training must be enjoyable, but it must also be demanding and within a strict military framework. We decided to aim at a high

Eton Again

standard of drill and turnout, but to balance this by using the weekly parades for a wide choice of courses, most of which we thought would be attractive. However, the real object of the exercise was to be achieved by replacing field days with 36-hour schemes, which occupied a weekend once a half. The purpose of these schemes would be to work up for annual camp in July, which would be compulsory, where the patrols into which the Corps would be divided would be able to 'go anywhere do anything'.

The idea of a patrol was unavowedly copied from Baden-Powell, who had devised his training methods in the Army long before he conceived the idea of transferring them to Boy Scouts. It would not have done to admit this, since it would have been regarded as childish by the Old Etonian lobby, but the idea was to create an organic group in which every member would make a contribution. Each patrol was commanded by a sergeant, whose task was challenging to say the least; although in essence the basis of almost all the tasks to be performed was simple: to turn up, with his patrol in good order, at the right place and the right time. The action which eventually ensued was often incidental to this task.

The patrols, about 12 to 15 strong, fitted the house system well: the stronger houses had a patrol to themselves, and other patrols were made up from two houses. They were rather large for a boy sergeant to command, but they related to a section in the Army, the basis of all infantry training. By a stroke of luck, the idea of using a trolley to carry an infantry section's heavier gear was orthodox military thinking at the time, especially for airborne troops. (David Callender and I built all the trolleys for the Corps, partly from second-hand materials, during one holiday.)

Accurate map-reading was vital. We evolved some ingenious ideas to make it difficult, such as cutting out some of the map squares altogether. The patrol had to learn the hard way to fend off hunger and fatigue, but the big problem was not to lose those patrols which had got the map reading wrong, but rather to put them back on course so that they could continue. By the standards of the time we had a good system of radio communication, but it was far from infallible. The planning of each 36-hour scheme involved a huge amount of work, because each patrol had to have a separate route out of sight of all the others. Sometimes with the permission of landowners we were able to use farmland and forest in the Thames valley or the Chilterns. We used the military

Eton Again

areas around Aldershot and occasionally went as far afield as Salisbury Plain.

Traditional Corps camps at the end of the summer half had been the most unpleasant experiences of the year: rows of huts, foul food, pointless parades, endless delays and elementary orthodox infantry training did nothing but provide a foretaste of National Service. They were interspersed with occasional demonstrations by a Regular platoon with much use of explosives, but even these were not always appreciated. On one occasion the general himself turned up and (forgetting perhaps his own schooldays) asked for opinions of a demonstration. Corporal Malcolmson put up his hand and said 'Frankly, sir, extremely poor.' You could have heard a pin drop.

'Greenfield' camps had just been invented for the Territorial Army, allowing them to avoid Regular Army training areas with their forbidding rows of wartime huts, and I formed the opinion by studying the rules carefully that school cadet forces were not specifically forbidden from using this idea. Much to the annoyance of the powers that be I took the voluntary Corps for its first camp to private land in North Wales where there was plenty of thick woodland. We ended the camp with the 'three day scheme' which was intended as the culmination of the year's training. The next year we were even more ambitious and took the Corps to Norway in four chartered aeroplanes, supported by two generous sponsors. We enjoyed superb weather and immense support from Heimevernet which, though named the Home Guard, was more like the Territorial Army. The terrain was superb and the event was quite adventurous: a spectacular success, in fact. The next year we chartered a train from Windsor to Achnasheen and then went by lorry to Loch Ewe, where some aspects of the camp were not merely challenging but hair-raising: however, everybody had an experience and everybody survived.

To the annoyance of the authorities I had insisted, again with Birley's support, on abolishing the Naval and RAF Sections of the Corps, but I assured the Admiralty that they would get more candidates as naval officers than before: this happened, and took the wind from their sails. It was essential that everyone should wear one uniform, and take pride in it. I took a great deal of trouble over the pep talk I gave to recruits, in which my objective was to point out that it was their Corps, and that to complain about it was disloyal, since if everyone tried hard there would be nothing to complain about.

Eton Again

I did get a lot of grumbling from other public schools. I had let the side down. Everyone would want to go voluntary now, and nobody would volunteer. Gradually over the years most of them followed suit, and eventually the Ministry of Defence did so also, reducing the emphasis on boring orthodox elementary infantry training and foot drill, and introducing adventure training. This is now universal in the cadet forces.

I have described the Eton system of giving boys responsibility in the running of their houses and for the day-to-day discipline of the whole school. It worked well but it did offer too much power without enough responsibility for the consequences. The Corps attempted to redress this for a large proportion of the senior boys in the school. If they did not turn up at the right place at the right time they were wet, hungry, uncomfortable and exhausted, and the sergeants were to blame. Each patrol, down to its humblest member, had to come to terms with quite a number of problems in order to succeed, in a very different milieu from that of the Latin verb or the playing field. A large number of Etonians continued to enter the armed forces. There was a period when four out of six ships in one frigate squadron of the Royal Navy were commanded by Old Etonians – and there weren't many squadrons. Many joined the Territorial Army and the Reserves, which were important in those days and continued to be so for many years. But the objective of the training we gave was much wider than this, and challenging adventurous training in the open air is now widely recognised as a Good Thing, spawning organisations like Outward Bound courses and the Duke of Edinburgh's Award.

Another institution owing its ethos to the era of Edmund Warre and ripe for reform was the Eton Mission. Its objective had been to provide, by the subscriptions of Eton boys, a church and a parson for one of the economically poorest districts of the East End (as it was invariably known) at Hackney Wick. This was High Church evangelism with a vengeance, not the Low Church evangelism of what is labelled the 'Evangelical' flavour of the Church of England. Once the church building had been completed, there was a mighty argument whether or not the next most important project was to provide the church with a tower.

As may be imagined, this painful dilemma provided a spirited (though clearly not a God-given) field of battle between those who supported it and those who didn't. The tower builders had the biggest

Eton Again

guns, but not the most telling arguments – and the result was that those who felt that it would be better to provide practical facilities for deprived children than to build a tower to the Glory of God broke away and formed a rival organisation which they called Eton Manor. They provided a splendid running track (perhaps influenced by the words of the hymn familiar to them from Chapel services, 'There is a book who runs may read') in an area devoid of facilities for sport or leisure. One of their leaders was Arthur Villiers, who not only put his money where his mouth was, but who actually put himself there, building a modest house in which he resided for the rest of his life. A hundred years later the area was to become the Olympic Park.

Arthur did not cut himself off from Eton. He had a gift for making money, as well as inheriting a pile which he devoted to the inhabitants of the Hackney marshes. It was he who invested the Farrer Bequest in German government bonds after the war, reckoning that the Germans would be good recoverers, and created such a cascade of money that, having paid the entire cost of a brand new boys' house at Eton, named Farrer House, he then asked if the school wanted another (which was named Villiers House); and finally used the small change to build a theatre worthy of a major city. But he and those who thought as he did cut themselves off from the Eton Mission.

The Mission in its original shape rumbled on, raising money for rather old-fashioned good works in the parish by means of obligatory collections held each half in boys' houses. One was expected to give half a crown which, of course, had to be provided by one's parent adding that amount to one's pocket money. The expenditure was in the hands of a committee of competent and well-motivated Old Etonians. The only master actively involved was the honorary treasurer, a job for which there was no queue, with the result that I was roped in. With Birley's encouragement we managed to divert some of the funds to helping old folks in Windsor and Slough with their gardens or their housework, or just chatting to the lonely ones. This idea, now known as 'community service' and more relevant to boys than simply providing money for a London parish, was just beginning to creep in at public schools, usually a soft option and an alternative to joining the Corps.

The work of a master at any boarding school was extremely demanding in the 1940s, '50s and '60s. It still is so, although it has been softened

Eton Again

by the creation of many new posts which remove much of the administration (now complicated by elaborate Government regulation) from the coal face, and spread the load in other ways. At Eton the requirement to take on boys as sixth-form pupils, and to play a full part in activities such as games (now called sport) filled up those parts of the day which were needed as breathing spaces in the exhausting life of attempting to teach academic subjects to a large group of mentally and physically boisterous teenagers. As I have explained, 'private business' ended only at 8 p.m. several days a week, and there were also numerous societies which needed a master to supervise them; and then after supper there was all the correcting and preparation for the next day which would begin with Early School at 7.30 a.m. However, the actual number of periods taught was fewer than today, and some respite could be obtained on half-holidays. One needed the school holidays as a rest cure.

In those days a large number of graduates from the best universities went into teaching, especially in the public, direct grant and grammar schools throughout Britain. In my opinion there is no more useful, fascinating and rewarding (though not in the financial sense) profession. True, it was regarded by some outsiders as being narrow, even cloistered, and it is true that it did tend to consume too much of one's being. Yet there were, on the spot, a large number of friends in one's colleagues and their wives and families, people admittedly working in the same milieu but with a very large variety of stimulating interests. It is not always recognised what remarkable groups of people form the staffs of our public schools. In both size and quality Eton was unusual, although even so large a school did have the narrowing influence of any profession, enhanced by the need to live over the shop. But one experienced the fascination of helping a stream of young individuals to grow up as sensible and civilised members of society. Few professions can offer anything as interesting or rewarding as that.

6
Lancing

I arrived at Lancing as head master in September 1961. It was a public school for some four hundred boys, all boarders, and had been founded in 1848 by the local vicar, Nathaniel Woodard, almost simultaneously and with remarkably similar objectives to W. E. Gladstone's foundation of Glenalmond in Scotland. In each case the founder's primary objective had been religious. Lancing was to be both a seminar for aspiring priests and a school for Anglicans, as was Glenalmond. In each case the project for the seminar never got off the ground, and was quietly dropped after a decent interval.

Woodard's objective was to educate the middle classes, bringing them up as Anglicans of the higher rather than the lower persuasion. Like Gladstone, he was influenced by the Oxford Movement and the Tractarians, who in the 1830s had revived the pre-Reformation 'Catholic' inheritance of the Anglican Church, rejecting the characteristically Protestant practices of the seventeenth and eighteenth centuries. In practical terms, in parish churches as in school chapels this meant the revival of the sacramental service of Holy Communion as the regular form of worship in place of Mattins.

Gladstone's objective was that Scottish boys should be brought up as Episcopalians rather than Presbyterian members of the established Kirk, whereas Woodard's was merely a change of emphasis within the Church of England; but Woodard's objective was a wider and perhaps a nobler one than Gladstone's in his mission to bring education to the rapidly expanding middle class. Lancing, queen amongst his schools, was for the upper middle class; the other two schools he founded in Sussex were for the middle middle and lower middle classes – a point which we were not allowed (whether by regulation or by good manners) to mention. Gladstone's objective was not purely denominational, however. He too had a noble ambition – that the Scottish gentry should have their sons educated in Scotland instead of sending them to English public schools. He realised by 1854 that this could not be achieved unless Glenalmond could 'obviate the Scotch accent'. The

Lancing

Scottish lairds would only send their sons there if they could be brought up to speak as the sons of English gentlemen did. These were local, or as we would now say regional, considerations. Gladstone applauded Woodard's efforts, and subscribed handsomely to the foundation of Lancing: so much so that his coat of arms appeared with those of other benefactors in a window in the dining hall. I felt at home.

I was not, indeed, entirely a new boy. I had been at Lancing during the war when it was a naval establishment – part of HMS *King Alfred*. I had been much taken by the chapel, then virtually unused. As a nineteenth-century Gothic revival church it is, in my opinion, unique: it has the inspiring spiritual quality of the real thing. It imitates, but not slavishly, the great cathedrals of the Ile-de-France. Of the many hundreds of Victorian Gothic churches in Britain, including some very striking examples, it is to me the only one which supremely and serenely has this quality. The way in which it has been done is indefinable: one can only say that, unlike most of their contemporaries, the Lancing architects, Carpenter father and son, 'spoke the Gothic'; they had the magic touch.

By the time I arrived at Lancing the chapel had been a-building for almost a hundred years, and was nearly complete. But I inherited a problem as to what went on in it. During the previous thirty or forty years the Communion service had been gradually taking over from Mattins as the regular Sunday service throughout the Church of England. Previously, it had been the custom for churchgoers to attend Communion, and take the sacrament, at least three times a year; and in very many cases 'at least' also meant 'at most'. There were many who did so more often, perhaps regularly once every few weeks: but to do so only three times was by no means a sign of slackness. Many people felt that the service would be devalued if indulged in too often.

In this much vaunted 'parish movement' the rest of the world was merely catching up with Lancing and with a minority of High Church churches, where the Communion service was the regular one on Sundays, and had been so as long as anyone could remember. However, it had not been the custom in these churches that all, or almost all, the congregation should actually take the Communion, in the form of the consecrated bread and wine: it was sufficient, except on special occasions, to be a witness. (There is a bit more to it than that, but the subtleties cannot in this context be allowed to detain us for a month of Sundays.) In that respect, it was up to Lancing to catch up. Yes, there was and always had been a Communion service every Sunday, attended

Lancing

compulsorily by the whole school, just as at most other schools there was compulsory attendance at some form of Mattins; but the boys did not take Communion. If they wanted to do that, they must make the effort to come to a voluntary service (more often than not early in the morning, involving the self-denial of a long lie in bed). So what was to be done?

My predecessor John Dancy had decided, in agreement with the provost, a High Churchman if ever there was one, that the only solution would be to make it possible – indeed easy – for boys to take Communion, but not of course to oblige them to do so. This well-meaning and perhaps seemingly innocent proposal put the cat among the pigeons. The chaplain would not comply: he thought that the whole solemnity and sincerity of the occasion would be prejudiced, and that boys would come to the altar merely to stretch their legs. Perhaps he was right. Anyway, he was asked to leave, and Christopher Campling was appointed in his place. This was the situation which I inherited.

Cuthbert Shaw, the sacked chaplain, a quiet devout man, was liked and respected by his colleagues, especially those who cared about the chapel. They came out in sympathy. Christopher did not have the support of the majority of the housemasters. So what should be done? There was no alternative but to suck it and see. After all, the new practice complied with what happened in most parish churches, and compulsory attendance at Sunday chapel was common form at public schools. If it had not been, few people would have turned up, as indeed they would have done to voluntary lessons, and it would not have been possible to educate them in accordance with the school's clearly promulgated and unalterable statutes.

The Sunday services of the new kind went very well, all considered, although the objection to them still rankled in a few conservative masters; which was important, insofar as these men really cared. Campling was an able man, a good organiser and a gifted and original teacher of divinity. As a chaplain should, he helped and counselled many boys in all sorts of circumstances. He had the ability to simplify without trivialising. He took the services well and had a good voice. The music, too, was both distinguished and unusual, under John Alston. Alston was a charming man and good company, but he had spent a great deal of time and effort getting the chapel music as he wanted it, and was not well endowed in the art of compromise. His reputation as a musician was second to none, and his choristers regularly won music or choral scholarships at Oxford and at Cambridge, especially at King's and St John's Colleges. He was a close friend of Peter Pears, Britten's partner and the most celebrated of Old Lancing musicians. I remember an interview with John in my study about the choice of music for some chapel services, which he ended by stating his case unequivocally: 'It is better music, Head Master. And that is not an opinion: it's a fact.'

The whole school sang plainsong, in both the Sunday and the weekday services. This was unique in public schools, or almost so. Its simplicity, rhythm and understated momentum carried the services along without the hearty approach and rousing hymns which were the popular features of many public school chapels. John Alston had achieved the half-voice singing, in which everyone or almost everyone took part, and the canticles and psalms were sung at reading speed as they should be, without all the artificial decorations and gear changes and irritating sluggishness which bedevil Anglican chanting. John Dancy, finding the plainsong tedious for the full duration of a long term, had insisted on Anglican chants for a fortnight. This was a revelation: it is the only time I have ever heard Anglican chants used as they should be, sung at the speed at which they would be spoken.

Another unusual but admirable custom at Lancing was that the compulsory daily service was Evensong, not a shortened form of Mattins. It took place when the main work of the day was over, and everybody could do with a few minutes of peace and calm, and perhaps of reflection and prayer. This was preferable to a morning rush between breakfast and lessons, when boys were struggling to organise their approach to the coming day and preoccupied with the imminent testing of the previous evening's inadequate preparation. Besides, Evensong in the Book of Common Prayer is a much more finely constructed service than Mattins, which is derived from several medieval services mercilessly strung together, with a surfeit of canticles. Evensong is entire of itself. The two canticles, the Magnificat and the Nunc Dimittis, flow well with phrases and images which are both memorable and, with a little help, easily understood. The former has grandeur, the latter is a fitting conclusion to a day's activity. The three collects are a perfect set of Cranmer's best, dignified, rhythmical and memorable. For the hymns, Lancing used the English Hymnal, compiled with more discrimination and scholarship than the common alternative, Hymns Ancient and Modern, and including all the best seventeenth- and eighteenth-century hymns with their refreshing simplicity, whilst not rejecting some of the more extravagant Victoriana.

The old order was represented by the other clergyman on the staff, Henry Thorold, a High Churchman with a good deal of style and eccentricity. In the school services Henry went along with what was ordained by the school. He never agreed to preach on a Sunday more than once a term, but his sermon was worth waiting for: witty and topical, memorable, simple and profound. There was a daily Communion service celebrated either by Henry or by Christopher, to which a few devout masters and boys turned up, so the old order was still present in Lancing chapel, even if as some mischievous commentators suggested Henry and Christopher used it as an occasion to pray privately for each other's departure.

Lancing had been founded in the tradition of High Church simplicity in contrast to the more ritualistic practices commonly summarised as 'smells, bells and lace' which suffused the Anglo-Catholic movement later in the nineteenth century. Bells and lace could be introduced by degrees, but incense was incense and a simple *casus belli* in many churches. It had been kept out at Lancing, thus reducing differences of opinion about ceremonial to skirmishes rather than full-blown battles. There was an occasional High Mass with a good deal of bowing and scraping, but in relative terms simplicity was the order of the day. Most of the public schools were firmly Protestant in their orientation, so the Anglo-Catholics tended to make for Lancing or one of the other Woodard schools for the spiritual education of their sons. However, by the 1960s Anglo-Catholicism as a distinct movement at the highest peak of High-Churchmanship had run its course, and only a very few people (parents and clergy) ever referred to it. With the Communion service now common practice in parish churches throughout the land, Lancing when I was there was able to follow the broad and fairly comprehensive Catholic tradition of the Church of England. The chapel had a strong and benign influence. There were always plenty of candidates to become sacristans or chapel guides.

I liked and supported Christopher Campling, and I admired his achievement, but he was unable to win back the support of the housemasters and of a few others who cared about his role, and it seemed to me that after about seven years it would be right to have a change. The appointment of the chaplain, however, lay in the hands not of the head master but of the provost. This was an unworkable situation, laid down by the Founder with the objective of giving the chaplain the desirable degree of independence. The arguments were not dissimilar from those used to support the parson's freehold, which presented the clergy of England with parishes for life; or with private patronage, which prevented the bishop from appointing the clergy in his own diocese; with disastrous results which I shall refer to under another heading.

The provost was a clergyman of standing, presumably although not essentially in the diocese of Chichester, who presided over the group of Woodard Schools. At an early stage of Lancing's history it became clear that the head master would have to agree, and would presumably have to be consulted, over the appointment of the chaplain. For the most part this anomaly, so typical of English institutions, was handled amicably and with common sense. The provost had appointed Campling, at Dancy's suggestion and with Dancy's support. During the seven years of Campling's chaplaincy he did not give the support he should have done, a matter about which Christopher felt strongly. Christopher also thought that I was more concerned with peace and quiet, or at least with good order, or even with what was possible, than I was with the matters which mattered most to him. Some kind of agreement was necessary, even if a compromise, and, not wishing to compare myself with a Roman emperor, I refrained from reminding Christopher that the Nicene Creed had been arrived at in similar circumstances. It was admittedly difficult to know what a successor would do, especially in the climate of the late Sixties when objections to compulsory chapel had to be faced.

The provost came up with a candidate, Paddy Smythe, an Irish Anglican. Now Irish Anglicans tend to be Low Churchmen, having been since the Reformation the alternatives to Roman Catholics. However, the provost assured me that Paddy was an exception: he was as high as anyone at Lancing could wish – and he had charisma, the gift of the gab and the ability to get on with all and sundry. I interviewed him at length, and agreed that he might be our man.

This was a mistake. Paddy turned out to be a trouble-maker. His mission seemed to be to sow dissension wherever he could, and to make life difficult for me, mainly over trivialities. He saw the task of the chaplain as being to keep the head master under control. His method of helping boys who were worried or unhappy or who disliked the regime was to face me directly with his interpretation of their problems, which he required to remedy forthwith as best I could. If a boy found a rule objectionable, I should remove it. If I pointed out that the boy's house master was the person to enlist, he said it was my fault for not having a more sympathetic regime. As to the masters, they were on the whole well aware that they could bring their problems to me, and would at least get a sympathetic hearing, so he concentrated on the scandal of their having to pay their own laundry bills, or on the quality of their coffee during the morning break. He beavered away at the problems of the domestic staff, and brought those along too. If I pointed out that they were in the domain of the bursar, he thought I should teach the bursar to change his ways. If these problems had been anything but trivial, or if they had suggested to me any actual unfairness, they might have engaged my attention. As it was, they exasperated me by wasting a great deal of time; for I could not refuse to see the chaplain, even at short notice or none, if he said he had something important to tell me.

So Paddy had to go. But how? Fortunately he had an inflated view of his own importance, so he might be found a promotion. I was not unaware that occasionally a bishop can find no way of getting rid of a misfit except by persuading somebody else to give him (they were all male in those days) a job. What more Christian way than to magnify the virtues of a colleague? Fortunately the governors of a choir school in Grimsby asked me specific – well, fairly specific – questions about his suitability as a head master, which I was able to answer, with a little charitable massage, to their satisfaction. Paddy was replaced by the steady and sensible Tom Baker, whose sincerity, firmness and good judgement were well employed dealing with objections to compulsory chapel.

Apart from this intractable situation, in which the majority of those who cared most about the chapel disliked the new Sunday chapel services which John Dancy had rightly introduced, making things difficult for the chaplain, the legacy of my predecessor was a welcome one. True, he had made one or two specific appointments which did not accord with what I wanted to achieve, and which were very difficult to unscramble. But he had succeeded in the main task which he had been given, namely to improve the academic standard, and had carried out the unenviable task of removing from the staff those whom he regarded, in almost every case correctly, as exhausted or incompetent, making himself unpopular with many of their old friends and colleagues. He had, on the whole, appointed very good men in their

Lancing

place. It was thought (correctly) that I would bring a gentler touch. John had, indeed, cut his teeth on Lancing, and later he was the first to volunteer that he might have been more diplomatic in his approach. When W. E. Gladstone was asked in old age what was the most important quality required of a prime minister he replied that he must be a good butcher. I had taken this on board, and I respected what John Dancy had done. It made my own inheritance easier.

The abilities of the staff were on the whole well matched to their tasks. Drama, art and music were well served, the two former by a liberal and the latter by a highly disciplined regime. There were some well-run societies or activities to encourage a range of interests from philosophy to woodwork, and the games played in the afternoons were played well, some better than others. Two games, soccer and squash, were played supremely well, giving the school a valuable reputation externally and an even more valuable standard of excellence internally.

The success in soccer was due to Ken Shearwood, and in squash to Sam Jagger, a genial Cambridge blue who had been recruited long ago to coach cricket and teach geography when geography was the refuge of the non-academic sixth former. Sam had soon become bored with teaching cricket, but having a keen eye for a ball and a tidy mind he had become fascinated by squash and taught it, rather as he taught geography, by working out exactly what the basic shots and the basic tactics should be, and teaching them by reducing them to their simplest elements and by constant practice. This enabled boys without much natural talent to become remarkably successful, and boys who did have talent to work out the refinements for themselves and excel. Sam's achievement was considered the more remarkable because the squash courts were very old ones with floors of cement screed, rather than timber, but in fact these slower courts encouraged boys to try to make unreturnable shots.

Tennis was quite popular and Eton fives was played well. Lancing was fortunate to have a full-length shooting range, neatly tucked in a little cwm in the Downs below the school, so that full-bore rifle shooting could be practised on the spot, with good results at Bisley. Again, athletics and cross-country (for which the Downs were ideal) were well performed, and the Ladywell game, with unlimited numbers on each side and no rules other than a code of conduct handed down by word of mouth, was a pleasant reminder of the days when sporting activities

Lancing

were dependent on local topography, as with fives and the Wall Game at Eton. It was not indulged in often, but when it was it made one of the best occasions in the year.

Games were important, but there was no cult such as bedevilled Eton. There was not quite enough steel or style in the boys' attitude, but on the other hand there was rather more appreciation of the fact that games were to be enjoyed and that the playing fields were not Spartan or imperial training grounds. The mixture of amateurism and carefully honed skill was about right. There may have been a vague understanding that games were compulsory, but it was not elaborately codified and there was no objection when I consented to boys who were by no stretch of the imagination athletically gifted occupying themselves in other ways, although I preferred them to be doing it outdoors.

The Corps was a shambles. John Dancy had appointed a Lancing old boy, a professional soldier with a good war record, to pull it together in view of the lack of volunteers on the staff, but he had told him that he must make allowances, which he did – indeed he overdid; so we were not really much better off for his presence. It was not his fault. Lancing was a most unmilitary school. Some admirable activities of which sailing was the most important were carried on enthusiastically and successfully by masters who, I suppose, may have been officers in the Corps, although there was no clue in their demeanour which would have led one to suspect it. There was a senior Scout troop, although its programme consisted almost entirely of 'community service', a worthy and worthwhile activity in which boys brought a breath of fresh air into the lives of some of the many aged people of the Sussex coast; so with the assent of Trevor Foulkes who ran it we allowed others to 'do' community service and the Scouts slipped into a state of suspended animation.

By the time I arrived for my first term, I had some idea about what I might hope to achieve, and my early experience of the school did not alter my views. The masters, good as they were at their particular jobs, needed to be given more scope and more responsibility to take their own decisions. That was the way, and the only way, they would grow. The same was true of the boys. They needed scope, including space and time. They needed more freedom to form and express their ideas, in spite of the fact that some of those ideas would be immature and silly, and indeed sometimes outrageous. They too needed to be encouraged to take decisions, and to be responsible for the consequences.

Lancing

I had received two opposite briefings as to my task, the first – from the Governing Body – more authentic than the second, and one which suited me well and encouraged me to accept the challenge, namely to maintain the academic standards which Dancy had begun to achieve, whilst enabling people to feel more at their ease and to develop their self-confidence. The second was delivered by Lieutenant General Sir John Evetts, president of the Old Boys Association, a man who as he said was utterly devoted to the school but unfortunately (as he didn't say) to the school as he remembered it some fifty years before. He wanted me to enforce short hair and good manners. Shortness of hair was to him the Law of the Medes and Persians, which changeth not. Manners to him were a matter of discipline, not consideration for others tempered by the conventions of society. I was considered at Eton to be a fairly fierce disciplinarian, so he thought that if I could be collared at an early stage I would be able to correct the slackness which had crept in under John Dancy. This was a bad start, making me very wary of the Old Boys' Club, most of whose devotees turned out in the event to be loyal, sensible and supportive athletes.

In spite of the magnificent surroundings of Sussex sea and downland, the immediate geography of the school buildings was not encouraging. In particular, all the boys' houses were arranged in the quadrangles, which had been considered by my predecessors, not without reasonableness, to demand a certain uniformity of rule and custom. The dormitories were huge (which had advantages) but privacy in every respect was at a premium. Individual or shared studies were few and far between, so much of a boy's life and work was in a house room. Here Dancy had made a major improvement by introducing private desks and shelves on the lines of the Toys he had known at Winchester. But this was not more than an alleviation of the system in which every boy lived in public.

The accommodation in two, or perhaps three, of the boarding houses had been made tolerable for married house masters, and I at once set about converting more, reaching a score of six out of the seven before I left. A good number of houses had been built for married masters at Hoe Court, and this we continued, but the bachelor masters all, or almost all, lived in The Tower in the upper quad, which also housed the masters' common room. This had the advantage that there were men on the spot, but it did foster a parochial atmosphere (or worse) and on the whole was not a Good Thing.

Lancing

Nothing, or nothing much, would happen unless the example came from the top. I was already well aware of the temptation of head masters to use and enjoy their authority without much thought about the consequences, and indeed with the passage of time to become indifferent to the views of others; which, consequently, these others ceased to bother to express. Unfortunately, the way in which power corrupts is an insidious one, partly because observers (if not victims) admire a strong leader. However, not much leadership is admirable unless it is by personal example. If you want people to think for themselves, don't think for them. That is why leadership solely by example is so rare, and where it exists it does not work in an obvious or measurable way. So I decided, as far as practicable, and in some cases further, to sit back and let people get on with it.

It was, however, only practicable within a broadly accepted framework, a framework in which the great majority agree what is done and what is not done. Outrageous thoughts and actions are then recognised by the majority for what they are, even if, in an ideal world, they are tolerated. The rules and customs not only of civilised society, but also of a particular institution with very clear objectives (such as a boarding school) have to be more or less universally recognised. It is within this framework that individuality has to be encouraged, and with it responsibility for one's own actions. This is obvious: the question is precisely where the line is drawn between discipline and freedom; and who draws it.

Unfortunately, I chose rather a bad moment to try out these ideas. The Sixties were to turn out to be a decade of student revolt, when the framework was rejected as being old and rotten, and nothing was proposed in its place. In fact, my ideas worked surprisingly well (perhaps it was surprising that they worked at all), but not many people were aware of this at the time. On the whole, I was criticised for being weak, except of course by those who suffered when I wasn't. With hindsight, and in the light of what happened at some other schools, perhaps a tolerant regime (even, as mine was thought to be, to the extent of slackness) worked as well in the Sixties as a more restrictive one would have done.

Almost all the public schools, old and new, were mainly or entirely boarding schools. Long before he dared to conceive the stupendous chapel, Nathaniel Woodard built the ambitious and authentic but

Lancing

austere Lancing quadrangle, to which a second less formidable upper quadrangle was added in due course. No expense was spared (Woodard was a model for fundraisers) in the masonry and, especially, in the superbly knapped flint, the authentic Sussex vernacular material, with which every building at Lancing was faced. Although it is predominantly grey, the flint also contains many warmer colours, giving the walls a softer and more varied texture than freestone. But the monastic plan with its two cloistered quadrangles did impose a certain uniformity on Lancing which it could well have done without.

There were seven boys' houses, mostly with around sixty boys. In the lower quad were the old head and second masters' houses, still preserving those names, and the School House which had spilt in to the upper quadrangle and had been divided into two, Olds and News, the latter renamed later after Lancing's best known head master, Sanderson. In the Upper Quadrangle were two more modern houses, the only ones built with individual studies for sixth formers, Fields and Gibbs's. Finally, a slightly detached head master's house built on a megalomaniac scale by Blakiston (of whom later) between the wars had been converted into a house for nearly sixty boys and named Teme House after the evacuated school's sojourn in Shropshire during the Second World War.

Nothing is more important for the head master of a boarding school than the quality of the house masters. They must have a good – ideally perhaps an intuitive – understanding of the minds of adolescents; they must have good judgement, and they must have qualities which lead their charges to respect them. I was fortunate in the group which I inherited at Lancing.

Three of the house masters were survivors of the Blakiston disaster of the 1930s which is well chronicled elsewhere: the school had been brought to its knees, and staff salaries and pensions had been cut. The disaster coincided with straitened times. All the public schools were hard pressed to fill their places after the financial crash of 1929–30 as a result of which (as one of my aunts neatly put it) nobody had any money. These three veterans were remarkable schoolmasters, although they naturally tended to like the old ways of doing things, and indeed Arthur Cooper soon left because he did not like clever boys. Patrick Halsey (an outstanding house master) and Monkey Chamberlain (his severity tempered by age and marriage) soldiered on, together with three very able men of the younger generation, Terry Kermode, Bernard

Fielding and Bill Dovell. Finally there were Ken Shearwood and Henry Thorold, each of whom deserves a few paragraphs here, although much can be discerned about them from their own publications. To say that each of them was difficult to handle when in a bad or stubborn mood would be an understatement, but each in his own way made an important contribution to the school: because they possessed, and exuded, qualities which were not common there.

Ken has written a long autobiography, in which he includes an analysis of the qualities he brought to house-mastering, concluding that the most important was his encouragement of the weaker brethren. This quality is not, perhaps, notably common among schoolmasters, and Ken possessed it to a high degree, but it was not what made him uniquely valuable to Lancing. Indeed it is odd that in all the pages he has devoted to his career as a schoolmaster he shows no inkling of what made him so highly esteemed by his head masters. It was the quality of single-mindedness, applied with the personality of a buccaneer, and it was brought to bear in his role as football coach.

One of the delightful qualities of Lancing was a sense of proportion, a mild distrust of enthusiasm in its cruder forms. It gave the school a liberal flavour in which individuals could establish their own sense of values, and not try too hard to be what they were not. But it was not quite that quintessential British quality of effortlessness in achieving success, for it had more of the effortlessness than the success. It did not extinguish the pursuit of excellence in those who had the capacity to achieve it, but it did not officiously encourage determination amongst those who did not. There was not enough ambition in the school's ethos, nor determination to succeed against the odds. Ken had the single-mindedness to inspire these qualities, and achieved what was needed in a very public arena.

The difference was apparent in the school's approach to cricket and to football. The approach to cricket was gentlemanly, but (to put it bluntly) wet. Cricket demands intense concentration, and above all the batsman must not throw away his wicket. These points did not prevail, with the result that the only school we could expect to beat was Westminster, whose approach was even wetter. The school's approach to football was not altogether gentlemanly, but it was stunningly successful.

It was important that boys should learn to be good sportsmen and good losers, and that there were certain things that simply were not

Lancing

done. One day the supporters at a football match booed the referee. This was totally unacceptable, and I told the assembled school so the next morning. I thought I had got the message across, but Ken let it be known that in his opinion I was talking 'a load of codswallop'. We had a good row over that, but he was unrepentant. However, he was worth his weight in gold.

Henry Thorold, to whom I have already referred in the context of chapel, was a very different man, and much more of a trial to his head master, but like Ken he provided a quality which was in short supply at Lancing, namely style. He had been a lazy classical scholar at Eton, and he had had to resort to the Scottish Episcopal Church to find a bishop who would ordain him; and it can only be said that his success in getting a job teaching at a good public school was against the odds. He taught Latin as he fancied he himself had been taught it at school, and he would have no truck with syllabuses or examinations: he could not be brought to heel except by being sacked, and he was too firmly entrenched for that. Indeed, in the ecclesiastical microcosm of Lancing he was the stalwart of the High Church party, who detested poor Christopher Campling's efforts to make a success of the new system. He was not perhaps the person they would have chosen for this role, but he was unmovable (and thus a reliable representative of his point of view) as well as irremovable.

Henry's method as a house master would nowadays be called laid back. It coincided happily with his disinclination to do what he did not enjoy, a quality commonly identified with laziness. But it worked. He encouraged the boys to run the house and he let them get on with it. He disliked heartiness, and once when asked by a parent whether the boys did Outward Bound activities he replied 'Madam, this is an Inward Bound house.' But it worked. His house was perfectly competent at games as well as work, and its inhabitants were proud of its achievements and its identity. He encouraged them in artistic pursuits, including drama. He was an authority on architecture, especially church architecture, and had a broad knowledge of art, coupled with excellent, if conventional, taste. He had a wide range of friends and acquaintances, with whom he corresponded in his fluent italic hand. He came of an old Lincolnshire landed and strongly clerical family, and retreated to his manor house for the holidays. He was not well off – he would not have worked as a schoolmaster if he had been – and he was not interested in money. What he did, he did in style. He bought a Rolls-Royce

Lancing

(albeit an old one) because it was the only car he could drive from Sussex to Lancashire, to visit his dentist in Bolton, without changing gear.

The teaching at Lancing was excellent. There were several stars, especially Donald Bancroft, a classicist who had turned to English literature and had a magic touch with the brightest sixth formers, always winning some scholarships to Oxford and Cambridge. Robin Reeve succeeded Roger Lockyer in the history department, and recruited in turn two distinguished colleagues, Christopher Storm Clark and Ted Maidment. Harry Guest in the modern languages department and Christopher Headington as a musician were a poet and a composer respectively, though their unconventionality in some respects made them unorthodox members of an orthodox institution. These particular men spring to mind, but there were other excellent teachers on the arts side, and science played a much more balanced part in the academic life of the school than it had done at Eton. There were good mathematicians, and a couple of high-flyers came for shortish periods in a field where recruitment was notoriously difficult.

There were also some more than competent teachers of the less academic boys. In this field Lancing was better equipped than Eton, where men with first class degrees in classics were teaching boys who would never be able to master the difference between a comma and a full stop. There were very few dull teachers or passengers.

The heads of departments were perfectly capable of running their own shows, provided that they had easy access to the head master when they wanted discussion or approval. The powers of organisation required were fortunately minimal, because almost without exception they were (to put it mildly) not good administrators. They all argued fiercely over the amount of time they should receive in the timetable, but once this was decided they had the timetable presented to them as a *fait accompli*. What they needed was flair and enthusiasm for their subjects, and this they had.

John Dancy had appointed Donald Bancroft to a new position as head master's assistant shortly before he left, and he thought that this would be a help to me. But Donald was not an administrator: his contribution was academic (and younger men could learn from this) and as a broadening and steadying influence in a parochial atmosphere. The head master of a school of Lancing's size (and indeed any size) needs to be in direct contact with the heads of the departments: a go-between is of no use to him. Where I most needed help was in introducing prospective parents. They need to meet the head master – and to get from him the answers to their most searching questions – but he simply does not have time to give them a full picture of the school. But Donald was not interested in becoming a house master, so he was of no value to me in that respect. I could not think of anything for him to do. Devising the timetable would have been too menial for the head master's assistant; and he would not have been very good at it anyway.

Nowadays public schools have directors of studies, senior masters, senior housemasters, second masters, deputy head masters, heads of year groups and two or three times the number of departments apparently requiring heads (some of them must be one-man bands). Most of these offices have been invented to give the older masters the possibility of promotion in an otherwise flat career structure. There are a few jobs too (such as registrar) to comfort the recently retired. We had none of this in my day. The timetable was made up by two people, Laurence Brown (an ex-colonial administrator) and John Higginbotham, who had a first in classics and an orderly mind. They would come in to my study and explain, in their very different styles, why certain combinations were impossible. We would decide the best solutions, whereupon John wrote the whole thing out with impeccable neatness and accuracy.

John was the only member of the staff who had the ability which would be required of an administrative grade civil servant, although he did not possess the tact to smooth his way to the higher reaches of such a career. He was therefore a valuable member of the staff, but his opinions were supported by a ruthlessly rather than broadly applied logic. When we had an argument he would conclude it by going to my study door, turning round, repeating his point of view and departing before I could reply. When Mark Morford left he became head of classics in a shrinking department.

I'm afraid I was very conservative in my support for the classics, which were under fire from all directions. Moreover my support was for the linguistic side of a classical education, rather than for the understanding of Hellenic and Roman civilisation, which on the whole could be taken as far as anyone below university level could take it by teaching it in English. My argument was that language is the most important element of any culture, and a great deal of understanding of the society in which an author lived would be obtained by reading what he wrote. Thus linguistic training, even at an elementary level, is cultural training.

Apart from English itself, Latin and Greek are keys to the understanding of most other Western European languages. Latin, the common language of Renaissance Europe, and Greek, rediscovered in the Renaissance, not only show us how they influenced the development of the vernaculars, but also enabled us to devise logical new vocabularies where they were needed, especially in science. (The fact that Welsh cannot do this assigns it inevitably to the second rank: the astonishing fact about Welsh is that it has survived at all, and is being learnt by more and more people.) With the demise of Latin and Greek, new technical vocabularies have no roots and no logic, making them impossible to master except by rote, and providing no logical routes for expansion. (What a pity that Greek disappeared a few years before computers became important.) Thus learning the mere elements of Latin and Greek provided the key to the understanding of ancient culture and its modern derivations.

The learning of Latin was a valuable tool in the educational locker, precise and economical. As with a musical note, a Latin word had to be correct in several respects. It was either right or wrong.

Latin and Greek were under attack from many sides. Their most virulent enemies were their nearest neighbours, the modern languages, whose teachers identified them as the easiest targets for plunder. Why not do less Latin, or none at all, and share the time between French and German? Thus the modern linguists slowly but systematically destroyed their closest allies: and now, far from having more time for modern languages, we have less and less. Every year the number of people studying modern languages at A level declines. This is not solely because there are no ancient languages to lend support to them, but it is an element. By insisting on abolishing the classics, the modern linguists shot themselves in the foot.

Alas, there was hardly anybody except a small group of classicists, and myself, to hold the fort. It was a hopeless battle, for the vast majority of parents were not on our side.

When I arrived at Lancing, Greek was under threat. How could I ever have imagined that this would happen in my lifetime, yet I was still under forty years of age! How could the civilisation on which we set so much store abandon one of its greatest cultural treasures and return to the Dark Ages? Greek was no use, I was told. Well, I thought, there

Lancing

would have been no Renaissance if people had thought that then. Yet they had not merely had to learn Greek from a grammar and textbook, they had had to unravel a lost language. We seemed to be on the threshold of a culture in which usefulness ruled supreme.

I thought up what seemed to me to be a clever idea. The top set of boys would give up Latin for their second year in the school and concentrate on Greek instead. This was universally thought to be eccentric, but I tried it. These boys had learnt Latin since they were eight. They could easily have passed the O level at the age of thirteen. So why not give them a year off, enable them to master the elements of Greek, and save a classical education in a sixth form: for a sixth form classicist with Latin and no Greek is a one-legged man. They would easily pick up Latin where they had left off.

My idea did not really work, or not for long, because the classical education was, as it turned out, in its death throes, and within twenty years classical sixth forms had been consigned to history. One reason for this was the lack of nerve of the classicists themselves. Their defence was to abandon (more or less) classical languages and teach instead 'classical studies'. This fashion swept through the classical world. It was, unfortunately, unconditional surrender, if only they had been able to see it.

Apart from their lack of 'usefulness' the problem with the classical languages was that they, especially Greek, really were too difficult for quite a high proportion of the boys at public schools. Eton was exceptional at attempting to teach about half its pupils Greek. Most public schools settled for less, and sensibly so. Latin was easier. Perhaps a half or even three-quarters of an average public school could have gained some benefit from it. The old education was indeed too strongly linguistic. The process had been self-perpetuating not merely since the Renaissance, when secular schools and colleges wrested the monopoly of literacy from the Church, but from the Middle Ages when Latin and literacy were almost synonymous. The teachers wanted to teach what they themselves had learned, and had learned to love. The war of attrition against this regime was long and bitter. But the intended tactical withdrawal of language-based studies turned out to be the death knell of the classics.

Lancing was not on its own, but a member of the Woodard Corporation. The Founder wanted central control of his group of schools and achieved it by a Trollopian hierarchy in which the grandeur of the office

Lancing

varied inversely with the importance of the job. The Divisional Chapter, designed to keep the four Sussex schools in line, consisted of a large group of well-meaning country gentlemen and retired clergy and schoolmasters, who met annually to indulge in an extravagant dinner at our expense. They had the alarming authority to cream off the money from the more successful schools to support the unsuccessful ones, or even to start a new one. They were kept to heel by a divisional bursar, the pipe-sucking Clifford Freeman, whose investment policy had been learnt in the golden days of Edwardian Britain. He summed up his policy in seven oft-repeated words: 'I do not believe in capital appreciation.'

Fortunately the authority of the Chapter to govern the schools was delegated for day-to-day purposes to the School Council, which was in practice more or less self-electing. We had a wise and helpful chairman in Charles Chadwyck-Healey, a publisher, and some very able and financially acute members including Sir William Lawson and Nicholas Browne-Wilkinson. Flying in the face of Clifford Freeman we invested our reserves in equities and made a killing when they reached a peak in 1968.

The secretary of the School Council was the school bursar, Bill Tydd, an old Lancing boy who had been in the Burma Police and who looked, and indeed acted, the part. He treated the house masters as natives, obliging them to queue outside his office after lunch if they needed a replacement light bulb, and complaining to me regularly about their extravagance as 'Your house masters'. I told him that they were not mine, and that they were not natives, but my remarks fell on deaf ears.

The longest argument I had with Bill (it never changed, and never ended) was over the chairs for Great School, the school hall, which had room to seat the whole school of about 400 boys. Bill would not buy stacking chairs, avowedly because they were more expensive but actually because he would only allow the school to possess precisely one chair per boy. Thus when chairs were needed in Great School, they had to be moved from the classrooms by a huge team of junior boys, who naturally introduced such light relief as was available into this tedious chore, with the result that (on account of the slackness of 'my' prefects) several were broken each time, and not replaced until the following term. This accordingly involved daily, or even hourly, furniture removals between classrooms. Bill refused to listen to the argument that a boy could only sit on one chair at a time, and that the chairs would last longer if we had more of them and did not have to move them so often.

The quadrangles and surroundings were looked after, under the wary eye of the bursar, by the gardener, Mr Passey, who had migrated from Shropshire when the school returned after the war, and who was allowed a small mowing machine but no wheelbarrow. The cut grass had to be piled on a tarpaulin and carried away by hand. One path, neatly kept, bore the notice 'This Path Not to be Used'.

In one sense the bursar shot himself in the foot. He was so good at saving money that we could afford a much-needed new Music School on the chapel building site, replacing a builder's yard, and next door to the Art School established in the chapel undercroft, now under the benign direction of the thoughtful and eccentric Tom Griffiths. We were able to include in the Music School a much-needed room for chamber concerts and lectures, there having been previously nothing between a large classroom and the Great School. My policy was that sixth form lectures should consist entirely of men of action talking about their own experiences. I thought that this would encourage boys to try their hands. Some of the lectures were unforgettable, either for reasons which pleased me or caused me acute embarrassment. The latter had the redeeming, indeed rewarding, feature of showing that Lancing boys typically had good manners, although not in exactly the way General Evetts would have wished.

Indeed, we killed three birds with the Music School stone, since it not only cleared up a building site of bygone times and provided a cultural centre, but it also enabled John Beeston to establish a small technology centre in the old music rooms above the science laboratories. He had a flair for letting technology demonstrate itself by creating examples of the principles involved by means of minimal technical gadgetry. We were of course still in the pre-computer age, and one of my final purchases was to obtain for the mathematics department a dozen desk calculators at £50 each, capable of producing logarithms, sines and cosines, and cubed roots by the deft turn of a handle. Within a decade or so these latest products of high technology had been consigned either to the dustbin or to the museum. John had the originality to show the first steps towards miniaturised electronics. In those days Art and Design were still enemies, or at least rivals, rather than allies. Much emphasis was by then placed on the importance of design, in the hope of persuading society that what worked well ought to look good; but the world of Art was poles apart from the worlds of technology, science, engineering, architecture and crafts. Some people think it still should be.

My main objective in getting money from the bursar and the very supportive School Council was to create more studies, known as 'pitts', for senior boys, and accommodation for married house masters. Since the boys slept in dormitories the pitts could be quite small, ideal for individual work and just large enough for three of four friends to enjoy improving conversation. I often wondered whether, in my quest for numbers of these pitts, I was making them too poky. I rejected out of hand the idea of making them bed-sitters, which would have been so expensive as to halve the numbers. We achieved good facilities in this respect in three more houses. Instead of two houses having their own pitts, and two others sharing (a constant source of trouble) the original Pitts Passage built for the whole school, six houses now had good facilities in this respect. For the seventh house I made do, probably wrongly, with some temporary accommodation. It is impossible to make an objective assessment of the benefits of this expenditure, which I regarded as so important.

The physical training instructor, the admirable Mr Deacon (who began every sentence with the words 'Up from there'), was hijacked by Bill Tydd to run the domestic staff, which consisted mainly of what would nowadays be called 'people with learning difficulties', whose wages could be minimal, housed in a building on the east side of the school under the severe aegis of the chapel verger. The hall staff were presided over by the delightful Frank Wood, who had become used to a paltry wage in the difficult 1930s.

Bill managed this mixed bunch with aplomb and with minimum expenditure. He was a brilliant bursar, simply by sensible housekeeping and the attention to detail which that demands. He always had the detailed figures at his fingertips, carefully dividing the expenditure into two categories: on the one hand what was both unavoidable and revenue-producing, and on the other hand what was not, which included all improvements. There were no endowments to complicate the problem. He understood the cash flow in detail (schools receive all their annual income in three dollops) and he could make projections at the drop of a hat. He was much in demand to help other schools which got into financial difficulties. He had a secretary, and he used the school's woodwork instructor, and the foreman of a small local building company, to do most of the maintenance of the buildings.

The management of an independent school's finances is difficult, and unlike that of a business, whose sole aim is profit and its sole constraint the market. Of course we were constrained by what the market would bear, but our criterion was to give value for money and to budget for a surplus which businessmen regarded as absurdly small, namely about 3%. Everything depended on knowing exactly where the break-even point came. Once the fee was set, there had to be a given number of boys paying the full fee. Every pupil in excess of this number represented a surplus. That surplus had to be used to help the less affluent parents with bursaries, to attract clever boys with scholarships, and to provide for all building improvements. To be fair to Bill, he did at least recognise that there was an argument that better facilities were essential to retain revenue in the long run.

Apart from the need to give both masters and boys the opportunity to develop their responsibilities as individuals, the school needed a thorough sprucing up. The north side of the chapel had been a builder's yard for a hundred years. People had got used to it, and it had spread right up to the eastern boundary of the school, which housed not only necessities such as lavatories (still known as 'the groves', apparently because the Founder had seen no necessity for anything more than a few trees) and Eton fives courts, but whole ranges of shacks, some used as garages and others as stores. The main school approach still featured the wartime static water tank, and the road, instead of aiming for the central cupola of the Hall as intended, wandered vaguely off to the right. Even on a sunny day, everything seemed just slightly down-at-heel. The magnificent buildings did not enjoy a worthy setting. The apparently interminable task of completing the chapel gave the impression that nobody had ever tidied the place up. John Dancy wielded a new broom in every respect but the literal one. It is well known that Wykehamists are so preoccupied with intellectual matters that they don't notice their surroundings. The paint and furniture in my study were porridge and dark green respectively.

7
The Scouts 1972–82

I A NEW SHAPE FOR SCOUTING

I was Chief Scout from 1972 until 1982. My name was put forward by a person who had invited me to give the main speech at a large Scout conference in Brighton whilst I was head master of Lancing. This invitation to speak came simply because Lancing was the best known school in the area, and not because I had any particular interest in Scouting. I accepted after receiving an assurance that there would not be resentment if I was critical of the Scout Movement.

I had been an admirer of Baden-Powell since I first saw him in 1929, when I was four years old. My father had explained to me what a great man he was, and I had seen him inspect and chat to a large number of Boy Scouts and Scoutmasters. Later at my prep school I had hugely enjoyed the experience of being a Scout myself. Then I had joined the Scouts at Eton, where they were popular with the younger boys and very well led, although at the age of fifteen, like most others, I had joined the Corps. (There was only one troop of Senior Scouts.) I enjoyed the camping and the cooking and the fieldcraft in Windsor Great Park, Burnham Beeches and Hedgerley, as much because we had a hilarious time as because of what I learnt.

I had little or no connection with the Scouts for the next thirty years. I regretted that they had not recovered their position at Eton after the war, there being only the senior troop and no juniors during the decade when I taught there. This was because almost everyone joined the Corps in view of National Service, but also because the Scouts had lost their appeal. They seemed old-fashioned, having preserved not only the uniform, which was becoming ridiculous after forty years, but also all the little customs and language which Baden-Powell had so successfully introduced before the First World War. Head masters in the interwar period had made big efforts to enlist imaginative and entertaining masters for the Scouts, but they gave up on it after the Second World War.

The Scouts 1972–82

The trouble was that Baden-Powell was a genius in giving the Scouts their stamp. He created such a powerful image and had such astonishing success, and remained so active and enthusiastic into a remarkable old age that he and his creation were regarded with reverence not only by the boys but by adults whose imagination had been seized. The world had changed between the days of Edward VII and the 1930s, but the Scouts had not. There was nothing wrong with the fundamentals, but the image was no longer fashionable, and certainly didn't appeal to young people.

When Baden-Powell died in 1941 he was succeeded by Lord Somers, who sadly died in 1944. Lord Rowallan succeeded him, and by the later 1950s he had been Chief Scout for as long as the majority of Leaders, and of course all the boys, could remember, and he had seen little need for change. This was surprising in view of the fact that during the Second World War he had been one of a group of distinguished and imaginative Army officers whose task was to improve the performance of candidates who had been rejected as almost, but not quite, good enough to be officers. There was a severe shortage of officers. They had to be trained very quickly. Some candidates had the vital minimum standard of education but were short on qualities of leadership. Following the method invented by Baden-Powell, they were placed in situations requiring those qualities, simple ones at first and more challenging ones later. But this experience does not appear to have rubbed off on Rowallan as one which might be applicable in the civilian environment of post-war Scouting.

The point is illustrated by Rowallan's foreword to the facsimile edition of the original *Scouting for Boys* of 1908, which was produced in 1957 to mark the centenary of the Founder's birth. 'Fifty years have passed,' he wrote. 'Edition after edition has appeared. It has been revised, but how little revision has been required.' It was not until 1967 that the Association produced a worthy successor in the form of the *Scout Handbook*.

As the twentieth century wore on, the training of both Leaders (Scoutmasters) and boys concentrated more and more on the tricks of the trade rather than the trade itself. Boy Scouts became known for their skill in tying knots: the reason why they should be taught that skill was left on the shelf. Thus from having been the very latest thing in the training for life of young people, the Scouts became old-fashioned and out-of-date. In a rapidly changing world the changes identified by young people were most obviously superficial – in fashion, driven by a new and profitable consumer market. This fact had to be recognised.

When Sir Charles ('Chips') Maclean succeeded Rowallan he realised that he had a problem. Towards the end of the 1960s he decided to take the bull by the horns and shrewdly appointed an 'Advance Party', with a very wide remit, to report directly to himself on the changes needed. It was made up from the cream of Scout Leaders under forty years of age. During my own time in office I met most of these individuals: they were of a very high calibre, and their report was accepted as a whole.

The Advance Party report brought about a change both of image and of substance, and revived the Movement. It gave the Scouts and their Leaders (no longer 'Masters') a new look, and although the new uniform lacked style (a sad loss, for after all style was Baden-Powell's genius) it was modern, normal, functional and inexpensive. The old hierarchy of Commissioners, distinguished by the cockades in their hats, was replaced by the doctrine that everyone had a job to do: there was no distinction of rank. The introduction of a retirement age (beyond which people could help in a great variety of ways, but not as warranted leaders in uniform) was important. The Rovers, including members continuing long into adulthood, were abolished, as were 'Senior Scouts' who could remain in the ordinary Scout section beyond the age for which it was designed; and a new section of Venture Scouts for older boys was brought in. 'Minimum standards' were introduced to prevent very small groups, usually but not always led by a single opinionated leader, living an independent existence. There were some slight modifications in the Scout Law and Promise to make them more plainly relevant to young people.

All the important elements of Baden-Powell's training, especially camping and fieldcraft, were preserved, but the actual programmes for the various sections were redesigned, and expressed in modern language. A number of challenging and enjoyable outdoor pursuits, which would not have been impossible under the old regime, were systematically introduced under the aegis of properly trained Leaders and instructors. There were to be three specialised National Activity Centres staffed by experts, although in time these turned out to be financially unsustainable and were slightly scaled down and administered more locally, with other county or regional centres.

In line with the programme, the training of Leaders was revolutionised, concentrating no longer on the teaching of practical Scouting skills but on the personal qualities required. There was a well thought out and representative structure of committees to keep all the new systems working and to ensure continuous updating.

These changes had a salutary effect on the Movement, turned decline into growth, and in particular made the prospect of becoming a Scout Leader a reasonable proposition for a very large number of parents. It was my good fortune to inherit this situation, which presented plenty of challenges but which dramatically altered the chances of success.

I vividly remember the circumstances of the speech I had made to the conference at Brighton. It is difficult to be critical of well-motivated volunteers who are obviously committed to what they are doing. In front of my modest lectern was a large gathering of gentlemen of all ages in shorts, their appearance the more formidable because of the theatrical seating plan. Of course the atmosphere was good-humoured. I did not lose my nerve, and my remarks, though bluntly worded, were kindly received. The theme was simple enough: that by living, and manifestly living, in the past as disciples of Baden-Powell, they had abandoned the spirit of his original and ingenious approach. I said that it was impossible to appeal to boys except in an environment and a language which they readily understood. Radical changes were needed, and needed soon. Unknown to me, this turned out to be more or less the view which Chips Maclean himself developed as Chief Scout during the 1960s.

It was difficult to estimate whether the politeness of my audience was any measure of their agreement with my theme, and I thought no more of the matter; but the preparatory school headmaster who had suggested that I be invited to make this speech also suggested my name as a possible Chief Scout a few years later. I had not served the Scout Movement as an adult, but the selection committee were open-minded enough to consider an outsider, and my career as a schoolmaster made me a credible candidate. Seldom have I been happier than when I was offered the opportunity to take up what I knew would be a challenging role.

It will be clear from what I have written that I saw the Scouts as a wonderful influence on young people in Britain, and that the Movement was facing a challenge to continue to appeal to them almost seventy years after its foundation. Provided that it could do so, I was convinced that its methods were relevant and successful. Its whole

The Scouts 1972–82

ethos was to be enjoyable, to be a game with a strong sense of challenge and adventure which helped groups of boys to work together, to develop their own talents and to recognise those of others in a very positively tolerant way. This sense of belonging seemed to me to be especially important when the traditional forms which had held society together were becoming weaker, if not disintegrating. The old moral barriers and conventions were being dismantled, largely because they were seen as unjustifiable, irrelevant and restrictive. Newness in itself was presented as an overriding virtue, as was 'freedom': freedom from past restraints, freedom from hierarchies and freedom from 'respect'. It seemed to me that Scouting was responding to this social revolution in a balanced and measured way, encouraging self-discipline whilst still suggesting a strong social and moral framework through its Law and Promise. I wanted to be a part of it, and I had the immense good fortune and privilege to have happened to blow in at an ideal moment of opportunity. I did not have any grand ideas about anything I might help to achieve: I just liked the idea of helping to keep the ship on course.

Some of those who objected to the Advance Party's measures stayed on in the Movement, and on the whole made the best of the situation. A very few left altogether, and some created little independent denominations of their own, including, typically, one which called itself The Baden-Powell Scouts. Unfortunately the Founder's widow, Olave Baden-Powell, felt hurt by some of the changes, especially the changes to the Promise and Law. She thought that they were unnecessary, that they were changes for change's sake, that they broke with tradition and that they implied that the individual genius and achievement of the Founder was no longer respected as it should be. Not being responsible for them, I was able to point out that they were considered important by the Advance Party and were not at the whim of an individual or a clique, and I tried to defend them by arguing that the Founder was an innovator with an instinctive sense of what would appeal to the young people of his own generation. With her characteristic generosity of spirit, she did not dissent.

Overwhelmingly the report of the Advance Party received an enthusiastic welcome, so the problems were confined to getting a comprehensive package of changes to work in practice, and to deal with the teething troubles. Fortunately the Movement was served by a large number of very capable leaders. It had one signal advantage over the Girl Guides in that both sexes were involved in the leadership, although in those days most of the female leaders were still involved only with the Cubs, aged eight to eleven.

It would be wrong to give the impression that the Movement was weak before Chips Maclean decided to take action. The need simply was to be bold enough to initiate the process of reform. In a large voluntary organisation which is suffering from inertia at the centre, it is very difficult for those who are worried to get together to concert a plan of action. If a 'party' is formed to promote a policy it is likely to be considered disloyal or disruptive; but the real problem is that it does not have the resources – especially the required amount of time to be devoted to its cause – to push through a programme of reform even if it can devise one. Most of those involved, at every level, were busy enough earning their bread and butter. (This was one of the problems underestimated in the new Leader training programme.) As for the professionals, whose job is primarily administrative, they are only too well aware of the limits of their function: a point often similarly underestimated, in spite of the vast resources available, even by governments. Governments tend to doctor the limitations of a Civil Service by bringing in either 'businessmen' or 'special advisers' to what are essentially administrative roles, adding to the muddle of the half-baked schemes euphemistically called 'initiatives', of which the long-suffering public are only too well aware. A voluntary organisation has no such luxury. And it cannot afford to reorganise itself every few years.

Thus, as soon as the Scout Movement began to operate the agreed changes, its strength became evident and it moved from decline to slow but significant growth.

2 ORGANISATION, LOCAL AND CENTRAL

Each Scout Group was within a District, presided over by a District Commissioner with a number of volunteer assistants in and out of uniform. On average there were about ten Scout Groups, or 1,000 boys, in a District. The larger, and effectively the largest, unit was the County. This varied in size between less than 1,000 boys in sparsely populated areas to 20,000 in Essex and in Hampshire and in some of the largest cities, of which Glasgow and Birmingham were shining examples. Other large cities – Manchester for instance – formed several

The Scouts 1972–82

'Counties', and London was inevitably a law unto itself (roughly speaking seven 'Counties'). As far as possible, for practical reasons we followed local government boundaries. Like the Districts, the Counties had virtually no administrative structure apart from the Secretary and Treasurer, who of course were volunteers, and a group of expert volunteers to assist the County Commissioner.

This organisation in Counties, Districts and Scout Groups may sound hierarchical and even bureaucratic, but it was not. It was both flexible and decentralised, and enabled each County to be run and organised according to its needs. The tasks of the County Commissioner for Orkney were very different from those of Hampshire or Birmingham. He could dispense with Districts altogether in presiding over the two groups in Kirkwall and Stromness. The resources available to run a voluntary organisation at the two extremes were also very different.

Mirroring the geography and demography of the United Kingdom, Scotland, Northern Ireland and Wales had their own Chief Commissioners with small headquarters offices in Edinburgh, Belfast and Cardiff. England was so comparatively large that it needed running slightly differently but, in such a decentralised organisation, only slightly.

Inevitably there were complaints about Headquarters imposing unnecessary regulation, and people wondering what on earth everybody there found to do. But on the whole I think we got it about right in deciding what had to be centralised. The boundaries of what was acceptable were defined by an elaborate volume entitled *Policy, Organisation and Rules*. The Training and Programme department dealt with What People Do, the programmes being periodically updated by large representative boards for the three sections (Cubs, Scouts and Venture Scouts) which met only once or twice a year with a tiny secretariat. In the wake of the Advance Party Report, which had produced quite radical changes after decades of inertia, all concerned were resolved to keep the Movement up-to-date, and there was a tendency to make changes too frequently to suit the digestive limitations of a voluntary organisation. Nevertheless it was striking how quickly programmes did get out of date, especially in the Cub Scout section: within the decade of my own involvement the range of knowledge and experience available to an eight-year-old advanced radically, thanks not least to some educationally slanted, but nevertheless popular, television programmes.

The Scouts 1972–82

There was also a huge advance in children's books. The Programme and Training Department provided an excellent choice of attractive material on activities. A centralised Public Relations department was essential to communicate with the national media, and the monthly Scouting magazine was also produced by Headquarters. Insurance obviously required the advantage of scale which only Headquarters could provide. And above all, perhaps, the people at Headquarters had to be available to answer a stream of questions from all and sundry.

The Movement's finance depended on the membership fee, which clearly in a voluntary organisation endeavouring to attract boys from all walks of life had to be as low as possible. The Advance Party had decided that this should be a Capitation Fee, which involved a useful annual census. Apart from the fact that Scouters were honest people, the temptation to cook the figures was moderated by the desire to be seen to be doing well. The necessary census provided useful statistics by which success or failure could be measured.

The Scout Association was governed by Royal Charter with the standard large and unwieldy Council consisting of the great and the good, which met once a year for the same purpose as a medieval parliament – to hear and confirm. All the decisions were taken by the Committee of the Council which met monthly. This executive committee was properly representative, with a majority of elected members who were mostly County Commissioners from all over Britain. In the classic pattern of similar organisations, the Committee had its three sub-committees for Finance, Programme and Training, and General Purposes, the last sweeping up everything not covered by the first two. The Scout Association had sufficient standing to recruit first-class advisers to join these bodies.

The Movement was as well served by its small professional staff as by its volunteers. Headquarters was divided into four sections: the Headquarters so called, and the hostel, Baden-Powell House, in London; the training centre at Gilwell Park, the Founder's Estate near Chigwell in North London; and the Trading Arm (primarily Scout Shops Limited) on an industrial estate at Lancing in Sussex.

The London Headquarters were in an old-fashioned office in Buckingham Palace Road, but fortunately with the aid of Charles Williams, a lifelong Scout and a successful property developer, a site was obtained in the Cromwell Road adjacent to Baden-Powell House, the hostel which had been built as the memorial to the Founder. Here a small but

The Scouts 1972–82

well-designed new headquarters was established, and opened by the Queen in 1974. As well as providing exactly the offices required, it was able to share the larger meeting rooms and the catering with the hostel next door. On the top floor there was some staff accommodation and a flat for the Chief Scout. Alas, financial problems have obliged the Movement to give up this ideal building and to use the White House at Gilwell instead. Perhaps modern communications have made this more satisfactory than it would have been in the 1980s, and Gilwell does have the advantage of being the Mecca of Scouting.

The Chief Executive Commissioner (the vestigial title of Commissioner, introduced by the Founder for all senior appointments, has now been dropped from the title) was Ken Stevens, a man of great ability with a lifelong experience of Scouting, mostly at Gilwell. There had been much debate by the Committee of Council, whether to appoint Ken as the 'natural successor' or whether to head-hunt an outsider to run the organisation. Ken not only had the required judgement and skill but his knowledge and understanding of the Movement was especially valuable in the wake of the Advance Party. I was most fortunate in having him in office throughout my tenure. He was positive and enthusiastic and a good adviser, and several times a year he used to come and spend a night at our home and we would use a couple of days exploring ideas (our own and other people's) for the future. He saved me from many pitfalls. In retrospect he was over-cautious, but he was a good foil for my ability to produce ideas without always showing the perseverance to push them through until they were 'thoroughly finished'. He kept the Movement on course and every year we could show a slight but welcome increase in membership, which over a decade amounted to about 15%.

One of the difficulties of his very demanding job was that many senior (in every sense of the word) members and former members expected (and for the most part deserved) to have personal access to him and he was not very good at terminating an interview when it was over. But this regular contact with people from all over the country helped to keep him in touch with what was going on and what people saw as their problems. He tended to accumulate too many minor problems rather than having the gift of 'clearing his desk', but in a large and complicated organisation which is sensitive to its 'users' there are always more loose ends than one would wish. If Ken had a weakness it was that he was not always a good judge of people in making

The Scouts 1972–82

appointments. Methods of selection were less sophisticated than they are nowadays.

The other pillar of Headquarters was Ted Hayden, the Secretary and No 2, who again was very capable and had a lifelong devotion to the Movement. He was an entertaining speaker who had the infuriating habit of telling a stream of jokes when he was meant to be introducing the main speaker at a meeting or conference. He was in charge of the various Headquarters departments – finance and property, insurance, programme, training, public relations, international – and the various camping and training centres scattered around Britain. Scotland, Wales and Northern Ireland ran their own headquarters under their Chief Commissioners with a professional staff of two or three people.

John Huskins, a clever and ingenious schoolmaster from Charterhouse, had been introduced to run the new regime at Gilwell. John created the new leader training programmes, and revolutionised the way in which training was approached. His was a notable achievement but, having a penchant for academic jargon, and being accustomed to abstract ideas, he did not always fit the training to the trainee. In this respect he lacked the flair of Baden-Powell to teach quite subtle points in a simple and practical way. Thus, although John was exactly the man to transform the whole ethos of the leader training, he was not equally good at modifying his ideas in the light of experience, and he was probably right to move on when he had accomplished his vital initial task – of persuading the Movement that its Leaders must focus their attention on the boys they were training, and not on the skills they were teaching. He put the Scout Movement back on the educational map.

There were about 75,000 uniformed Leaders in the Movement in Britain at any one time, some serving for just a few years and others for a lifetime. Many courses were run at Gilwell, but there were also a number of training centres around the country, a few run by the largest counties and cities and some by groups of counties, so that it was not necessary, as it was for a Gilwell course, for a Scouter to take a full week off. Training courses could be fitted in during evenings and at weekends, but Gilwell set the pace and provided all the literature for the training programmes. It was there that the trainers of Leaders were themselves trained.

As well as the Scottish, Welsh and Northern Ireland headquarters some of the larger English counties employed one or two professionals, but it was Headquarters which employed the important group of Field

Commissioners (there were seventeen of them in my time) who covered groups of counties throughout Britain. All of them were volunteer Scout Leaders who had decided to give their professional life to Scouting. Paying for them was the largest single expense incurred from the central budget, but they played a crucial part, particularly in two respects. First, they linked Headquarters with the remotest areas, maintaining standards and communicating problems; secondly they acted as a lifeline for the County Commissioners, who virtually ran the Movement in their counties but were busy people in their own walks of life. It was very often a Field Commissioner who made a County Commissioner's job sustainable by giving advice (or simply 'talking over' problems) and support. Inevitably there were sometimes gaps between appointments when a Field Commissioner would temporarily take on a District Commissioner's role. The three National Activity Centres and about a dozen national campsites were also run by Headquarters.

The commercial operation at Lancing (Scout Shops Ltd) was run by an expert retailer who was one of the five or so 'Executive Commissioners' (though not in uniform like the others) – together with Stevens, Hayden, Huskins and the No 3 at headquarters, Robbie Robinson, one of whose main jobs was to run the Field Commissioner service.

Hitherto Scout Shops had been a mixture of small units run by the Association either centrally or in districts, or of privately owned shops. The Advance Party rightly identified the advantages of a centralised service which could both procure and sell the new uniforms cheaply to members, and which could sell other Scouting and camping equipment profitably both to members and to the general public. We had the advice of a senior Marks & Spencer manager as a committee member, and a suitable appointment was made to run the central store and office at Lancing and a small chain of about eight shops. The annual profit was a welcome addition to our budget, opening up the possibility that the business could gradually expand and perhaps pay for all the Headquarters costs. This was in the days before camping and outdoor shops were common. We had a head start, and although some shops were more successful than others the prospects looked good. Then the executive left and a poor appointment was made – in fact a disastrous appointment. Our trade was expanded by too much siphoning off of the retail business to others, a process not carried out in an entirely disinterested manner: this problem should – and easily could – have been identified sooner.

It has to be admitted that, even at its best, the business suffered from some common shortcomings. The catalogues were better than the supply of the items they advertised. Whilst we had our head start we also suffered somewhat from the common malaise of British commerce and industry in that era – complacency and a general acceptance that what was easy to achieve was good enough. Stock was not efficiently controlled. Nevertheless we were doing well and if the right appointment had been made we could have continued to grow. As it was, we still made a profit but the business slumped into the doldrums.

Almost without exception, the professional staff of the Association were dedicated and efficient, and many had a notable flair for their roles. Some served for a lifetime, others came and went. Writing some thirty years later, I am happy to record that two of the most promising young men appointed during my tenure, Derek Twine and David Shelmerdine, rose to become the Chief Executive and the Secretary.

3 ROBERT BADEN-POWELL

Baden-Powell's assumptions were based on his experience at school at Charterhouse and in the Army. Much of his energy in the Army was expended in the orthodox manner, on specifically military training at the tactical level: in the use of weapons and equipment, and on the rigid hierarchical organisation of the regiment, supported by strict discipline, drummed in by endless drill. To every soldier the regiment was the institution in which he lived and moved and had his being, given to creating and nurturing his morale, the most important element in war. Officers and other ranks were poles apart; not by then so much for social reasons, which alone had kept them poles apart in days gone by, though still with a strong flavour of arrogance and snobbery; but for well-tried reasons of military discipline as well.

In this military environment, bred of a fairly simple set of assumptions, Baden-Powell became something of a maverick. In India in the 1880s he taught his men map-reading and fieldcraft (teaching them to track both men and animals), and devised a series of lectures for them. He encouraged them to think for themselves and to take decisions to get out of a scrape. His was a cavalry regiment, where these skills were more appropriate than in the infantry, and much more relevant in India than in orthodox European warfare. As it happened, his ideas were vitally relevant in the Boer War which began so disastrously for the

The Scouts 1972–82

British infantry in 1899, using European tactics against the roving bands of Boer mounted countrymen; men born to fieldcraft and to accuracy with the rifle. In fact it was the volunteer British Yeomanry Regiments, farmers and countrymen like the enemy, mounted infantrymen rather than formal cavalry, who saved the day.

Baden-Powell honed his ideas twenty years before the founding of the Boy Scouts in 1905. In 1884 he wrote *Reconnaissance and Scouting*, based on his series of twenty lectures to his men: 'A scout must be a man of intelligence and pluck, and a good horseman, with confidence in himself, that is to say, one who will not lose his head in a sudden emergency, but can trust himself to get out of all difficulties, and who is full of "dodges" to meet every kind of incident or accident that may occur.' This is vintage *Scouting for Boys* material. That book appeared in parts, at 4d each, starting in January 1908.

Much has been written about the incubation period of Scouting between the end of the Boer War in 1901 and the Brownsea Island Camp of 1907; and about Baden-Powell's thoughts and his conversations with leaders and supporters of other youth organisations, especially the Boys' Brigade and the Church Lads' Brigade. Field Marshal Lord Roberts, who had been pulled out of retirement to retrieve the disastrous situation in the early days of the Boer War, was worried about the shortage of future officers for the Army. Baden-Powell recognised this and knew how he could help, but from the start he emphasised his aim to train young people in and for 'civil life' rather than the armed services, and he did not click either with the military parading or with the starkly formal evangelistic spirit of the Boys' or the Church Lads' Brigade. He also shied away from new youth organisations in both Canada and South Africa whose macho ethos he disliked and distrusted. Before he started the Boy Scouts there were already three small organisations in England which, without his leave, were using not only his ideas but also his famous name – a name which had become a household word on the relief of Mafeking.

It has often been pointed out that Mafeking was not of major military importance, and that the siege owed its fame to the need for any kind of victory. Critics have shown that Baden-Powell's actions in the war were not universally chivalrous – to put the matter mildly. But what caught the public's imagination was his ingenuity and his ability to improvise – that most British quality which has so often (although the First World War was a notable exception) turned defeat into victory. Soon after he started the Boys Scouts he was almost overwhelmed with its 'mushroom growth'.

Baden-Powell wanted to mix boys from different social backgrounds 'like plums in a pudding', and the mixture was an early and successful example of group dynamics. Boys were to help one another and each had a contribution to make to his patrol. This idea of the small organic unit was one of his most important and original ideas. They were to plan their own ventures, to think for themselves and to overcome difficulties. His notes for instructors, printed in italics, were larded with little ingenious ideas not so much to provide solutions as to present small problems: puzzles which could be solved by ingenuity or, most importantly, by observation. Boys were taught (not by lecture, but by doing) that they could learn to hear and to see things which others did not hear and see. But there was more to it than that. By looking outwards boys learnt to think less of themselves and more of others, to widen their horizons and to acquire 'a multitude of small interests outside themselves'. This was at a period when almost no elementary school had any such aim or method to lighten the grind of the Three Rs, nor any concept of teaching its pupils to think for themselves. For most children, the elementary school was the beginning and the end of their education. The great majority had never seen a field, let alone a cow.

Scouting, said Baden-Powell, was a game. It was to be enjoyed: 'because if one is happy, one has it in one's power to make all those around happy'. He was as good as his word, for many of the lessons he taught were learnt through games. In the twenty-first century Scout and Cub programmes are still liberally larded with games.

Baden-Powell's ideas were enlarged and consolidated during the early years of the Boy Scouts, and the moral, spiritual and social training which he wanted to impart were represented by the formalised Scout Law and Promise. Surely he has a claim to be recognised as the greatest practical educationist of the twentieth century, perhaps also the twenty-first. The Girl Guides owe their existence to him as much as the Scouts do, and he was a pioneer in creating a passionately anti-racist international organisation. Those were the days when gentlemen would not see tradesmen's children in their children's schools, nor would tradesmen see working men's children; and when the idea of including black or coloured children in a group of white children was unthinkable. This is not judgemental. It is simply a statement of fact. It justifies the suggestion that Baden-Powell was 'ahead of his times'.

The Scouts 1972–82

I might be taken to task for saying that in using small groups as organic units and virtually inventing modern group dynamics, in teaching boys to use their eyes and ears to perceive what many would miss, in learning by doing and by problem solving, especially by improvisation; in broadening horizons and teaching social responsibility, Baden-Powell was a trainer rather than an 'educationist'. But this would be perverse, for those who train rather than educate depend on instructing their pupils rather than drawing the best from them. Indeed, contrary perhaps to most people's perception today, the elementary schools of the late Victorian and Edwardian era, disciplined as they were, contributed almost nothing either in teaching their pupils to think for themselves or in social or moral education. Religious teaching was inhibited, not to say in many cases prohibited, by late Victorian legislation. That Baden-Powell should run contrary to this tide – especially in the Army with its rigid hierarchy and strict discipline – marks him out as a pioneer of modern education.

By the time when that bane of education, the educational theorist, began to appear on the scene, Baden-Powell's system was already helping hundreds of thousands of boys and girls at any one time. The Scout and Guide Movements quickly became the largest youth organisations in the world, as they still are today. His emphasis on developing powers of observation – and the games he used for the purpose – were starting to become subjects of mockery (as was his best idea in social education – doing a good turn every day). Yet in spite of the legions of theorists who have influenced our schools, little attention has been given to the needs of clever children who lack academic ability, by which I do not mean children affected by those (common) types of dyslexia which are now recognised. The solution to the social problems posed by variations in academic ability, aided and abetted by political interference, has been to lump everyone together and dumb down the academic rigour required for success – or, rather, for the avoidance of failure. Those in opposition to this policy have not invented an alternative academic syllabus but have suggested that non-academic pupils should be sidelined into 'vocational' training, a euphemism for teaching them how to succeed in a manual occupation. It is my firm belief that the education which most benefits school 'failures' is to teach them to use their eyes and ears and to find some topic and skill which grips their interest..

Education in Britain since the 1960s as promulgated by the theorists

The Scouts 1972–82

has been, broadly speaking, powerfully anti-Establishment. In other words it has tried to rid itself, and its victims, of conventional restraints. Its approach to discipline has been governed more by hazy idealism than by practical common sense. This change took a long time to work its way through the system, because the vast majority of teachers who set out on that career (or, rather, vocation) stick to it. Meantime it has, needless to say, invented its own conventions, its own framework, and indeed its own establishment, in the form of 'political correctness' which has now filtered through to adult life.

All this reflects the far-reaching and largely beneficial social changes which have affected Britain (and much of the developed world) since the 1960s. But a social (or a political) revolution is like a cavalry charge. It is easier to start it than to stop it. The loosening of the old social restraints, the system which supported and was supported by the 'Establishment', the permissiveness which replaced the old 'liberalism', have brought in their wake the forms of undesirable behaviour which governments now wish to reverse. The problem is that they try to reverse them by treating the symptoms rather than the disease. I am tempted to say that the Scout Movement, still inspired by the Founder's imagination and initiative, has nurtured education and social reform and is one of the comparatively few institutions in Britain which has not only 'got it about right' but which is still a benign and powerful influence. It is a fine example of the continuity of British institutions, based on their ability to adjust themselves to the needs of the times.

4 THE SCOUT GROUP

The key to the success of the whole Movement lay in the quality of the Scout Group Leaders. The Scout Group was the essential unit, and it had the merit of being about the right size. This was variable according to demographic circumstances. The rural groups were often quite small, with just one Scout troop and one Cub pack, but the Advance Party had decided that they must not be too small, or they would not be able to provide an adequate programme and maintain a satisfactory standard. There were many cases where a small village or a hamlet could raise just one Scout patrol or six Cubs, or even fewer. They travelled to the local market town for their weekly meetings as part of a Group. This system worked well. There were also a number of successful small Groups in towns or cities where a strong tradition had been built up – strong enough to ensure continuity of leadership when people left the Group for one reason or another. This continuity was greatly helped if a small Group had its own Scout hut – by then rather grandly referred to by most people as its Headquarters. Sometimes these small Groups also had long-established contacts providing camp-sites and other useful forms of support. But on the whole it was the large Groups which were the most successful and which made the running for the whole Movement.

A typical large Group would have three Cub packs (each of up to about thirty boys aged eight to eleven), two Scout troops (up to the age of fifteen) and a Venture Scout unit (which had a minimum size of nine members). It might have about 150 boys in all, and at least twenty uniformed Leaders, a treasurer and a secretary and a band of instructors and helpers. The majority of the Cub Scout Leaders would be women, and most of the Scout Leaders men, but more women were involved with the Scouts and the Venture Scouts as the 1970s wore on, and quite a number were becoming Commissioners, a rare occurrence before the Advance Party report. But Scouting was still a boys-only movement, apart from the odd girl who crept in unnoticed by the authorities, often a Leader's daughter. Most of the large Groups had their own headquarters, and local authorities were quite generous with grants to help with building costs. With three Cub packs and two Scout troops, as well as a Venture Unit, the building would be used every evening of the week.

The success of many of these large Groups could be attributed to an individual Leader who had managed to build it up until it was more or less self-generating. The secret was that the Leaders should enjoy their role. Although for the most part they came to Scouting after a day's work, they found good company and plenty of mutual support. Nobody had to be jack of all trades. Money was no worry: there were people to do the fundraising, and with the Group so strongly connected with its neighbourhood this was not too difficult. Parents were in many cases the best source of Leaders. In a family with two or more sons, one or both parents might help, and might stay on after their boys had left. Expertise or skill of one kind or another was available for the asking.

The Groups often had a long history, and often included Scouting families in which everyone had been involved with the Movement for several generations: Scouting was one of the most important features of their family life. These families were always full of cheer and they formed an invaluable hard core of the Scout Movement. But there were also Leaders who, perhaps, would just give their time for a few years. The consequence was that the programmes were of a very high order. There were plenty of indoor and outdoor activities, expeditions and camps, and a strong sense of belonging. The boys enjoyed themselves and often those who started as Cubs went on to be Scouts and then Venture Scouts, and remained in the Group until they were twenty or twenty-one years of age or left home for university or a career. The Queen's Scout Award was of long standing and carried prestige. The Advance Party had devised an excellent and varied programme for the Scout section, leading to the Chief Scout's Award, and this too was highly valued. Some of them would soon become Leaders, forging an important link between generations.

Another virtue of these Groups was that their membership covered a wide range of backgrounds. There were some from predominantly working class communities and some from leafy suburbs but, because of its inclusive nature and its particular, and indeed unique, flavour, Scouting was a good leveller from the socio-economic point of view.

I visited a large number of Groups each year and I made it my objective to find out what their problems were. This was not too difficult because there were several common difficulties – raising money and recruiting Leaders being amongst the most typical. There was quite a range of possible problems which were either obviously likely to be identified, or which I soon learnt about by asking questions. But when I asked the question in these extended successful Groups the answer simply was that there weren't any. This gave a clear indication of what we should be aiming at.

The Association had a long tradition of including boys with what is now known as special needs and was then known as a handicap. The idea of integrating physically disabled boys and those with learning difficulties into ordinary Groups was already well under way and was of benefit to all concerned. There were also a number of excellent Groups associated with special schools where integration would not have been advantageous. There was an adequate supply of well-trained adults, whether at Group or district or county level, to give support.

Many Groups were connected, strongly or loosely, with churches and chapels. The Founder had emphasised the importance of spiritual values, which were a vital element of the Movement, cemented by the Law and Promise. Many of the church and chapel Groups had been started in the early days before the First World War. In those days parishes had been well staffed with curates, many of whom became Scoutmasters. This was in decline by the 1960s, and the shortage of clergy was beginning to be felt; so in most of the church Groups the leaders were lay members of the congregation and, indeed, in some cases the Group's connection with the church was tenuous. Many other groups had a clergyman as their chaplain, who could be called upon to turn up on appropriate occasions and to hold the St George's Day service in his church or chapel. It was a pity that the Church didn't do as the Scouts (and practically every other institution in Britain) did, and form larger units.

The Scout Handbook (first edition 1967) and the *Cub Scout Handbook* were first-rate, admirably edited and produced. They were written specifically for boys, but were also splendid programme guides for leaders. In most cases Scout troop or Cub pack meetings were very lively affairs, governed in both shape and content by the ethos of the Movement, with just enough of its cheerful eccentricity to prevent earnestness from taking over, but not enough to become crazy. There were collective activities, including always games, group activities by patrols or sixes, and individual or Group activities learning this or that, often from an instructor who had been roped in, and often concluded by the award of a badge (but sometimes the number of badges achievable devalued them, especially in the case of Cubs). Much – one might almost say everything – depended on the training and aptitude of the Leader, preferably delivered with a strong enough whiff of personality to make it interesting without being exhibitionist.

This ethos was caught rather than taught, either by Leaders who had been members in their youth, or simply from getting the feel of it. The post-Advance Party training courses for Leaders were effective, showing them how to concentrate on the people they were leading rather than the material they were teaching. In this respect, however, they went rather too far and one of the main problems which had to be solved during the early 1970s was to get the balance right between theory and practicalities for the Cub and Scout section Leaders.

The Venture Scout section was different, both in itself and in the leadership required. The Advance Party had reached the right conclusion, namely that it needed to be self-governing, without the Leaders occupying the front seat. In truth, it tended to be a social club, indulging in periodic activities, some of them very adventurous and demanding. The 'minimum standard' required at least nine members, and on the whole it was only in the larger Groups that nine or more boys wanted to stay on after the age of fifteen: there were so many other demands on their spare time, and moreover many other organisations and many families were taking up imitations of the Scouts' programmes for themselves.

The requirement for a successful Venture Scout Unit was therefore a Group large enough to continue to want to enjoy not only the ethos and activities of Scouting, but also each other's company. True, in theory only two or three recruits were needed each year, but in practice most Venture Units had a hard core of perhaps nine or ten boys who were all roughly contemporary. Once that was established, then it would be viable to recruit a few new members each year, but on the other hand when the hard core left the Unit tended to collapse, and the Scout Group had to start to form one all over again. Probably the commonest cause of collapse was the departure of several members to colleges or universities away from home, and very often at the same age others would start full-time work and lose interest.

As in other contexts, it was often outstanding leadership which led to continuity, especially in a Unit which took the Queen's Scout Award seriously. Over and over again this became evident at the presentations which we held two or three times a year, preferably in a grand or special building: relatively few Units had just one Queen's Scout. More often those who had any had several, and members of such a Unit would keep turning up year after year, until for some reason the chain would break.

The idea was that if a Group did not have enough candidates to form its own Venture Scout Unit, there would be a District Unit, and this did sometimes work well: indeed there were a few District Units which might have a membership of fifty or sixty, and which made an outstanding contribution to their communities. Once they had reached that size, like large Groups they were self-generating; but to get to that size they had to have an inspiring Leader. To most boys, however, the District was amorphous or even unknown, except perhaps on the occurrence of the occasional memorable event when an ocean of Scouts

The Scouts 1972–82

appeared before the eyes of those accustomed to see a pond. On the whole, if boys became Venture Scouts it was largely because they could continue to enjoy the company of their friends.

In the early Seventies there was still a strict agreement with the Girl Guides that the Scouts would recruit males only, except in the case of Leaders. (Most of the female Leaders were in the Cub Scout section, although this was starting to change.) At the same time it was obvious that Venture Scout Units were more likely to be formed if girls as well as boys could join. I devoted such diplomatic skill and patience as I could muster to trying to persuade the Girl Guides to join us at the older age Group, and to form joint Units, and we very nearly got there; but in the end they drew back. They thought that men would try to dominate. At the time I did not think they were right: I thought we would be capable of forming a balanced partnership. But now I am not so sure. The problem was not a particularly subtle one. It was mainly that most of the top Guiders were only too well aware that it was still the men who had the money; and he who pays the piper calls the tune. Of course there was more to it than that: much more. But that was, I believe, the deciding factor when the proposal we had arrived at was put to the vote by the Guides.

Venture Scouting played an important part in the lives of many young men, and served them well. But from the Association's point of view it was never quite the success the Scout and Cub sections were, and the numbers never rose much above 20,000, when the two younger sections were growing quite successfully – even after we introduced girls unilaterally, to the great benefit of the section, which they sharpened up no end.

John Huskins, as I have mentioned, masterminded the transformation from knowledge-based to person-based training, but he underestimated the difficulty experienced by numerous Leaders in coping with theoretical and abstract language. It was not the material he devised which had to be modified, but the way in which it was expressed. The second problem had similar roots: it was thought wrong to serve up the training syllabuses on a plate, as had been done under the old system. Rather, the Leader should think out suitable programmes for himself. This too posed a problem for the Leader who was not accustomed to designing his own material. But it also made things more difficult for Leaders who were familiar with this kind of challenge, but who simply

The Scouts 1972–82

did not have the time or the mental energy after a hard day's work to devise a programme from scratch. What was required was a series of menus, for which the Leader had to invent his own recipes; or, perhaps, a series of recipes from which the Leader had to invent his own menus. It was too much to expect a Leader, other than one who either had plenty of experience or an undemanding day-time job, to invent both. This difficulty was redressed by an increasing stock of excellent programme material, some of it in *Scouting* magazine and some on special (and very well illustrated) sheets.

The other difficulty we had to alleviate in the 1970s was what was then coming to be known as the Management of Change. This, again, was a question of trying to get the balance right – for a voluntary organisation – between too many changes and too few. The Movement was by now very conscious that in the future it must evolve, making revolutionary change unnecessary. But those responsible at the centre had a different view from those at the coal face, to whom every change was a potential irritation. Changes were considered by large and fully representative Boards, but the members did tend to be people for whom the concept of regular updating and modification were familiar. Through the eyes of an over-taxed Leader devising weekly programmes, things looked different.

During the 1970s the pace of change was most rapid in the Cub Scout section. This was due largely to improvements in television and the growing popularity of playgroups. During the course of less than a decade the experience of a child of three or four years old was transformed, provided that there was parental participation. Alas, by that age a deep divide was forming between children with educated parents and those without. Moreover, children from a home where they would be encouraged to watch Blue Peter and some programmes about the natural world, and where there would be a few Ladybird books lying about, were already streets ahead of contemporaries who were deprived of these experiences, most of whom would never catch up – unless they were unusually gifted. Sadly, it was the deprived sector who were least likely to join the Cubs.

The Scout Association spotted these processes, and took early steps to keep the Cub Scout programmes in tune with them. It took the Association some time, however, to abandon the urge to impose on volunteer Leaders a constant stream of modifications (now termed 'initiatives' and the bane of teachers), and to introduce changes only by

The Scouts 1972–82

a carefully considered system. The same problem affected the Scouts, but without similar pressure. They were becoming more sophisticated in a rather different and less fundamental way.

The big question was whether to reduce the age of entry to the Cubs below eight, or indeed whether to introduce a new junior section. Throughout my time as Chief Scout there were endless discussions as to whether the age ranges of the Sections were right. If the Cubs should start younger, should they end younger too? Should boys join the Venture Scouts at fourteen rather than fifteen? Should a Senior Scout section be inserted? I think the general conclusion was probably the right one – namely that the section should adjust what it did, and how, rather than that the Association should change the ages of transfer. The system had the merit of coinciding with the national system of school education. But if boys (and girls) were now so much more advanced before they even reached the age of eight, ought we to cater for them at a younger age, when they could digest most of the former Cub Scout programme? We did lower the age of entry, but we decided against a junior section for the time being.

There were two difficulties. First of all, in spite of the fact that there were 30,000 Cub packs throughout Britain, there were massive waiting lists. The Movement, as I have explained, had about 75,000 uniformed leaders in all, and although some served for thirty years or more, the average turnover was rapid and the resources for Leader training – the human resources in particular – were limited. How were we to increase this vast volunteer army? We might simply have said that it was hard enough to stand still, but in fact we managed a small increase year upon year. If we started a junior section, perhaps it would be led mainly by our present leaders, aggravating the problem for the Cubs, which were really a huge success and making a massive contribution to the training of young people. The second problem was more intractable. There was clearly a measurable period of time for which the average boy remained in the Movement. There was some leakage between the Cubs and the Scouts, some during the years in the Scout Section, and a great deal towards its upper end.

There was of course the argument that this was the trouble: that the problem we should address was how to keep boys in the Movement for longer. The answer is simple enough: this was exactly what we were trying to do, and always had tried to do. The solution would not be discovered by being blind to the facts. The question we should be asking was not – or not only – how we could maximise numbers, but where was Scouting making its most valuable contribution?

There was some degree of consensus that this might be at the age of Scouts, roughly between eleven and fifteen. If we were to bring boys into the Movement sooner, might we not lose them sooner, and cease to contribute so much in terms of the things we were best at? We did not want to make the whole Scout Movement more juvenile, and it was in the age range which might vaguely be described as adolescence that we could do our most valuable work. After all, adolescence means the threshold of adulthood, in spite of its connotation as The Difficult Age (as Peter Sellers aptly put it, 'too old for Mother Goose and too young for Lolita'). It is indeed the age when children lose their innocence; but more realistically it is the age at which young people begin to come to terms with the responsibilities of adulthood. Scouting had a clearly identifiable contribution to make to that.

Apart from the fact that a junior section could have made an important contribution to society, there was the difficulty that other organisations were starting to jump on the bandwagon and recruit children straight from the nursery. Should we respond to demand, whatever the difficulties in a changing world? On balance, I was in favour of a change towards the end of the 1970s, although for the reasons I have mentioned it did not take place until the late Eighties. The Scout Section did indeed suffer more leakage in its older ranges, but the relationship between cause and effect is impossible to quantify.

5 SCOUTREACH

In the early days a group of boys who wanted to form a Scout troop had simply to find an instructor and apply for registration to the manager at Baden-Powell's London headquarters in Henrietta Street. They were given their name and number. The numbers in a large town, or indeed any town, were not always consecutive – gaps were deliberately left in the series – but were cherished, and many are still in existence today. The organisation into Districts and Counties followed shortly afterwards. Baden-Powell had clearly demonstrated by his camp on Brownsea Island that he intended to appeal to all social classes. The programme he devised appealed to boys from every sort of background but the benefits were greatest where no experience of the kind now offered by the Boy Scouts had previously been available.

The Scouts 1972–82

Those of course were the days of massive manual employment, both in industrial towns and in the countryside, and indeed of massive white-collar employment too, for those who could aspire to push a pen rather than to mind a machine.

Fifty or sixty years later the Movement could still claim with some pride to appeal to all sorts and conditions of boys, although it is obvious that middle class areas were more adept, and had more of the resources required, to run a Scout Group, than areas where no residents had experience of organisation or management. But the old distinctions between social classes were changing. They had never been simple, with their distinction between unskilled, semi-skilled and skilled workers. The distinction between white collar and blue collar was by no means meaningless, nor was the distinction between manual and non-manual jobs, but the blurring between the concepts of working-class and middle-class occupations meant that the old labels were no longer helpful. (They are still used for the purposes of government statistics, where they say more about people's perception of themselves than they do about economic or social facts.) What was alarmingly obvious was that a new underclass was being created in our 'inner cities'. Indeed the phrase 'inner city' came in to common use by the 1970s to describe not a geographical but a social environment.

The first of the new slums – the tower blocks which at once started to replace the serried rows of back-to-back terraces – were identifiable by those who had eyes to see them as early as 1954. The concrete jungle was on its way and, although the new flats were palatial in comparison with the old slums, the old social cohesion which created communities in the poorest areas of industrial towns was only too often obliterated.

There was nothing new about urban regeneration. 'Improvement schemes', following Birmingham's lead, had become common by the 1880s. 'Slum clearance' had got under way before 1939. What was new was decamping whole townships to new sites, and housing them in towers where neighbourhood communication was impossible; or simply building towers in areas cleared of redundant factories, or by German air raids or by slum clearance for its own sake.

Unfortunately this national disaster was not apparent to the bureaucratic or the political mind, and the ponderous machinery of urban change rolled on unchecked. What was obvious to any detached observer was undetected by politicians until at last Michael Heseltine took a coach tour in Liverpool in 1990 and declared that he had identified a problem. It was too late.

Scouting flourished most strongly where there were large Groups, and in simple terms these tended to be in middle class areas; but the disappearance of neat boundaries between 'classes', especially between 'working class' and 'middle class' (white collar workers were saying that 'the real money is earned on the shop floor') meant that many boys from simple homes were able to join the finest Scout Groups; and, as I have mentioned, there were many very effective Groups in areas which, if they were anything, were working class. These were mainly areas with large factories employing many thousands. There were many 'one works towns' in those days. The problem did not lie there, but in the new disadvantaged areas, the 'inner cities', where there was no social diversity and no social cohesion.

Schools were getting bigger and bigger, and further and further away (and the old system of discipline, reinforced by parental support, was disappearing); as were shops and hospitals and all other kinds of institution. Here and there an ancient pub on its own little island had survived: for adults only, of course. Here and there stood a lonely Victorian church, served now by only a single vicar fighting a good but hopeless fight. There were a few youth clubs, but they hardly scratched the surface of a rapidly growing problem. Baden-Powell would have expected the Scouts to do something about it, or so I thought.

It soon became apparent to me that I was optimistic in hoping that Leaders could be found to take on such a challenge. They had enough on their plates without travelling to and trying to start a Group in an 'inner-city' area. Besides, it was clear that the Movement would have to accept some dumbing-down of its admirable but perhaps rather high-flown ethos if it were to make a start in a modern deprived urban area. An ominous sign was that not only had it failed in the post-war scene to invent anything on the lines of the Duke of Edinburgh's Award scheme, but it had actually refused to run that scheme when His Royal Highness had devised it, because of its secular ethos. The Scouts were different: different from everything else; and so they would remain.

Perhaps in a culturally diverse society they should have been more flexible. Perhaps not.

On the other hand, the Scouts had a unique genius for enjoying themselves whilst pursuing an ultimately earnest purpose: Baden-Powell had, as I have said, even described Scouting itself as 'a game'.

The Scouts 1972–82

Scouting had shown its ingenuity in modifying old games and inventing new ones, and although it had lost its prominent place in the public eye it was the largest youth organisation in Britain and was on a growth curve to its largest-ever membership. If it was prepared to stoop to conquer, surely it could do something to alleviate a growing social problem where almost every other surviving institution – including the police, who were starting to lose the respect of young people in these areas – was struggling.

There were, then, two problems facing my idea of 'Scoutreach', a name devised by one of the Field Commissioners at a meeting at Gilwell where we debated my ideas. The first was that some outside support had to be found to help to finance it. A few dedicated volunteer Leaders could be found here and there, but not enough to make a national impact. Perhaps more could be found, especially from the youngest, as yet uncommitted, age group: but they would need professional support. They would need plant and equipment, but the Movement was fully preoccupied in providing its own.

There were plenty of open spaces – clearings in the urban jungle – where boys could be seen wandering aimlessly or causing mischief. Violence and gang warfare had been endemic in the worst of the old slum areas, but they were phenomena which could be, and were being, tackled. There was no 'yob culture' yet. Given a certain amount of mobile play equipment one could make a start. The Scouts were brilliant at inventing such equipment. They had learnt an unpleasant lesson or two from serious accidents, but safety rules were still reasonable and nobody minded a bruise or a graze.

The Association was supportive, and there was a good deal of enthusiasm, not least from the Field Commissioners, one of whom, Tony Allen, was seconded to support me, mainly for Scoutreach. I lighted on a brilliant volunteer to run the show: an old friend who, however, sadly soon became ill, for whose enthusiasm and charisma I never found a replacement. *Scouting Magazine* provided excellent publicity. All we lacked was money, and there was plenty of that sloshing about in the government coffers in the early 1970s, if only you could get your hands on it. (The 1970s were days of crazy unbridled government expenditure, with little regard for value for money, driven by political will – the duty of the Socialist state to provide – and by a muddled interpretation of Keynes's dicta about reinvigorating a moribund economy.) Moreover, it was not difficult to enlist some political support, either from back-benchers or ministers. But we came unstuck on one issue: there could be no funding unless it was jointly for boys and girls. We had a strict agreement with the Girl Guides that we would not recruit girls; and the Girl Guides were not interested.

Could we make an exception and say that for this purpose we would recruit girls as well as boys? I came to the conclusion that since Scoutreach would anyway have to earn willing acceptance for doing things which were not within mainstream Scouting, we could not do so. Was this Scouting, or wasn't it? The question had to be answered convincingly, without too many 'Yes, buts'. Nobody was preventing another organisation, new or existing, from doing the work I proposed. After seeing three government ministers, and talking exhaustively with their civil servants, I accepted that we would not be able to launch an effective national scheme. Thereafter our efforts were worthwhile, but modest.

One of the most admirable projects undertaken involved Cub Scouts who lived in tower blocks, but in spite of perseverance and making 'allowances' it foundered on the inability of the families concerned to have any concept of an activity which was voluntary, but which involved some measure of continuity, and indeed some measure of turning up at a given place at a given time. This was an example of the need to start in an entirely unstructured (or at least apparently unstructured) way – simply by providing a single experience which could be enjoyed, and which then happened to be repeated. It also suggested to me that my hunch was correct that we should start with roughly the Scout section age, say 10 or 11 to 14 or 15. It was indeed mainly within that age group that we had such success as we did. However, without in any way diminishing the projects which were carried out, sometimes with local government support and almost always against formidable odds, Scoutreach as a national project was not a success.

We paid a good deal of attention to the immigrant communities from Commonwealth countries, which were then growing rapidly. Scouting had had an immense international appeal, but that was a very different matter from integrating immigrant communities into home-based Scouting. Many if not most of those which were best attuned to Scouting preferred to operate on their own, within their own cultural base. I did not discourage this, because I felt that in most cases the best road towards cultural integration would be a long one. It was perhaps a big enough first step to form a Scout Group at all within the Scout Association, adhering to its policy, organisation and rules. If this was acceptable, and becoming part of a British Group was not, so be it. Whether they came as individuals or as Groups, most of such success as we had came within the Asian rather than the African communities.

6 THE CHIEF SCOUT

As Chief Scout I had a unique opportunity, and responsibility, to help to keep the Movement on course. The position had prestige, and it could be said that the Chief Scout had influence rather than power. But in political terms he did have power, the power to select the Chief and the County Commissioners. In one important sense he had to be a politician: he had to set his sights on, and to help to achieve, what was possible; which involved the arts of persuasion. But in another sense, the party sense, the Scouts were not political, and it was an important part of his responsibility to see that things stayed that way. Policy should be formed by consensus if possible; if not, by vote. What had to be avoided was the formation of parties as the only practical means of deciding policy. So the political role of the Chief Scout was to prevent major disagreements of policy from arising. He needed to be a diplomat, a negotiator; he needed to be not confrontational but irenical: to avoid contest, to promote peace.

In this context the power to make the key appointments – the power most sought by politicians – was not power at all, but simply a matter of exercising good judgement: which, in a large organisation, generally means accepting the judgement of others.

The Chief Scout was no longer the Chairman of the Committee of the Council, which was the executive body of the Association. This relieved him of a burden: it was not easy to find a good Chairman, especially one who lived far from London, because the role was a time-consuming one, requiring regular contact with sub-committee chairmen and lengthy briefings before meetings. A Chief Scout who was not in the chair could contribute to discussion, and he was always invited to air his views before decisions were taken. He was in regular contact with the Chief Executive, and although it was the job of the Chief Executive to keep the Chief Scout on the rails, it was also important that the Chief Scout should look after the Chief Executive, whose position over difficult or contentious matters would otherwise have been a lonely one. The system probably worked best if the Chief Executive had a long and detailed knowledge of the Movement and of its people, as Ken Stevens did then, and as Derek Twine does now, rather than that he should have been appointed as a breath of fresh air. The effectiveness of what Ken and I attempted, and the way we went about it, depended very much on our regular discussions.

With so large a parish there was inevitably pressure on the Chief Scout's time, but it was important that he should be able to stand back and form a view of the whole picture: nobody else had the same opportunity, coupled with the same degree of influence. But the view of the wood would be two-dimensional unless he also had a detailed understanding of the trees, and this took time. An effort had to be made to master the committee work, and to understand how the parts of the Association held together; but to achieve an understanding of the British scene as a whole in such a comparatively decentralised organisation took time. I laid it down unilaterally that I could not possibly do justice to my role as Chief Scout of the United Kingdom and Overseas Branches and at the same time pay attention to the international scene: I would not take part in international Scouting.

The Overseas Branches were the British Colonies or former colonies which were not large enough to organise themselves independently. The number of them – there were a dozen in my time – was diminishing as they became self-sufficient, but they could choose whether or not to apply for membership as a 'Country' in the World Organisation regardless of their constitutional standing. Much the largest of them was Hong Kong, which had chosen to hang on to the apron strings although fully capable of running its own affairs. It soon decided to become independent. Marc Noble was the Overseas Commissioner: he enjoyed travel, and looked after the Overseas Branches admirably during my tenure.

My predecessors had been Chief Scouts of the Commonwealth, but it was questionable whether this should continue. All the Dominions had been members of the World Organisation in their own right for many years, as were an increasing number of former colonies, now independent states, each of which had its own Chief Scout. A Chief Scout of the Commonwealth could not expect to have any form of primacy over such a person. The Commonwealth did not have any actual role in Scouting – in fact member countries were within several of the five Regions of the World Organisation. The Commonwealth countries did, however, have common roots because Scouting had been developed in most if not all of them by resident British leaders. Many Scouters in Commonwealth countries retained close personal associations with Britain.

The retirement of Chips Maclean seemed to present a good opportunity for ending the office of Chief Scout of the Commonwealth, but we wanted to retain a club, and we held meetings to exchange opinions and experiences, as well as for social reasons, at the World Conferences. This was approved by The Queen, and our meetings which were enjoyable and interesting occasions were convened by the Overseas Commissioner of The Scout Association: Britain, as founder country, was allowed to keep this nomenclature, uniquely without the national name.

Whatever grand ideas I might conceive about understanding, and influencing, the Association as a whole, the essential ceremonial activities throughout Britain were enough to fill my plate. Of course the two ran together, and to me the opportunity to use a visit to find out what made a county tick, what were its special strengths and its weaknesses, was just as important as the ceremonial role. But the ceremonial role must not be underestimated: its purpose, clearly, was to give recognition, thanks and encouragement. To do this well was extremely difficult.

English counties which were good enough to invite me to visit them usually chose an occasion which had involved much preparation, such as a county rally, jamboree or camp, often with visitors from other parts of Britain or overseas. Counties also used to arrange conferences for one group or another, perhaps for instance for District Commissioners or Group Scout Leaders, and I would be invited to play a part in these, and perhaps to combine it with visits to one or two groups and an award presentation. The invitations arrived soon enough for me to make a diary for the forthcoming year. They were mostly at weekends, and it was sometimes possible to visit one county on a Saturday and another on a Sunday. This was likely to involve a good deal of motoring, an early start and a late homecoming. In spite of traffic problems, Saturday evenings were comparatively quiet on the roads, so movement from one event to the next was not a problem.

The programmes tended to be intense, with a series of distinct events included, and often involved me in making as many as six or seven

The Scouts 1972–82

speeches on different subjects to different audiences: perhaps a so-called keynote speech to a small conference, one at an award ceremony, one at a dinner, one to potential donors to a fundraising campaign and two or three to assembled groups of varying size (from several thousand to a dozen) and varying makeup (boys, Leaders, parents or all three) and in varying circumstances (particularly with regard to weather). The first and most important lesson I learnt was to be well prepared, but not too well prepared.

However many preparatory questions had been asked, it was seldom possible to predict the exact circumstances in which one might have to speak. There were of course some occasions when it was appropriate not to address the whole audience: for instance, it might be best to speak just to boys even if Leaders or parents were present. But the problem was that it had sometimes not occurred to the organisers that the 'preparatory' questions had been asked for a purpose, or that it mattered if arrangements were altered. One simply had to be flexible, and moreover it might sometimes be necessary actually to rescue an occasion by making an impromptu or unscheduled speech. The techniques of the camp fire might be more useful than those of the orator. Oddly enough, the more difficult the circumstances, the easier it is to succeed. For instance, I remember one occasion when the entire population of a county rally was driven into a huge marquee by a thunderstorm: I got on to a chair and ad-libbed a speech. It was not done well, but it was surprising that it was done at all. The mere attempt was enough to earn genuine plaudits. The sense of relief that someone was trying to rescue the situation released the tension.

It was best to speak without notes if possible, and certainly not to try to adhere to a written text. Surprisingly, this is easier than it might seem. For those to whom it does not come naturally, the best way is to think out three or four paragraphs, and then to get the headings into one's mind. If one is liable to forget them at the last moment, four words on a postcard will serve as a reminder. Here again, an advantage of speaking without notes is that one's audience immediately give one credit for that. True, the credit given is more for cleverness than for hard work: the assumption being that one was speaking off the cuff, rather than that one had learnt one's speech verbatim, neither or which are true. Another advantage of this method is that it is easier to shorten a speech if the summary is expressed by four words than if it is summarised by four sentences or lengthier notes. This may be necessary if an audience who were supposed to be seated were in fact standing up, or if there has been a great deal of tedious and superfluous introductory matter.

Another useful principle is that a speech should be as short as possible, and not as long as possible; unless it is avowedly a lecture or dissertation on a given subject, when the rule is that it should be about half as long as the given maximum time, especially before lunch – although an English breakfast helps in that respect. On the other hand, one had to be careful not to give short measure.

A speech might be billed as an important item of a day's programme, often in the open air. The larger the audience, the easier it is to 'lose' a section of them, especially of young people in unfamiliar surroundings. The message needs to be extremely simple. It is pointless to try to deliver it unless this is done in a vivid way; but it doesn't do to try to be funny, or the audience will remember the joke and forget the substance. Jokes tend to make themselves, if one lets them; and that is quite enough.

Public address equipment in the open air is more a hindrance than a help. What one needs is a loud voice and a following wind. The following wind can only be obtained if one is able to move to the right quarter, and it often helps to make everyone turn round or crane their necks. The best, and preferably the only piece of equipment needed, is a chair, not to sit on but to stand on. It is much better than a soap box, as it is more easily carried around. Anyway, soap no longer comes in wooden boxes. Short indoor speeches to large audiences are not practicable: getting in and out takes longer than the speech itself, and any element of surprise or improvisation is suffocated.

Much harder than making set speeches is talking to large numbers of individual boys formed up in lines or coming up to receive an award. On a large parade it is almost impossible to do it well. With small parades the only technique is to break them up and get small groups to gather round one; it then becomes easier to get some sort of conversation or dialogue going, instead of asking a few obvious or trivial questions such as 'What's your name and where do you come from?' That question does at least have the advantage that the person asked often knows the answer, whether or not it is audible. It is much better to go round a campsite when people are doing something. It is possible to offer advice on almost any activity, regardless of whether or not the advice is sound, and you may just occasionally have the good fortune to be able to show somebody how to do something without making a fool of yourself. The greatest credit I ever got was from showing a boy how to gut a duck. Unfortunately the so-called raw materials of camp cooking have usually nowadays been processed and perhaps even packaged before use.

I developed a reasonably satisfactory technique for award ceremonies. Attempts at conversations with individuals as they come forward tend to be both fatuous and embarrassing. I would therefore start with a brief explanation of the symbolic nature of an award presentation, and there was a photographer at hand to record every presentation for the family album, mantelpiece or (in rare cases) grand piano. I said that I would like to meet everybody afterwards, and it was often possible to have a pleasant chat with their parents, Leaders or friends. Again the photographer was present to take a group, and there were numerous snapshots by family cameras. The only problem was that one could come away blinded by hundreds of flashes. We tried to hold the ceremonies for the Queen's Scouts in grand buildings in various parts of Britain, usually two or three each year, and the owners were always helpful and welcoming.

All these occasions, although demanding in their own ways, were highly enjoyable. Not only was one with volunteers who were working for a good cause, they were also there because they enjoyed what they were doing. It was fascinating to see what made them tick, and to meet so many people from different walks of life, all doing the same thing. I also enjoyed getting to know Britain better than ever I had done before. It is a land of endless variety, even nowadays when people move about so much. There are still local ways of doing and saying things, and people who move into an area often absorb the local flavour.

Apart from visits in England, I used to do a Scottish tour in the summer every second year, and a tour of Wales probably every third and of Northern Ireland every fourth year. These were organised by the Chief Commissioners, all men of charm and strong personality to such an extent that these tours were certainly highlights in my experience. George Pound, a retired captain in the Royal Navy, used his ingenuity to take me around Scotland – the Commodore's Barge, a Sea King helicopter, a borrowed light aircraft – so we managed to get to Orkney, Shetland and the Outer Hebrides as well as to all the large cities including of course Glasgow and Edinburgh, and visited almost every area in two tours. We managed Wales under the genial touch of Chris Cory, also in two tours: some of the old counties were truly rural, based on a modest market town, where the villages although small still had strong Scouting, unlike many of the villages of the Home Counties where Cubs (and village schools) had simply disappeared in the course of the last twenty years as the old rural families were displaced by commuters or pensioners. My Northern Ireland tour was less frequent because we could cover all six counties in a few days. Scouting was one of the few organisations in which Catholics and Protestants joined the same group: a most valuable contribution to neighbourly tolerance.

The ceremonial highlight of the year was the St George's Day parade at Windsor Castle, to which every Queen's Scout could come either in the year he received the award or later; and the magnificent service in St George's Chapel, which we planned carefully each year with the enthusiastic support of the Dean. The Queen usually took the salute and conducted the inspection. There were parades and services all over the country, as indeed there still are, but any attempt at drill and marching tends to be embarrassing and a walk past works better than a march past. The Queen always provided the band of one of the regiments of Foot Guards at Windsor, and there was some rehearsal, so this was an exception; and there were a good number of excellent Scout bands throughout the country, which certainly helped.

The Association had its own system of awards devised by the Founder for adult leaders as well as for boys, and these were generally accepted as an appropriate way of acknowledging exceptional service. Apart from commendations, and awards for long service, there were the Medal of Merit, the Silver Acorn and the Silver Wolf. They were all awarded very selectively and each was subject to an unwritten but customary time limit, so that even if there had been doubts as to the suitability of a candidate for a particular award, it was supported by a remarkable length of voluntary service, in the case of the Silver Wolf normally at least thirty years. There were no national occasions for the presentations, but they could often be worked in to a significant event.

I used to meet with the Chief Commissioners twice a year in my flat in London above Headquarters, usually in the evening after one of the monthly meetings of the Committee of the Council, and I found these informal chats most valuable, especially in identifying what was going right and what was not in the big picture.

There was only one Chief Commissioner for England, Bernard

Chacksfield, an able and energetic Air Marshal who was a good chooser of people. The most important subject which had to be dealt with between myself and the individual Chief Commissioners was the appointment of County Commissioners, which was sometimes easy and sometimes difficult. In this respect the rather grand network set up by Baden-Powell was invaluable, as we got a lot of help from the County Presidents, many of whom were Lord-Lieutenants of their counties: they needed to be good judges of people, and could often help us to find and select the most suitable candidate where there was not an obvious successor. I thought that England was too large for one Chief Commissioner and that, however capable Bernard Chacksfield was, he could not hope to know the background in all the counties and – not least – help to find and bring on promising people for the future. He did not really agree, but we soon had three Chief Commissioners, Will Lestock-Reid of Northumberland taking on the North and Robin Stayt of Gloucestershire the South and West. As for London, that presented its own problem. The admirable Lord Ranfurly had been made a Chief Scout's Commissioner by Chips Maclean in the rather vague hope that he could help him in this respect, but that did not really work since an intimate knowledge of London Scouting was required. My next candidate soon retired to the Channel Islands, but nevertheless without a system we mainly succeeded in finding suitable people, some of them outstanding.

Chips had had the idea of creating a small and select group of Chief Scout's Commissioners to assist him, but unless they were really in the swim they were not often able to deputise satisfactorily, and anyway if people invited the Chief Scout to a particular occasion they did not want a substitute. The exception was Robert Baden-Powell, who was enthusiastic and dutiful and did an immense amount of valuable work, more it has to be said in his own right than as a deputy for me, especially in international scouting. The two new Chief Commissioners for England, and somebody to help me with Scoutreach, could play a more valuable part and I let the idea of Chief Scout's Commissioners lapse in its own good time, without preventing my successors from being able to revive it if they saw fit.

A problem I had to face was how much I could get involved in individual correspondence in an organisation with 600,000 members, not to mention parents who were one of the most likely groups to raise their concerns, probably without the faintest concept that I could not do them all justice individually. Ken Stevens rightly pointed out the dangers at an early stage, both in terms of sheer weight of numbers and also in the advisability of not getting involved in controversy; especially because controversy was often about personal issues, a point often not clear in the early stages of correspondence. The difficulty of course was to persuade and train the people writing on my behalf about this matter or that to do so tactfully, and if possible positively. Since this is a problem which has still not been solved by large organisations with their call centres and 'customer services' departments, I feel no shame in admitting the difficulty. Unlike a bank which cannot afford to distinguish its important clients from its small fry, and therefore writes them all a rude letter instead of a polite one, or which prints entire standard letters by computer, we did at least try to untangle disputes in a civilised way. As far as I was concerned, most of my letters to individuals as such were letters of thanks or congratulation, a big task but a pleasant one.

I used to make two routine visits to Headquarters, each lasting two days, each month, and since I had my flat in the penthouse over Headquarters I could pack a lot in by working long hours, as well as spending one train journey reading the preparatory material and the other the aftermath. I was able to meet all the senior professionals at least once a month.

One of my visits had to coincide with the Committee of Council, which met every month except August. There was always the question whether we could manage with fewer meetings, as there are with many committees, but the answers seldom take into account the intangible factors, which is not much different from saying that the morale of a committee is as important as the morale of every other institution. There has to be a feeling of continuity, with the opportunity for members to get to know and trust each other within the limited timespan of their membership, and in order that they may achieve enough grasp of long-running issues to make a worthwhile and confident contribution to discussion. These matters are seldom given enough weight in the urge for short cuts in committee work, which sometimes result in poor decision making or with too much power being given to sub-committees with the responsibility still laid at the door of the main committee.

There were of course other visits to London for particular reasons, including meetings with other organisations, especially the Girl Guides, with whom dialogue was important, and occasions for 'media' interviews masterminded by Jack Olden who was in charge of our public relations. I was not very successful at the latter, not least because I found it difficult to simplify the kind of complicated issues the media are interested in.

I was fortunate in having Ron Meyer, a lifelong devotee of Scouting, as my personal secretary and assistant. He was a brilliant stenographer and interpreter of what one wanted to say (he had received the BEM for serving Field Marshal Montgomery in this way during the war, so he may have found that doing the same for me was child's play), a good administrator when it came to matters of detail (such as finding the best way to get to the right place at the right time, or getting the wording just right in ceremonial matters) and he had an intricate knowledge of Scouting people. Fat envelopes arrived at my home two or three times a week and I could spend a couple of mornings dealing with them without having to travel to London. These of course were pre-E-mail days, when correspondence moved at a more moderate pace and people were more economical with words than now.

7 THE WORLD ORGANISATION

My determination to play no part in international scouting in view of the size of the task in Britain was worn down by Ken Stevens's insistence, first that I must attend World Scout Conferences, and soon afterwards that I must be willing to stand for election to the World Committee. I did my best to resist, but with hindsight I could see that he was right. Britain was the founder county, and it was essential that its Chief Scout should turn up.

At my first appearance at a World Scout Conference in Nairobi, I was a fish out of water. It was certainly a remarkable experience, the fruit of two years' organisation by the World Scout Bureau and a massive effort by the host country. Everybody except me seemed to know everybody else. The atmosphere was both friendly and lively, the programme was well put together and there were plenty of sideshows. The administration of the agenda was efficient in spite of the cumbersome nature of an international voluntary organisation with about a hundred and twenty member countries. With everybody dressed in Scout uniform it was colourful and it had its share of very determined people, some of whom were only too accustomed to going through their hoops.

The Founder had laid it down at an early stage that only two languages would be allowed, English and French. There was a good deal of canvassing for the admission of another language – particularly Spanish and Arabic – but to have admitted one would have been to open the floodgates. This did somewhat limit the membership of each nation's delegation, but then it was desirable for delegates (with six votes for each country, whether for the USA with six million members or for a small island with a thousand) to have some expertise in the matters to be decided, and on the whole the core membership of most of the delegations consisted of people who could get along in English or French, some of whom turned up time after time. That, indeed, was the best if not the only way of achieving enough continuity to make sense.

I am not sure that even nowadays it would be easy to have simultaneous translation into a very large number of languages at the centres in all the countries which hosted World Conferences. It was considered an important matter of prestige to host such a Conference: both the rich and the poor countries wished to do so, for slightly different reasons, and one session on the final day was taken up with presentations by the countries which wished to act as hosts for the next-but-two Conference. The delegations had to decide between the temptation of luxury in, for instance, Munich or Quebec, and sympathy for the simplicity of Dakar.

The situation was further complicated as a result of many countries having more than one Scout association, particularly the early joiners like France or Germany. Most of the associations within a single country were denominational – for instance many countries had a Catholic association – rather than regional or ethnic. But the associations had to agree on the membership of a single delegation at the World Conference, and this seemed to cause few problems – except in one or two Latin-American countries where there were two rival Catholic archbishops. Some of the poorest countries could only afford to send one or two members anyway, often helped by richer countries or, especially in Africa, by their governments: not always providing good value for money. In practice cohesion and continuity were achieved by having five regional organisations which met during the intervals between World Conferences, because many of the issues raised tended to have a regional flavour, or at least had been sifted at that level.

The Scouts 1972–82

The Founder had laid it down that a 'country' could be a member of the World Organisation without defining precisely what he meant. It was a typically British pragmatic arrangement, and it probably worked better than a legalistic attempt to define the criteria. His main reason may have been to avoid a problem within the British Empire, so that, for instance, self-governing Dominion status was not a requirement. India might not have qualified before Independence, but it had qualified without argument, although (one of the eccentricities of a typical British institution) its delegation had the name of The Bharat Scouts and Guides, which happened to be the most successful association in the sub-continent, and to which others tagged on happily enough. With partition, Pakistan was at once admitted without argument, and then Bangladesh. Former or surviving colonies could become members more or less on application, and, although there were some stirrings when Hong Kong was admitted, the organisations hopeful of qualifying (however unlikely to do so) probably served their cause better by keeping quiet than by being vocal.

Baden-Powell did make one serious mistake: he admitted the Armenians exiled in Paris after the Russian revolution to membership of the World Organisation in their own right. They were not called Armenia but Armenian Scouts. Sixty years after the revolution there were not very many of them left. After a couple of generations' assimilation, most of them were joining their host country's own Scout associations, and eventually they would lose their separate identity and disappear; but the problem was that a precedent had been created. The Polish Scouts in Britain, and the Estonian Scouts mostly in Canada, expelled by the Soviet Union, many of whom (or whose fathers) had played a valiant part in the war against Fascism, were fiercely proud of their national identity. The answer had to be that they must join the association (or an association) of the host country, where they could keep their identity as Scout groups.

It was a difficult answer to give people who had suffered so much in their noble cause, but compared with the difficulty which would have been created by compliance it was minor. The Palestinian Scouts offered a *casus belli* for the whole Arab world, had Scouts been belligerent people.

Whether or not the Secretary-General László Nagy (for he was the moving force) was wise to have allowed the creation of an Arab Region as one of five regions covering the world may still be a matter for

The Scouts 1972–82

debate. Compared with other regions, the population was insignificant – less than 100 million people – and I suppose it is true to say that the Arab countries between India and the Atlantic embodied only a small minority of the world population of Islamic people. Yet they were – extraordinarily – served by a single language (admittedly with variations) by a world-class religious identity (again with variations), and they were the representatives of one of the most remarkable cultures of world history. They were given a regional identity equivalent, for instance, to that of the whole of 'Asia-Pacific' or Europe, although they represented fewer people than the largest country of any of the others. But László, who acted not exactly on impulse, but perhaps more on intuition, or on instinct, than on pure reason or logic, was probably right. He gave the Arab world, and the Islamic world, a distinctive voice through the Arab Region. Besides, it has to be stated that the Scouting world was not the demographic world, for the Soviet Union and the People's Republic of China could not have been admitted under the Founder's criteria, whether or not they had wished to be. The big growth areas in Asia were in Japan, the Philippines, Indonesia and in Formosa which insisted on labelling itself 'Republic of China', a name not officially accepted.

The original offices of international Scouting had been in London. They had been transferred to Geneva but needed redesigning in the 1960s for their modern task. A remarkable Hungarian refugee, an academic, László Nagy, turned up in Geneva where he had been taken in by a kindly banker. His first academic task there was a dissertation on a new framework for international Scouting, and he was then elected Secretary-General to put his own scheme into practice. His proposal, amply fulfilled, was that the headquarters of WOSM, the World Organisation of the Scout Movement, must be small and select. He had soon collected a few professionals of remarkable talent, the few remaining members of the old staff being relegated to second line tasks. One of the most remarkable new men was Malek Gabr, a gentle Egyptian with exceptional linguistic talent and a firm grasp of the way in which international constitutions could be operated effectively. Malek was the classic chief of staff, never in the way and never out of the way, organising meetings, tactfully promoting solutions, smoothing squalls and calming the mercurial personality of László without compromising his contribution

The result of László's policy of 'small but select' was a very high standard of administration in Geneva in departments ranging from finance to public relations, and the five regional committees were effectively staffed. The city was a honeypot for people wanting to work for international organisations, and those who had the talent, administrative, diplomatic and linguistic, to work with over a hundred member countries, commanded high salaries, but it was better to have a handful of those than an army of second-rankers. The committee structure was, perhaps, over-elaborate, and one or two of the minor committees were not quite as might have been wished, but WOSM had to work with the volunteers whom the countries had elected, and the very positive way in which this was handled – people who might have been sidelined were encouraged into participation – was outstanding and gave the whole organisation a happy and friendly atmosphere. Moreover, László was cunning enough to ensure that anyone who criticised a particular sub-committee was promptly induced to become a member.

The executive was the World Committee, consisting of twelve members, one third of whom were elected at the World Conference every second year. The system worked out well enough to make the Committee as a whole fairly representative. No country could have more than one member. The United States, on which there was tacit recognition that the organisation depended for its solvency, in practice always had a member. Britain as a founder country usually did, but not as a matter of course. That is why Ken Stevens was so anxious that the Chief Scout should be active: in the circumstances he rightly felt that when a vacancy came up he would stand a good chance of election. At that moment we did not happen to have an International Commissioner who had been around for long enough to have earned a suitable reputation. When a long-serving person retires, there cannot by definition be another such waiting in the wings to succeed hm. Sure enough I was roped into the organisation, and five years after becoming Chief Scout I found myself as a member of the World Committee for six years. I regretted the additional commitment but the work itself was interesting – indeed fascinating – and enjoyable.

The first task I recollect being thrown into was membership of a 'working party' with the remit of revising the Law and Promise to fit the modern scene. As each country had joined, it had tended to adopt Baden-Powell's Law and Promise as a whole, or where that was impossible with minor modifications. There were no fundamental difficulties because the Founder had pragmatically allowed some latitude in the wording of 'Duty to God', and countries where such a phrase was peculiar or irrelevant had happily accepted this or other (to them) eccentricities of British culture. However, after the huge expansion of two or three generations, people here and there who cared about this aspect of the Scout Movement were becoming more scrupulous, or at least airing the perceived problem.

The problem of rewriting the 'ten commandments' of the Scout Movement in internationally acceptable form was a diplomatic and intellectual challenge; and suitable people were appointed, which tended to refine and highlight the difficulties. The cultural diversity of Europe alone (or the 'Western World') would have been quite enough to occupy us. The French argued for the recognition of a secular society, and the application of reason, with intense respect for the state. The British accepted that the Founder's moral imperatives were religious, preferred a pragmatic approach, and were happy to denigrate their own political system unless it was challenged by foreigners. The Americans had no idea what was being discussed. The Indians were willing to accept 'duty to God' although it is meaningless to Hindus.

In the Committees which met in Geneva, as well as at the regional headquarters, delegates who could not manage in English or French were able to have interpreters at hand, but those most remote from European culture tended to express no more than puzzlement at the various wordings suggested. I suppose that their frame of mind was that they had taken on board a 'Western' institution and were willing to comply with it and fit it to their culture as best they could: 'when in Rome'. It did not matter too much if some of the doctrine was not fully comprehensible. Some of the member countries were more or less totalitarian, and ran their Scouting as they thought fit: the mild patriotic flavour of Baden-Powell's language suited them very well. Anyway, we eventually came up with an acceptable wording and, although the debate at the next World Conference was to say the least a difficult one, the great majority of countries were happy to agree to what was suggested.

Later I spent many years as a member of the Constitutions Committee, vetting the constitutions of aspiring members and amendments to those of existing members. To me, this task which would have seemed dry to many was an interesting one, since the objective was to agree what was proposed with minimum alteration. It was not always easy to understand why a particular wording had been chosen; but there was nearly always an answer if one looked and listened.

The Boy Scouts of America were much the largest in membership, reaching about six million. Scouting in the United States was unrivalled as a youth organisation and received huge financial support as a charity. Baden-Powell's ethos fitted the American ideal of manliness like a glove. Moreover, there was an author in William Hillcourt (in partnership with Olave Baden-Powell) who was to become the Founder's more or less official biographer and an artist in Norman Rockwell who accurately reflected the programme devised by a British cavalry colonel for the moral and sentimental American.

Yet it was in Africa (where, after all, Baden-Powell's training devised in India had been put to practical use in the Boer War) that Scouting, conveyed by British missionaries, teachers and civil servants, perhaps had its clearest and most direct appeal. Like Christianity, it seemed to suit the African continent as it emerged from darkness even more directly than it appealed to its native Europe. The 1970s were still within the age of great expectations for sub-Saharan Africa, in which (against all the odds) the newly emerging nations were on the road to good government, thanks to the influence of the British. It became clear to me that in this age of change on a gigantic scale, the influence of Scouting as the basis of a way of life had been even more important in the political formation of the new Africa than had been the spread of the Christian religion. It had affected the whole generation of Africans (the fortunate few) who had benefited from attending British-run schools. Scouting is still a major influence in Africa, but less seminally so, and – sad to say – the commanding heights of political power have been captured in many states by corrupt regimes.

In the age of apartheid, South Africa was excluded from every organisation in sub-Saharan Africa except Scouting: the presence of a South African delegation at the World and Regional Conferences was unique. It was not permitted in any other pan-African or even regional institution. Black and coloured people were admitted to Scouting in South Africa, in spite of the draconian laws of the apartheid regime, as the equals of whites. Obviously these people were, at least in an informal sense, attuned to some extent to the white regime; but nevertheless the fact that Scouting was able not merely to survive but to flourish within the hostile and indeed (with its banning orders) ruthless political system was remarkable.

The Scouts 1972–82

Scouting flourished, too, in francophone Africa, that is to say in much of West Africa from the Mediterranean to the Gulf of Guinea, introduced by the French, and was as much an influence for good in the areas coloured green on the map as in those coloured pink. It flourished in Cameroon, and existed almost everywhere, although obviously it was thin on the ground in the hinterlands and in the Portuguese and Belgian colonial areas.

Insofar as emergent British and French Africa had a colonial past, this had a firm constitutional and legal framework. In most cases representative government was in its infancy, but an intellectual infrastructure had not only been introduced, but was highly respected, on which it could potentially be built. In the Asia-Pacific Region, an even larger growth area for Scouting, this was not so generally the case. The old European colonial influences there (with important exceptions including Australia, New Zealand and Malaya, the American influence in the Philippines and of course the intensely imitative culture of Japan) had been the commercial interests of the Portuguese and the Dutch, which were uncompromisingly rejected by the unavowedly totalitarian new regimes. WOSM, led by the pragmatic László Nagy, decided to go along with them: otherwise there would have been no Scouting at all. It is perhaps to stretch a point to say that, paradoxically, in a totalitarian regime not devoted to the triumph of evil, there was by definition nothing to quarrel with. Even where law was enforced by a military framework (the top leadership of Indonesian Scouting, although they were civilians, had the nomenclature of Generals!) the Scout Movement, heavily subsidised and supported by the government, was an important agent not only of civilised values, but in the practical sense of civilised value, such as clean water, literacy and agricultural development.

It was easy to identify (and perhaps condemn) a 'country' such as Indonesia, with its huge and diverse territory, some highly urbanised and commercial, and some primitive, areas, ruled by a new nationalist regime far from scrupulous about its methods of achieving and maintaining power, by the European label 'totalitarian'. If, however, one was willing to look scrupulously at Africa, one would certainly not find – in 'countries' only just emerging from British, French or other European colonial regimes – anything that might or could have been honestly described as 'democratic'. And what of most of South America, unable 150 years after the removal of imperialist power to

The Scouts 1972–82

arrange for government by any kind of election? If Scouting was indeed to be a worldwide movement it had to be content, as do all other worldwide organisations, with what was given.

On the whole, therefore, the particular regime of a member country, provided that it was willing uncompromisingly to accept and promote the Scout Law and Promise, had to be accepted. The crunch came in Iran where, supported by the immense wealth of the Shah's government, the coveted privilege had been won of hosting the World Conference and the World Jamboree in 1979. (Immense numbers of trees had been planted and irrigated in the sand.)

It did not need a genius to realise that Iran's delegations to the Scout world Conferences were the servants of the Shah's regime; and that their methods of getting where they were had not been altogether as gentlemanly as Baden-Powell might have wished. Nevertheless they were going to put on an impressive show, and their Scouting was well organised, well supported and popular with young people.

Then the balloon went up. A matter of months before the long-planned World Conference and Jamboree (there was a Conference every second year, a Jamboree every fourth) the Shah and all his works (including the leader of the Scout delegation) were violently removed and an uncompromising theocracy took their place. What was to be done?

The founder country came to the rescue as best it could. We were in the nick of time to find one conference centre in Britain which could accommodate the Conference. We booked the whole new hotel and complex at the Birmingham National Exhibition Centre. The problem was solved by a telephone call. A good deal of hard work and improvisation followed.

What we could not do was to host a World Jamboree. These magnificent events, the Founder's brainchild, occupied an iconic place in the world of Scouting. Nobody knew about World Conferences. Everybody knew about World Jamborees. Less than twenty thousand Scouts attended them (about one Scout in a thousand) but they required a huge and costly infrastructure, and seven or eight years' preparation. Finding a site was difficult enough, for it had to have room for at least twenty-five thousand people (including staff and Leaders) to camp, with good communications for getting there and back and within reach of almost every imaginable kind of Scouting activity – rock climbing, sailing and parascending to cite but three – at the most sophisticated level. That was a start. Then the infrastructure had to be established: clean water at one end and sewage at the other, fire engines and ambulances. This was not the sort of camp where a friendly farmer would allow his tap to be used, and a hole to be dug in a corner of his field.

Once the basic facilities had been prepared, and expert volunteers found to man the administration and the numerous activities to make up ten days' programmes for twenty thousand people, sites of suitable sizes had to be planned for every national delegation and all the necessary instructions, rules and notices drafted. Opening and closing ceremonies, elaborate items in the obligatory ritual, were meticulously planned, liberally dosed with sentimentality: there even had to be some sort of rehearsal for these two massive parades. They consumed an immense amount of time and energy, some of which might have been better spent. Then home accommodation had to be found, freely offered, to give all these Scouts in ones and twos a week or more after the Jamboree itself to experience something of the life of the host country; and then to bring them all back to the right airport at the right time.

Anyone who had had the luck to attend a World Jamboree – one of the fortunate few – found it an unforgettable experience. These people were asked afterwards to spread the word by speaking and lecturing, with whatever graphics they could devise, to audiences at home. But in my opinion World Jamborees did not offer value for money or for effort. There was certainly no chance of organising one at a few months' notice to take the place of Iran. I have sometimes wondered what happened to all those trees.

Regional Jamborees were organised instead, each taking up to about five thousand Scouts, not only from their own Regions but drawn from the delegations which had been going to Iran. Many of the volunteers (served by a tiny band of professionals) who were booked for the World Jamboree were diverted to their Regions, where the WOSM offices, with a good deal of improvisation, could organise alternative events. In the particular circumstances of 1979 they obviously could not cater for all the delegations or provide substitutes for all the activities, but it is simply a matter of experience that a quantum leap is needed between a camp for five thousand and a camp for twenty thousand. Perhaps at a guess a mere one twentieth of the effort is required to provide four camps, each of a quarter of the size of one World Jamboree.

A Jamboree spread over several hundred acres is a mind-boggling experience for the most hardened of Scouters, and there is no question of any one participant meeting his contemporaries from more than a handful of other countries. A young mind simply cannot comprehend the scale of a World Jamboree any more than a Cub Scout attending a county rally can understand how there can be so many Cubs in the whole wide world. Much better value is obtained by a single Scout Group forging a friendship with Scouts of perhaps two or three other countries who are invited to each other's annual camps, and who then meet each other's families by staying in their homes; especially if there is a language barrier to help make the point that people in different countries do things in different ways. Here is an example of Small Is Beautiful; preferably using the farmer's standpipe and the hole in the corner of his field, and cooking unprocessed food on a wood-burning fire: because the best way to get two young people together is to give them a problem to solve.

The World Conference, thanks to the heroic efforts of Ted Hayden and a large team, duly took place at Birmingham. Everything worked to our advantage. The arrangements could not be perfect, but it was surprising that the Conference took place at all, and everybody was not only grateful but appreciative of the British knack for improvisation. The use of a massive modern conference 'complex' was un-Scoutlike, but what it lacked in character it made up for in convenience, because everybody was housed under one roof. The atmosphere of improvisation and making the best of things added interest and called for the kind of ingenuity which would have pleased the Founder. All the agenda for Conference business were of course already in place. As Chief Scout of the host country I was able to indulge my prejudices by reducing the pomposity of the ceremonial and simplifying whatever procedure I could. The formal dinner on the final evening nevertheless provided me with the unusual experience of the emperor receiving tribute from the nations: one delegate after another made his way to the high table and presented an often expensive, often decorative, and probably useless gift, accompanied by applause. My family were suitably impressed when they helped to unload my car, and I eventually distributed a few of the more curious items to my children, emphasising that they were not owners, but curators on my behalf.

For me personally the Conference had an entirely different and unexpected result, pitchforking me into the Chairmanship of the World

The Scouts 1972–82

Committee. Four of the twelve members were elected for six years at each World Conference, and the Chairman was normally elected (for two years) from the senior group. There was a consensus that the best person would be the very able and delightful member (a government minister, incidentally) from Cameroon. He would have been the first African Chairman, and an ideal choice. Unfortunately, although he spoke excellent English, he did not come up to the mark when chairing sessions at the Birmingham Conference. The Chairmanship was always allotted in turns to several members of the Committee, partly in view of their knowledge of particular aspects of the work. What I had not foreseen – and clearly I was not alone – was that Chairmanship of these sessions required not only a good knowledge of English (or French) but the ability to understand what passed for English from the tongues of many nations. This can be hard enough (to put it mildly) for native English speakers: alas, it was beyond – but only just beyond – Solomon.

I pointed out that the ability to chair a session at the World Conference was but a small part of the work of the Chairman of the World Committee. I argued that Solomon could have been put in to bat, most appropriately, at formal sessions where there would not be many verbal exchanges. I pointed out that we had a rare chance to elect a suitable African; but my words fell on deaf ears.

There were one or two other circumstances which reduced the potential candidates virtually to one, and under pressure I felt obliged to shoulder a burden I would have wished to avoid, and not only that: to take it after only two, rather than four, years of membership of the World Committee; and when I was already Chief Scout of Britain. It seemed absurd, too, that this was a job which many people would have given their eye teeth (whatever that means, or at least almost whatever that means) to get: a fact which became painfully real at the time of my successor's election two years later. Of course it was a wonderful opportunity for me, a fascinating experience, and a flamboyant feather in my cap; and the candidate whom I had sincerely and enthusiastically backed was a big enough gentleman to bear no resentment when I displaced him.

Every World Conference had a Theme which was given a great deal of thought by the Powers That Be, and a keynote address by a famous speaker. Although I regard such manoeuvres as window-dressing, they gave the worldwide Movement something well-defined to aim at – whether conserving wildlife, providing clean water, planting trees or saving babies. Most of our effort was the usual commitment to keeping the ship afloat and, preferably, on course. There were plenty of problems to solve, financial, administrative and political. Producing fertile ground for growth depended largely on finding sensible responses to these problems. So it was just as well to introduce a manifestly idealistic flavour at World Conferences.

Financing the World Organisation presented similar problems to those at national level, in heightened form because of the extreme differences in wealth between the rich and the poor. Marc Noble, our own Overseas Commissioner, headed the committee which dealt with this and produced a workable system which based the subscription to the World Organisation on each country's GDP. Like the local Scout Groups at national level, countries were torn between the desire to cook their census figures upwards to demonstrate success, or downwards to reduce their contributions, and it has to be admitted that some of the figures we worked on may not have been accurate. But the real difficulty was that even the richer countries were not very happy to fork out money to support worldwide Scouting. It was hard enough to raise money for one's local Group. Scouting in the Third World was undoubtedly a Good Thing, but the money would have to be found by someone else. This opinion was common at every level from Scout Group to National Headquarters, but in the event every member country adopted a responsible attitude and paid up. This assured WOSM of the bare minimum: almost everything else depended on the Americans.

It was easy to say that money was forthcoming from well-heeled Americans because in the United States money was the only thing that counted; and that, because as a youth organisation Scouting in America was unchallenged, torrents of dollars were directed through that channel in the hope of enhancing the prestige of the donors. It is true that this did lead to a certain amount of jockeying for position, but the fact is that the sincerely motivated immense generosity of American millionaires, most notably Bill Campbell who owed his fortune to General Motors, enabled WOSM to operate effectively and to be a massive force in spreading civilised values around the globe.

It was evident that we could not live hand-to-mouth hoping for another helping from a generous American, so the World Scout Foundation was established to endow the whole operation. Gustavo Vollmer, a Venezuelan with strong US financial interests, was the most dynamic of the Scouters at WOSM level whose enthusiasm and

The Scouts 1972–82

generosity made it happen. The Foundation collected 'Baden-Powell Fellows' from all round the world at a minimum of $10,000 apiece, and buttered them up as best it could at prestigious receptions. Generously, the King of Sweden became President and turned up at many of these occasions. The income provided a regular subsidy for the Organisation and enabled it to support Scouting in countries which could not provide from their own pockets.

In my innocence, I received a rude shock when it became my turn to give up the Chairmanship and preside over the election of my successor. A member of the World Committee – in his first two-year term – canvassed some of the members with unscrupulous hints about the unsuitability of others, and his conspiracy came quite near to success. He knew very well that it was Not Done to canvass, let alone denigrate rival candidates unfairly, but he was cunning and ruthless enough to try. Fortunately his plot was foiled. Mercifully we were not subjected to many people of his sort.

8
The Church in Wales 1972–92

I DISESTABLISHMENT

This chapter is about a particular small part – a province – of one of many varieties ('denominations') of the Christian Church during the second half of the twentieth century. I describe that province as an institution in the everyday and easily understood meaning of that word, and give my interpretation of the way in which it has coped with the challenges and opportunities of separation from the province of Canterbury and the Established Church of England. I am not writing about the generalised and more abstract concept of the Church – a subject on which countless pages have been written by theologians during the last two thousand years, the first of them, even before the four Gospels as we know them were recorded in written form, being St Paul, in his letters or 'Epistles'.

Paul's letters are part of the New Testament; not quite all the Epistles which have found their way into the Bible, for a few of them were concocted by other authors, but the majority of them. They look upon the Church in its proper sense, as the whole group or sect of Christians who were the earliest followers of Jesus. They met in their home towns – Corinth, for example, or Ephesus – and it was to these congregations or 'Churches' that Paul addressed his letters. The idea of constructing special buildings – what we call churches with a small 'c' – came later.

The Church in its proper or original and more abstract sense exists for two purposes: first, to pass on the message, often called the 'Good News', of Jesus Christ, the unique cosmic preacher born into the Jewish society of Palestine around the year AD 4; and secondly to use and pass on the authority which it claims to have received from Him to forgive sins; and to perpetuate itself by the performance of received rules and customs in order to do so. This continuity is achieved by the consecration of bishops by other bishops, perpetuating the authority given by Christ to St Peter (who in this context is believed to have become the first Bishop of Rome) and known as the Apostolic Succession.

The Church in Wales 1972–92

Jesus Christ left no written record of His teaching, but reports of His life and resurrection took an extraordinary grip in what can broadly be described as the Hellenistic world, covering roughly the vast post-Greek but still Greekish empire of Alexander of Macedon; and later also of much of the Roman Empire. When Christianity became the official religion of that empire, the difficulty was to decide and define how Jesus could be both God and man, and that within a monotheistic religion. Eventually after several abortive attempts a creed (misleadingly known as the Nicene Creed) was agreed on, in a spirit of reluctant compromise, at the Council of Chalcedon in AD 381, and this is still the creed which defines the beliefs of the Church today: that is to say of the 'Western' Church, notably in its two largest manifestations, the Roman Catholic Church under the authority of the Pope and the Anglican Church, which together form the greater part of the Christian Church in a single worldwide religion; indeed, the only worldwide religion that has yet existed.

The American Episcopal Church (which is the Anglican Church in the United States) derives its continuity from a technically more complicated source, in that by a quirk of history its bishops owe their authority to a bishop of the Episcopal Church of Scotland. This Scottish Church is Anglican in its doctrine and (by yet another quirk of history) it is the only remaining part of the Anglican Communion whose official liturgy (although often set aside in favour of permitted boring modern versions) is virtually that of the Book of Common Prayer, derived and revised from the Scottish Prayer Book of 1637 – which came to grief as a result of Charles I's clumsy attempt to enforce it in 1641 (or what we would now reckon as 1642), but was revived in 1737.

This essay is not about the Church in that proper sense, in the middle of the twentieth century. It is simply about the way in which a small part of the Church – the new province of Wales – has coped with the challenges and opportunities of separation from the province of Canterbury and the Established Church of England.

The Church in Wales was disestablished by Acts of Parliament which were passed in 1913 but not brought into force until the end of the First World War. This meant that the four Welsh dioceses were no longer a part of the Church of England which, because it was set up and shaped by Acts of Parliament in Tudor times, became the established or official Church of the nation, the Queen being its head 'as far as the law of Christ allows'. Henry VIII had abolished the power of the Pope in

England and replaced the authority of the Pope by his own authority as King. Thereafter the Church of England was regulated by Acts of Parliament, its own parliament in the form of Convocation meanwhile gradually losing its authority. The doctrines and the services and the organisation of the Church, and various measures to make them more or less rigorous over the course of centuries, depended on a variety of documents, including the Thirty-Nine Articles of Tudor times and the Book of Common Prayer, both enforced by Parliament. Bishops were appointed by the Crown and the clergy were sustained by endowments and taxes.

The Church of England was given the character of a Broad Church, meaning a Church in which people of varying shades of belief and practice can feel comfortable, during the reign of Queen Elizabeth I, when it was settling down after the traumatic changes of her predecessors' reigns, and on the whole this is a characteristic which it has retained. You can attend a parish church one week in which the beliefs are close to those of the Roman Catholics and the worship characterised by 'smells, bells and lace', and then the next week go to one at which the clergyman (or, nowadays, woman) wears a simple surplice and there is a minimum of ceremony. There may be a couple of candles on the Communion table but the keynote is simplicity. The congregation do not kneel for prayers nor turn towards the altar to recite the Creed. Nevertheless, the Church of England is by no means broad enough to satisfy every shade of belief and practice. A variety of other 'denominations' have been founded and the growing value placed on freedom within our national culture has tolerated their right to exist. This toleration applies not only to the Protestant or 'reformed' non-conformist denominations but also to the Roman Catholic Church from which all the restrictions imposed at the Reformation, both for the Church and for individual members, were gradually removed.

There was a surge in the growth of nonconformity during the eighteenth and nineteenth centuries throughout England and Wales, especially in Wales and the industrial north of England; and in Wales its influence and its difference from the Established Church was enhanced by the Welsh language. The reasons why the Established Church in Wales lost so many of its adherents are too complicated to deal with here, but a few generalisations can be made without fear of contradiction. The Church of England is divided into two provinces, headed by the Archbishop of Canterbury and the Archbishop of York – and Wales was part of the province of Canterbury. The four bishops of the Welsh dioceses were often Englishmen, and in some cases they hardly bothered even to visit their patch. Their revenue was very modest compared with that of an English bishopric. There were many conscientious Welsh parish priests, including a large number of Welsh-speakers, but there was no coherent leadership. Churches were in a state of disrepair, and some of the parish clergy were lazy and ineffective, perhaps pluralists or absentees who had put in a poor curate to do their job. The nonconformist ministers, on the other hand, were local people whose beliefs were passionately held and often supported by scholarship, especially their knowledge of the Old Testament, with which they vividly presented to their congregations a compulsively relevant world. Their influence spread beyond the confines of the chapel, often a fine building provided solely by local subscription, for they were both the educators and the moral and cultural leaders of their flocks.

Nonconformity was tolerated by the Church of England and, on the whole, by Parliament. The Liberal Party in the nineteenth century accepted that the Established Church could expect no more rights and privileges within the growing orbit of State-supported education than nonconformists could. But the stumbling block was the parish system which obliged householders to pay the church rate, and farmers to pay tithe, whether or not they adhered to the Church or were nonconformists, to support the Anglican parish priest (the vicar or the rector). The Church in Wales continued to shrink, and the nonconformist chapels continued to grow and flourish, with the result that a minority was being compulsorily supported by the majority. No wonder there was a powerful popular campaign to get the Church disestablished.

Ironically, this stumbling block was already being hacked away: the church rate and the tithe were already on their way out, and attention had thus to be diverted by the campaigners to the ancient endowments of the Church. It was natural enough that in those un-Christian moments from which Christians are not exempt that they should suffer a tinge of jealousy because these endowments supported people who were certainly no better Christians than themselves. As the campaign for disestablishment gathered force, the injustices which had inspired it had melted away. It therefore had to become a matter of principle, and there is nothing like a matter of principle for driving a political campaign.

The Church in Wales 1972–92

The Welsh Wizard, David Lloyd George, a politician in the right place at the right time, was the driving force who ensured that disestablishment would come about. Twenty-three years earlier, as a brash young man on a Methodist day out to visit the home of the venerable Mr Gladstone, he had impudently tried to persuade the Grand Old Man to commit himself to the disestablishment of the Welsh Church. Gladstone explained that the time was not yet ripe, and when contradicted he silenced the young radical by exposing his ignorance of the relevant statistics. But Gladstone was a carefully selected target because it was he who, in 1869, had set a precedent by the disestablishment of the Church of Ireland. The Anglican Church of Ireland, like the Anglican Church in Wales, was an Established Church in a land where the majority of Christians did not adhere to it. The case was very different. The vast majority of Irish were Roman Catholics, and their resentment at having to provide financial support for a Protestant Church imposed on them by conquest was one arm of a political campaign to rid themselves of an aristocracy of English landlords (even if they had been Irish for centuries), many of whom exploited their impoverished and sometimes starving tenants. But a difference in degree does not always amount to a difference over a matter of principle and, after all, why should the Established Church be the Church of a small and still dwindling minority? In Wales a bishop had become a caricature, recognisable only by his propensity for postprandial port.

Lloyd George transformed twentieth-century Britain, although it may not have looked like that at the time, by introducing the old age pension as Chancellor of the Exchequer in Asquith's government, and had effectively negated the power of the House of Lords to veto legislation by the Parliament Act of 1911. He helped to create the climate in which the disestablishment of the Church in Wales became a reasonable act of justice. There were Anglicans in Wales, both clergy and lay, who far from opposing it thought that it might be a 'Good Thing'. Making the Church in Wales an independent Welsh entity which had to stand on its own feet might do it a power of good.

The Welsh Church Acts removed the four Welsh dioceses from the province of Canterbury and enabled them to elect one of their bishops as archbishop. He would not be translated to a special diocese, but would remain in situ, just like the Primus of the Episcopal Church in Scotland (which had ceased to be the Established Church in Scotland at the time of the Reformation). The first Archbishop of Wales was the then Bishop of St Asaph. The diocesan bishops were to be elected by a committee known as an electoral college, made up of clergy and lay people from the province elected for the purpose. The acts also abolished private patronage and the parson's freehold. The former means that the parish parson (the vicar or the rector) may be appointed not by the bishop or by any committee or group of the Church, but by a private individual who happens to have inherited the right of appointment and requires no other qualification. This came about because most parsons' incomes (livings, as they are appropriately called) were originally endowed by the local landowner, who very probably paid for the building of the church as well. He was entitled to appoint any clergyman he chose. The parson's freehold means that the parson cannot be removed: he is there for life – unless he is found guilty in an ecclesiastical court of some heinous offence. This originated in order to protect the clergy's independence: a clergyman could not be sacked for preaching a sermon which might annoy his patron, or his bishop, or (worse still) the government of the day.

The ancient endowments of the Church considered surplus to basic requirements were confiscated and – believe it or not – handed over to county councils to dispose of the income as they thought fit to 'good causes' . Again, the precedent for this form of legalised theft lies at the hands of Mr Gladstone, who saw to it that the endowments of the Church of Ireland were removed when that Church was disestablished. It seemed a good idea at the time to oblige the Church to stand on its own two feet, but it randomly scattered financial support which had been specifically bequeathed by generous Christians in the past, in a fortuitous and indeed fatuous way. If that is not a breach of trust, what is? But democracy often involves the acceptance of decisions that we do not like. Even more importantly it involves respect for those who are not in the majority. Ironically, the Church in Wales did stand on its own two feet after disestablishment, and thirty or forty years later it was the largest denomination within the Principality.

The endowments were seized, but the churches and parsonages, and even here and there a patch of the glebe farm, were not. An entity had to be established to own and manage them, and this was called in the legislation a 'Representative Body', in which there were to be twice as many lay people elected as there were clergy. The legislation also permitted the Church in Wales to set up a 'Governing Body' if it wished to do so. We all know nowadays – or we think we do – what a Governing Body is, but the label is quite a recent invention, and like disestablishment it was devised by Mr Gladstone as a tool of reform, primarily of universities and schools.

The label 'Governing Body' was and is used as a general description, and any institution which is obliged to have one can invent a special name, or dredge up an ancient one. The characteristics of a Governing Body are that its members (or most of them) must be elected periodically, and that they must, at least in a loose sense, be representative. Neither the Representative Body nor the Governing Body of the Church in Wales selected a name which might give a better clue to its function, and the relationship between them is not easy to grasp. The Representative Body is responsible to the Governing Body, but it also has vital trustee powers which it alone may exercise, and if the Governing Body does not endorse its recommendations it has no method of obliging it to change them. Thus, although created by Act of Parliament, refined by a distinguished group of Welsh lawyers (including a Lord Chancellor and a Lord Justice of Appeal), the constitution of the Church has something of the anomalous characteristics of many an ancient British Institution which has evolved pragmatically over the course of time, often with more regard for practicalities than logic. The advantage of this is that it does not suit the style of legalistic nit-pickers, who, however, were amply furnished with opportunities for wasting time by the Governing Body's obligation to follow parliamentary bill procedure whenever it wanted to make a change. This obliged the Governing Body to examine every clause line by line, enabling a single individual to hold up business for the sake of a comma.

Disestablishment was regarded by many Welsh Church people, both lay and clerical, as a release and an opportunity, or at least a welcome challenge. The biggest practical problem was shortage of money to pay the clergy, which became severe after the inflation of the Second World War and the years which followed it. They tolerated it with a mixture of resignation and their perception of the place of worldly goods in their vocation, but many of them were married and it was hard on their wives, some of whom were expected to work in their parishes as 'unpaid curates', to live in poverty. It was some consolation that all the clergy were in the same boat, because the differences in stipends between 'plum livings' and the rest had been abolished. There was a scale of remuneration favouring large populous parishes over small ones, but the differences were fairly marginal. The tradition of parish giving was sixpence in the alms-dish at the offertory – traditionally to support the parish poor – and the Easter offering for the parson.

2 WELSH CHRISTIANITY

It used to be thought that Christianity had disappeared from Britain when the Romans left. One would imagine that a considerable residue would have been left behind in the indigenous, or at least the permanently resident, population, and archaeology has now shown that this was indeed the case, although what survived was in individuals or groups of people and not in the form of institutions. Nor was the Latin used, for instance, on memorial stones quite up to 'A' level standards of orthodoxy. The subsequent revival of Christianity in Britain came from two main sources. After the Roman Empire had been overrun by the peoples they called barbarians, many of the old transcontinental routes were too dangerous for trade and travel from the south and the east towards the north and the west of Europe. Goods and ideas from the Mediterranean world reached Britain by way of the western seaways: from southern France, from Gibraltar and Spain, by way of the Atlantic and the Irish Sea. It was by those seaways, which had been used off and on since the Stone Age, that what we now know as the Celtic brand of Christianity reached Ireland, Wales, the south-west of Scotland and probably Gloucestershire. Even the celebrated monasticism of Northumbria got there via missionaries from the west coast of Britain. This was the Christianity of St Patrick, St David, St Columba and the many other Celtic saints, charismatic individuals, most of them ascetic monks whether they lived in communities or in solitary cells like St Cybi who occupied his cubby hole at Holyhead.

Hundreds of Welsh parish churches are dedicated to local saints, some of them hardly known beyond their villages, their names often preserved to this day as local Christian names. Amongst them were the founders of the four Welsh dioceses, although the idea of a diocese with recognisable geographical boundaries came much later and owed its origin to the second route by which Christianity arrived in Britain, the route across Europe followed by the emissary of the Pope, St Augustine of Canterbury. Christianity coming from Rome was an altogether more organised business than the Celtic brand. It had been the official religion of the Roman Empire from the fourth century, and gradually adopted some of the organisational nomenclature of the Empire itself, including the term 'diocese', originally an area of civil government.

Augustine brought a grand plan for twelve bishoprics in Britannia (which of course included what we now know as Wales), but during his lifetime it was not much more than a plan. One of his successors, Theodore (oddly enough a 'Greek'), got further, but it was centuries before anything like Augustine's plan was fulfilled. When eventually the Welsh bishoprics became dioceses in a recognisably modern form, they were inevitably part of the province of Canterbury.

A vast programme of archaeology in France south of (but including) the Loire, beginning just before the Second World War, has gradually disentangled the customs and cultures of the barbarian tribes, who had settled partly with the permission of a Roman Emperor (or, one might say, the gracious acceptance of a *fait accompli*) and partly without. The Christianity which reached Ireland and Wales, and then south-west Scotland and parts of England, came by sea from the parts of France occupied mainly by the Visigoths, and embraced some of the cultural and religious modes of thought and the brilliant technical skills of the 'Thracians' (who occupied modern Bulgaria and created wonderful artefacts five centuries before Christ) and the Syrians of the early Christian era. The Visigoths picked up their Christianity from Syria too, and incidentally they were Arians asserting the 'one nature' of Jesus. Syrian Christianity in France and Spain may have been reinforced by Syrian refugees fleeing from the barbarians who were overrunning the eastern provinces of the Roman Empire, sailing across the Mediterranean and landing at Narbonne. The Visigoths from south-west France reached the Atlantic by the valleys of the Garonne and the Loire. Along the lower Loire they developed the special flavour of Christianity of St Martin of Tours.

It is many years since it was first recognised that the Christianity which reached Ireland and Wales by sea contained a strong dose of Visigothic culture; and many years since it was first suggested that Visigothic ways of thinking suited the mindset of the Celts. This is the evidence for the overwhelming monastic characteristics of early Celtic Christianity, both in small communities and in solitary ascetic monks. It was this that the Visigoths picked up from the Syrians. Perhaps the strongest single piece of evidence for the late cultural transfer – that is to say after the Visigoths had arrived in France – is to be found not in

The Church in Wales 1972–92

Ireland nor in Wales, but in Gloucestershire: it is evidence of church-building and church dedication, and of Syrian iconography. As to church building, the best potential evidence is still under a yew hedge in Cirencester, and as to iconography there is the extraordinary survival of the three strongly Visigothic carved stones in a small parish church, originally perhaps a reredos, which were rejected as out-of-date, and indeed even shocking, and used face inwards as building stones when the Anglo-Saxons came along. Eventually they were rediscovered and once more revealed to the common gaze; then, in the late twentieth century, their origin was at last recognised, raising for the first time the notion of the transfer not merely of ideas and useful objects but of images.

The Church in Wales, at least through its leaders, makes quite an issue of the differences between Celtic and English Christianity; but when pushed to say what those differences are the response is vague, if confident. Not many Welsh people are aware that the ascetic lives of the Irish and Welsh saints owe a debt to St Simeon Stylites – who lived at the top of a stone pillar and is generally regarded as something of a joke in the Anglo-Saxon world. But that is where it all came from. These solitary saints are often thought of as 'Egyptian'; but it was in Syria, especially the areas of northern Syria connected with Edessa, that the small monastic communities (based on the example of the dozen apostles) and the anchorites in their solitary cells first took root. So influential were their concepts of monasticism that they spread over much of the Ancient Near East: some of their most notable monasteries were in Egypt.

This earliest Christian monasticism was very different from that of the great orders of medieval Europe. It was inspired by the totality of the dedication to God of individuals, bishops and others, who sacrificed their lives to their Lord. It developed from the first congregations of Christians worshipping in churches which were specifically designed for the particular services performed in them. The isolation of monks from society was merely a product of this totality, not a rule or principle in itself, and these early monks were admired and respected for their sacrifice, just as in a humbler way the daily work of a farmer was regarded as his own sacrifice in seeking the bounty of God in the form of his harvest. Monks, then, were the leaders and initiators of Christianity in Syria and later, extensively, throughout much of the Ancient Near East, and then in the Visigothic lands of western Europe whence they came to Ireland and Wales. That is why the ancient Christian saints of Wales were such vital figures in the early Christian centuries: and that is the big difference between the Celtic and the Anglo-Saxon traditions. The main dispute between them was over the date of Easter, finally settled at the Council of Whitby, but anyone who wants to understand the real difference must set that aside as a mere incidental.

During the 1980s the Welsh bishops became very keen on keeping alive the Celtic traditions of the Church in Wales, and held regular meetings with the bishops of the (Anglican) Church of Ireland and of the Episcopal Church of Scotland. Yet what Church could be further from – or could have travelled further from – the Celtic traditions than the Episcopal Church of Scotland? The restored Iona Cathedral is not and never was one of the medieval or modern Scottish diocesan cathedrals. The Episcopal Church in reality is the standard bearer for the Anglican Episcopacy of the Reformation, the Anglicanism of the Stuart kings. What was discussed at these meetings is not clear: seemingly they formed a sort of club of the minority Anglican provinces, keeping their end up in the face of the massive provinces of Canterbury and York.

Early medieval Wales, or even Wales in what used to be called the Dark Ages, had the same four diocesan centres as did Wales at disestablishment in 1921: St David's and Llandaff in the south, Bangor and St Asaph in the north. Many of the English cathedrals were founded in villages, that is to say virtually in the countryside, because the Anglo-Saxons were almost as difficult to urbanise as the Romans had found the Celts, but most of them were later transferred to the towns which are still England's ancient cathedral cities. In Wales this did not happen. St David's and St Asaph are still more akin to what we think of as villages than cities. Bangor with a strategic position on the Menai Strait is now a considerable town, the more so since it became a university centre in the twentieth century; but its cathedral still sits modestly in its valley, concealed from Viking pirates and sea raiders, just as do the cathedrals of St David's and Llandaff. Llandaff still has the feel of a village, although it is now within the urban spread of Cardiff, and of all the catherals of Britain it is, I think, the most remarkable for being a soaring Gothic building hiding at the bottom of a steep valley. Thus the cathedrals and also many of the parish churches of Wales have a different feel from those of England, and it was easy for the Church in Wales of the twentieth century to establish its special new identity, embracing both the Welsh-speaking and the English-speaking parts of the Principality.

The Church in Wales 1972–92

St David's Cathedral is also hidden from the view of ships at sea. It is built on an awkward site of sloping rock so that the floor at the east end is higher than at the west; for this is the shrine of St David himself. Next to his cathedral stand the stupendous ruins of the medieval bishop's palace. They were abandoned because the bishop could not live at one extreme corner of his massive rural diocese with any reasonable chance of carrying out visitations of his parishes, or travelling without intolerable inconvenience to and from London (where he had a seat in the House of Lords). Most bishops live near their cathedrals, but as far as running the cathedral church is concerned this is not necessary, because the cathedral is run by the dean (with the assistance of canons). The Bishop of St David's' new palace was built at Abergwili, nearer the geographical centre of the huge diocese.

From the time of Henry VIII until the later part of the nineteenth century there was no way of forming new dioceses in England and Wales, either in order to reduce the size of old ones or, more specifically, to serve new centres of population; except by abolishing old ones and transferring their endowments. In the early nineteenth century it was decided to amalgamate the dioceses of Bangor and St Asaph in order to found a new diocese at Manchester. The proposal was abandoned after Welsh protests that one diocese for the whole of North Wales would have been unmanageable – just as St David's in the south already was. But after disestablishment the province could create as many dioceses as it thought fit – and afford; so the two new dioceses of Monmouth and of Swansea and Brecon (with its cathedral at Brecon) were formed from territory mostly in St David's, and also in Llandaff. There was debate as to whether Swansea and Brecon should be separate, but it was felt that six rather than seven dioceses could be sustained, and thus it has remained. The division of each diocese into two or three archdeaconries (the archdeacon has a sort of inspectoral role of the parish clergy and their churches), and the boundaries of parishes, many of them ancient enough to follow (and thus now to identify) the routes of Roman roads, were already in place.

3 THE NEW PROVINCE

The new province had to create its entire administrative framework and to write its own constitution. It duly elected its Representative Body in accordance with its statutory obligation, and decided to create a

Governing Body as its legislative authority. Its founding fathers were wise men indeed, although obsessively legalistic in their approach. The Governing Body was to consist of three 'Orders' of bishops, clergy and laity, and although the Body could proceed by simple majority, any 'Order' could require a vote by Order instead, in which case a decision required a majority in each. This was an ingenious and logical way of getting the safeguards of a bi-cameral or tri-cameral legislature whilst allowing the Governing Body to debate matters as a single entity. The latter advantage was important, because it gave the bishops, especially the archbishop, opportunities to give a lead to the elected representatives of the whole province, and to some extent to steer the debates; and, indeed, it gave every lay and clerical member that same opportunity. It also enabled clergy and laity to hear each other's point of view, and it created an essential sense of collective identity in the Body as a whole. The veto which it gave to each Order did tend to stifle reform. In that respect a simple majority would have been an advantage. But in an episcopal church the bishop has a special authority, and it would have been wrong for the Governing Body to be able to carry measures against the collective opinion of the bishops.

It might be thought that the system of voting by Order would encourage divisions in the province, but actually the opposite is true because it prevented the lay members from outvoting the clergy on important issues. For instance, during the time I was involved in the work of the Governing Body, both the Order of Bishops and the Order of Laity voted in favour of allowing women to be ordained as priests, but the Order of Clergy voted against it, although only narrowly. To those who, rightly or wrongly, thought of themselves as enlightened reformers (including many clergy) this seemed an undesirable and perhaps unwarranted veto of a change which, in fact, had already been voted some years previously by the Governing Body as acceptable (or, to be precise, not objectionable) in principle. Yet to impose it on a Church in which more than half the elected representatives of the clergy objected to it would have been divisive to a degree which might have put the Church of Wales in turmoil.

In a 'free country' with a representative (and nowadays typically a democratic) form of government, patience is an essential virtue. New ideas take a long time to achieve general acceptance. On the other hand, if they are good ideas, it is probable that a number of people will have them at roughly the same time, and that general acceptance will follow

The Church in Wales 1972–92

after a period of years. This is known as evolution. It is the characteristic – almost by definition – of every long-surviving institution, and it is preferable to revolution. The similarities or differences between the evolution of species and the evolution of ideas is a subject for endless debate; which is a cogent reason for not embarking on it here.

The disestablished Church in Wales has two significant advantages, but whether it has used them to good effect is another matter. The first is that it is about the right size. The provinces of Canterbury and York are so large that it is impossible to make any kind of change in them without the formation of political parties in their synods. This is compounded by the fact that the Archbishop of Canterbury is the Primate of All England, so that the two provinces have to work as one in matters of legislation. There is an obvious parallel in the development of the power of Parliament, especially that of the House of Commons. An individual member without a party base can achieve very little. The so-called two-party system, stoked by first-past-the-post elections, is a different animal from the make-up of parliaments which have some degree of proportionality in their voting: they spawn a larger number of parties, but nevertheless the creation of or adherence to a party is the only way to make a difference.

It is true that a single vote on a particular motion may transform a majority into a minority and vice versa, but no government could be formed merely with the hope of retaining the support of a few individuals wayward enough not to attach themselves to a party, nor could a one-man band launch a political programme with the faintest chance of success. The best illustration of this fact lies in the history of our own Parliament.

The power of medieval English Parliaments, such as it was, was the power to pull the purse-strings. When Parliament began to be used by the Tudors to reinforce their policies by the force of legislation, then, provided that the Crown's leadership was efficient and forceful, there was no way that the members could organise an opposition, because Parliaments and parliamentary sessions were of short duration. Even if a group of members formed what might be considered as a 'party', they were soon dispersed around the country in their constituencies until, perhaps a few years later, another Parliament was called. And it was only when parties were formed that legislation could be devised by any other organisation than the government.

The Church in Wales 1972–92

The way in which the first party to oppose Crown policy was formed in what became the 'Long Parliament' in Charles I's reign presents a question which has kept historians happily occupied for generations. So much detailed evidence is available that new theories follow one another with the passage of years, but they turn out to be no more than variations on a theme. The one thing about which all are agreed is that both in the Lords and in the Commons there were hard cores of members, capable of drawing others into their orbits, which effectively dished the royal policy of governing the country without the restraining force of Parliament. Like it or not, we have had a two-party system since then. Small parties come and go, but ultimately they have to decide to support one or other of the two largest parties. There has not been even a name-change for almost a century, since Labour supplanted Liberal. There are many other sorts of system available, but without parties representative government of large entities cannot be made to work.

In small entities, parties are not essential, because every individual member of the legislature who is bold enough to get on his feet and face the audience has an opportunity to express a view. A motion can be put provided that a few members will support it, and debated, and individuals can then vote as they think fit. There is no need to follow a party line, either in debate or in voting. The motion can be amended, and by the end of the session everybody has heard all points of view and a resolution can be put. This encourages a far higher standard of debate than you ever hear nowadays in the House of Commons, and it enables every point of view and every argument to be considered. It has the advantage of enabling individuals to make up their own minds, and it prevents a sense of the back-bencher being sidelined by the Establishment. It thus helps to create a sense of collective responsibility. Even in a small entity, however, there has to be some tacit understanding of a convention that some 'party methods' are not tolerated. For instance, it is 'not done' to canvass support by circulating partisan literature before a debate. Conventions of this kind can only be sustained by the support, tacit or other, of a large majority. One argument against canvassing is that everybody can follow suit, driving up expense and allowing money to push debate off the forum. This is an illustration of the important part which convention plays in making institutions work. If convention is not strong enough, the alternative is to write more rules.

This is not to say that in large institutions parties are not essential. All it says is that in smaller institutions they are not. And this is a reason for considering how big or small an institution should be if there is a choice. Another way in which small institutions work better than large ones is a sense that everybody knows everybody, not literally, but in a general way. This induces a better collective atmosphere, more willingness to accept views contrary to one's own and to express one's opposition to them in gentlemanly (or ladylike) terms, a more positive approach to compromise and a more tolerant attitude to minority opinion.

The Church in Wales consists of six dioceses, so a Provincial Committee made up of one cleric and two laypeople to represent each of them presents eighteen members. This is rather big. One cleric and one layperson might be better, but at any rate it is manageable and keeps the lines open between the diocesan committees and the provincial ones. The problem is to find capable people who are willing to give up their time. Too much continuity on a committee tends to lead to the stifling of new ideas. As soon as you hear a member of a committee saying 'We tried that before, and it didn't work', perhaps it is time for that person to go. Times change, and an idea which didn't work twenty years ago may work now. It needs perhaps to be considered on its merits rather than its history.

The Governing Body and the Representative Body were both rather large, especially the former, and every few years somebody got the feeling that they should be smaller on the grounds of saving money; in other words, on the grounds of efficiency. You can certainly get the same decisions from a small body as a big one, and less laboriously. The problem is that you become less representative, but that is hard to measure in pounds sterling. You tamper with a subtle network of communication: the Committee's decisions filter back on paper, but the minutes of a meeting should be laconic, if not lapidary. The most important reason for allowing representative institutions to be larger than 'efficiency' demands is that people who were actually present at a meeting can explain verbally why decisions were made to their diocesan committees, and can indeed be asked by these committees to make a point at the next meeting. Moreover, provided that a diocesan committee knows that its views have been presented, it is much more likely to accept their rebuttal with good grace.

In a commercial or industrial undertaking 'efficiency' takes the front seat, even though in a large firm a prime objective of each layer of management is to prevent the layer above from knowing what is going on. (This is one explanation why non-executive directors of large companies are ineffective. It is almost impossible even for the full-time people to know what is going on, for they have no evidence beyond what is fed to them from below.) But with non-commercial organisations, most especially those manned by volunteers, what is important is that people feel that their work is valued and that they can play a part in decision-making. In any organisation large enough to need a committee structure to take executive decisions, morale at every level is one of the most important considerations. There will always, or almost always, be a feeling of 'Us' (the so-called grass-roots) and 'Them', the central organisation which makes the decisions, but it has to be a prime aim of the latter to eliminate it.

The Representative Body, concerned with the property, finance and administration of the Province of Wales, worked almost entirely through committees, and only met as a whole once a year to receive, amend and approve its committees' reports – holding in effect an Annual General Meeting to decide what should be handed up to the Governing Body for its approval. The Representative Body worked as well as it did because most of the members were involved in its committee work or, if not, they were at the receiving end of the committees' minutes in their dioceses and could comment on them to their members. But the Annual Meeting was not a mere formality or 'rubber stamp' because it was also an occasion for summing up objectives, and methods of achieving them, drawing together the work of all the committees and exploring new ideas and new policies. This was necessary in itself, but it was also necessary because the Representative Body had to present its report to the Governing Body for its acceptance. By the time this happened it was history, and could not be rewritten, but it was an opportunity to explain, and a useful indicator of temperature for those who could benefit by reading it. I vividly remember one occasion when the Governing Body was meeting in the great hall of Aberystwyth University, and the Chairman of the Governing Body for the session was a respected Judge. The Representative Body's investments had done very well that year but the Representative Body was resolved not to cream off any of the capital profit and use it as income. The judge thought that we should use the capital profits to give the clergy a bonus, and even asked an alternate to take the chair whilst he made his plea. However, the Chairman of the Representative Body refused to budge, and even dared to tell the judge to 'come off it', which resulted in the audience drawing an audibly deep breath. But the Representative Body stuck to its guns, and carried the day. This anecdote illustrates that the existence of 'grey areas' in the interpretation of constitutions can work quite well, final decisions depending on a convincing case being made in debate rather than on a splitting of hairs during a constitutional impasse.

The Governing Body was numerically much larger than the Representative Body, because it included representatives of each deanery (a group of parishes forming a subdivision of a diocese); and it had a much wider remit than the Representative Body. Like the Representative Body, it had to consider its own committees' reports. These often led to some of the best debates.

Dealing in detail with the committee stage of bills, a chore which since the days of my own participation has been delegated, was tedious, but apart from that there were often interesting debates on matters of policy. The subjects were mostly suggested by the Powers That Be, but back-benchers could put down motions, as long as they could find a few people willing to add their signatures.

At each meeting the Archbishop gave (he still does) a 'keynote' address, and individual bishops were the chairmen of some of the important committees, so the bishops took a leading part in debates and its members became known to the members of the Governing Body as a whole. Other chairmen might be lay people or senior clergy with particular expertise, and there was thus a very real sense that the Governing Body was genuinely representative, that it was deciding the policy of the Province, and that the lead was being given by the bishops.

One third of the Governing Body and of its committees was elected every second year, and after six years members of committees had to stand down for a time. This provided a satisfactory mixture of experience and new blood, coupled with a sense of continuity and, perhaps most importantly, a feeling that everybody did to some extent know everybody else. This is the key to a sense of common purpose and an atmosphere in which passion and prejudice are cooled by friendship and humour. The most important task of a Chairman is to nurture this atmosphere and to encourage every speaker and would-be speaker to feel that their contribution matters.

Wales suffers from its geographical division into north and south, with more sheep than people in its rugged and mountainous wasp-waist.

The Church in Wales 1972–92

The communications between north and south are nothing short of hopeless, whether by rail or road. Every ten years or so somebody has the bright idea of an air service between Hawarden and Cardiff. The latest version is coming up in 2013. The only time this has survived for more than a few months was in the 1970s when civil servants in the north were falling over each other to take seats on the plane and waste a day in conference with kindred spirits in the capital, but in the end even they ran out of subjects to discuss and the service was closed for lack of support. Wales has one long frontier – with England – and it is across this frontier from North Wales and South Wales (and mid-Wales for that matter) that communications work well and naturally. Welshness has survived the centuries in spite of this disadvantage, but one of the problems for the Governing Body was to decide where to meet. Having tried a number of inconvenient meeting-places, the Representative Body unashamedly decided to meet in Shrewsbury, and the Chairman wrote to *The Times* over an assumed name saying that Shrewsbury should be annexed to Wales and that most of the objections to this idea seemed to have been dropped by Salopians; but, in spite of nine follow-up letters, before the Editor ended the correspondence, an exceptionally long series for *The Times*, nothing was done.

The Governing Body felt that it ought to stay within the Principality. Until the 1970s it usually met at Llandrindod Wells, an ancient place which had become a delightful Victorian spa town and which had the merit of being equally inconvenient for everybody. There were magnificent hotels there, and a parish church, enlarged in the nineteenth century presumably to accommodate the spiritual aspect of healing, where the whole Governing Body could hold its services. Then the Governing Body became for a time peripatetic between north and south. Once we met in Llandudno and the mayor made a comical speech of welcome, claiming that Noah's Ark had touched down there ('Have We Landed? No.'). But there was no other argument in favour of this northern resort, however delightful it would have been for non-ecclesiastical junkets.

For a time the meetings were held at Aberystwyth University, which in many ways was convenient, but the sleeping accommodation was rather dispersed and the eating centralised, and in the end the Governing Body fetched up at the University of Lampeter. Lampeter was a unique small university qualified to confer its own degrees, established specifically for the training of Welsh clergy. Admirably though it carried out the task, the problem was that the students missed the opportunity of a broader kind of university education, and never left their native land before beginning their life's service in a Welsh parish. (The most select did get scholarships to Oxford or Cambridge, it is true, but they were a minority.) After the university expansion of the late 1950s and 1960s, Lampeter increased in size and broadened its base, and during its vacations it was the ideal place for the Governing Body to meet, with a large hall and dining rooms, but compact enough for social as well as ecclesiastical intercourse; one of those delightful small towns which were gradually being eliminated in rural Britain, complete with its independent specialist shops, grocers and ironmongers with modest fronts but cavernous interiors, veritable Aladdin's caves.

The Governing Body's meetings involved two nights away from home except for those who lived near at hand, and two meetings were held each year. There were always people who thought that we could manage with only one meeting a year, but this would have meant that committees could only report once a year, by which time many of their decisions were historical *faits accomplis*, thus reducing the function of the Governing Body to that of a rubber stamp. If the Governing Body did have a positive function, then reducing its meetings to one a year would have meant that more committees had to be invented to fulfil part of its function. Besides, committees do not spend much time questioning their own policies, let alone their *raison d'être*. They have plenty to do completing their agenda. Time spent on waffle means a later train home, or driving through the rush hour. Moreover, there would have been only one opportunity each year for each committee to keep abreast with other committees' thinking.

'Well, anyway,' one can hear people saying, 'half the members never open their mouths.' But that does not mean that they don't have ears? It is only too easy to destroy a subtle network of communication and of responsibility for reasons of economy. Moreover, if you meet only once a year you lose much of the collective feeling of the institution because people do not get to know each other. But that again is something you cannot measure. One of the keys to the effectiveness of a deliberative and legislative chamber, not least in encouraging people to put forward new ideas, is morale. The biggest damage you can do to such an institution is damage to its collective sense of purpose. This operates best if there is the right balance between new blood and continuity. If you are a new member of a large group like the Governing Body, it is twice as hard to get to understand the business in hand, and to get to know your colleagues, if you meet once a year rather than twice. You can only decide that it does not have to be three, or more, times a year if you have been granted the gift of common sense. Oddly enough, people who measure things by statistics know that statistics unaided by common sense are often worthless.

People will say that this argument may have been valid twenty or thirty years ago but that with modern communications a smaller membership and less frequent meetings are more appropriate. In that case why is the Government bent on spending £32 billion on the first phase of a high speed railway which will no doubt have cost £100 billion by the time it is finished? Imagine all those civil servants of the 2050s knowing that they can get up half an hour later and enjoy an English breakfast in a first class carriage in order to spend a day chatting with their colleagues in Birmingham, or a decade later in Salford. Better still, the exiles from London will be able to travel to their old stamping grounds in the opposite direction. Early in 2013 the chief executive of a very large but faltering company has decreed that working from home must stop. People need to knit together (as a 'team' no doubt) by working in the same place.

4 A MODERN STRUCTURE?

In its early days, the question of the Governing Body meeting only once a year hardly applied, because nobody had thought out a way of filtering its business. It is obvious that you do not need a meeting of two hundred people to decide whether or not to insert a comma. The Governing Body in those days not only had to do all its business, including minutiae, in plenary session, but it had to do it without anybody having first tried to knock it into shape. Archbishop Gwilym Williams was the first to take the bull by the horns and he set up an Archbishop's Commission on Boundaries and Structure to propose a more efficient *modus operandi*, without prejudicing the principle which gave the Governing Body the ultimate executive authority. The Chairman was a very able and engaging academic sociologist, Chris Harris, so the Commission's report was sure to be the result of professional fact-finding and logical argument. Eventually it came up with the idea of inserting an additional layer between the Governing Body and the dioceses in the form of a Council, much smaller than the Governing

Body but much larger than a Committee. The Commission's proposals were debated by the Governing Body which rapidly came to the conclusion that it would compound the problem rather than solving it. The Report was torn up in a single session and the poor Archbishop was back to square one.

The Archbishop made one mistake: he asked his Commission to deal with boundaries as well as structures. An experienced Parliamentarian would have realised that unless there is strong sentiment in their favour, boundary changes will seldom be accepted willingly by those who are their victims. The Commission, after painstaking research, proposed some logical alterations to diocesan boundaries. Nobody wanted them, and almost nobody would speak in their favour. They merely added fuel to the bonfire.

One of the many sensible things the Archbishop had done was to abnegate his sole right to chair the Governing Body and to establish instead a small panel of Chairmen who could take the job by turns, consisting of two or three bishops and two or three lay people. (Apart from anything else, this enabled him to play a part in debates without having to go through the procedure of getting the Governing Body to appoint a temporary alternative Chairman.) In the hope of salving something from the wreckage of the Commission's report he asked one of the panel of Chairmen to get a small group together and come up with a better plan.

The Chairman was asked by the Archbishop to suggest suitable members, and based his choice on the need for a pragmatic attempt to achieve maximum effect with minimum apparent disturbance: in other words, not to produce a blueprint, but to reform the kind of structures with which people were already familiar. This was the classical method of nineteenth-century Parliamentary liberalism, being evolutionary in approach and endeavouring not to challenge vested interests if this could be avoided. The group soon came up with a more practical idea than the Commission had proposed, the basis of which was simply to filter the business of the Governing Body. This required an Executive Committee to which all the existing committees (or whatever more fancy names they might have adopted), both of the Representative Body and the Governing Body, should report. If there were several committees dealing with one aspect of the Church's life, then there must either be some amalgamation or they must become sub-committees, whichever seemed the simpler and more efficient.

This major committee was to be called the Standing Committee in order that its name should not either reveal or disguise its function. It did have to be fairly big. In addition to the bishops, the main Committee Chairmen had to have a place on it and it had, too, to be manifestly representative. But it did do the trick in as simple a way as anyone could think of. It gave the diverse business which the Governing Body had to deal with some kind of coherence. It obliged the Representative Body to create one small committee (virtually its own Committee Chairmen) to speak for it to the Standing Committee, which in itself made it possible for the first time for the Governing Body and the Representative Body to coordinate their policies, and had the incidental advantage of encouraging the Representative Body's committees to work together. The creation of the Standing Committee provided, too, a channel through which future proposals for structural or constitutional reform could be considered.

The working group also gave the Archbishop a useful political tool in the form of the Business Committee – again, its name did not reveal, or conceal, its function. Since this function was merely to decide the 'order of business' at the next meeting of the Governing Body, it could be very small. Its unavowed objective was to give the Archbishop the opportunity to shape the Governing Body's agenda as he thought fit rather than leaving this in the hands of the Standing Committee and the administrative staff at the office. It was in fact a second filter for the Governing Body's business, enabling the Archbishop to set the priorities. Archbishop Gwilym appreciated that this was a valuable tool in his hands, but subsequently the problem was that (at least in the Church in Wales) archbishops and bishops are not political animals, and they did not perceive the advantages which the Business Committee offered them. Perhaps they were and are just too other-worldly in the way they try to get things done

5 THE REPRESENTATIVE BODY

The Representative Body of the Church in Wales established its office in Cardiff – appropriately in Cathedral Road. For the diocese of Bangor this involved (as it still does) a long and tiresome journey, but for others it was as convenient as anywhere else, because it could be reached by tolerable roads or railways, which is more than can be said for people coming from the north or the south to central Wales. During the 1950s and '60s the whole administrative machine was run by W. R. Jones, an accountant, as Secretary to the Representative Body, with Glyn Ellis managing the office as Administrator and a minimal staff. Graham Jones, the solicitor, was the only other professionally qualified member. The Representative Body, as the business arm of the Church, also administered the Governing Body, and for a time W. R. appeared capable of running the whole show. Totally dedicated to his role, with a remarkable understanding of the character as well as the nuts and bolts of provincial government, he was a master of economical administration. But it was more than even he could manage, and periodic attempts were made to provide some support for him by the Governing Body appointing its own Secretary. Unfortunately the succession of people chosen were not of the stamp of W. R. and the task was performed inadequately. It required a person who had the imagination to understand the Church as an institution and who had the energy and the sensitivity to help it to achieve what the Archbishop and the bishops wanted; but this it did not get.

It was clear that W. R.'s retirement would mark the end of an era. It was decided to appoint a 'Secretary-General' to administer both the Governing and the Representative Bodies, and that a person of the standard of the administrative grade of the Civil Service would be required – and paid accordingly (more generously, that meant, than the Archbishop and bishops, let alone the rest of the clergy). This was not a popular move, but it was essential. David McIntyre, who had considerable experience at Church House, Westminster, the headquarters of the Church of England, was chosen, and although he may not have satisfied everybody in all respects, he had a proper understanding and appreciation of the Church as an institution and he masterminded the establishment of an appropriate secretariat to run it. What he did need in this difficult and potentially lonely task was a mentor, a role which fell on the Chairman of the Representative Body.

The Secretary-General was to be Secretary to both the Governing and the Representative Bodies. He therefore needed the support of an accountant in the place of W. R. himself. The solicitor was already in place. But who was to manage all the Representative Body's property? We discovered that there was no complete record or terrier of all the churches and parsonages and other property owned by the Representative Body, and although they might or might not be properly maintained by the dioceses there was no set of rules and every chance that a building here and there might be neglected, or might even disappear. Title deeds were not indexed. The archdeacons did have an inspectoral role, but no training or expertise in looking after buildings. So we appointed a chartered surveyor as our Property Manager. The small team consisting of the Secretary-General and the three professional executives enabled the Representative Body to fulfil its responsibilities.

At about the same time the Governing Body established a means of coordinating its policy and that of the bench of bishops in the form of the Board of Mission at Penarth to steer and coordinate its policy with a carefully selected senior cleric to run it. Unfortunately this person considered his authority to be superior to and independent of the Secretary-General. This caused the fur to fly and, as may be imagined, war between two senior people in a small organisation does spoil the atmosphere, to put it mildly.

This is a good example of the fact that two senior people with very different functions working within an institution, especially a small institution, have to be able to get along together, and that the only element which is certain to cause trouble is a lack of self-confidence. Unfortunately neither of them was willing to get on with his job without finding grounds for testing his superiority over the other. The only solution to this sort of problem is to be found in the departure of one or both of them. The bickering had to run its course until, mercifully, the tenure of one of them expired. It might be argued that in a well-designed institution this would not happen. Perhaps the Church is not well designed in this respect. Certainly as an institution it is organic in nature, and if one part of the body does not work satisfactorily you have to mend it rather than to redesign it.

The Church's endowments having been confiscated, the Church was short of money to pay the clergy. In the early days the financial experts on the Representative Body were unaccustomed to inflation and frightened of the risks of investing in what we now call equities, largely because the idea of a balanced system of investing in a wide range of enterprises had not yet been devised, either for institutions or for individuals. Still prominent in the minds of the older generation were memories of the great slump of 1930, when people had lost everything but their shirt overnight. The value of money, though subject to ups and downs, had remained more or less stable for many decades before 1914, and after the First World War the big question was how to keep it so: to get back to normal – just as everyone had wished to do after the

Second World War. Equities were seen as 'speculative' investments, too risky for trusts: it was still not legal for trusts to invest in more than a given proportion of them. If indeed the value of money was still stable, a good return could be obtained from gilt-edged investments: Government Securities (now referred to as bonds), issued to fund the National Debt, which had been a feature of national life since William Pitt the Younger consolidated it in 1797, and on which the genteel middle classes and the majority of the idle rich had lived for more than a century – roughly from Jane Austen to P. G. Wodehouse. As the idea of capital appreciation crept in to cope with the new phenomenon of apparently endemic inflation, the generations were divided between those who believed in it and those who didn't. There was thus a long time lag between 1939 and the late 1960s before the Representative Body grasped the nettle and succumbed to what was then a modern investment policy. Meanwhile inflation had sapped the value of stipends until, as mentioned above, the clergy were living in poverty.

It was David Vaughan, Chairman of the Representative Body's Finance Committee, who bought Bush House for less than £2m. Its eventual sale for £18m transformed the finances of the Representative Body and of the Church in Wales. Meantime a modern balanced investment policy, split between gilt-edged securities (guaranteed by the Government, but subject to inflation), equities and investments in property, stood the Church in good stead for many years. The difficulty was, however, that the clergy, regarded as being 'like everybody else' in this respect if in no other, had to be given the chance to retire, and to retire with a pension. Since most of them were not ordained until they reached their upper twenties or their thirties, their retirement covered a larger proportion of their life than was the case with 'everybody else', with the consequence that, as people would say nowadays, the sums did not add up. For many years the Representative Body, with the help of actuaries, simply set aside sufficient investments to pay for pensions, but in the end it was obliged as a trustee to fund the entire pension scheme as a separate entity.

David Vaughan's was a difficult act to follow, but Raymond Cory masterminded the investments successfully for many years. We did much better than the Church Commissioners, who held the investments of the Church of England, but that was not saying much and we submitted ourselves to a select league table every year, and came out very well. But we did not have the resources to fund both the pensions and the upkeep of the parsonages and the stipends of the clergy in the face of inflation, especially as there was a long and arduous climb to get back to tolerable stipends after post-war inflation.

Dr Glynne Jones, who was Chairman of the Committee responsible for stipends, came up with the policy of doubling them in real terms over the course of five years. The continuing inflation which had made this necessary also made it very difficult to achieve. It involved for the first time the necessity for parishes to contribute to the payment of their clergy. For many years the parish quota was only a small percentage of the total stipend, in spite of inflation, thanks to the Representative Body's successful investment policy. This enabled a new and unwelcome idea gradually to gain acceptance, and of course it revolutionised parish finances. It brought the clergy out of poverty and enabled the principle to be considered that their incomes ought to be equal to those of teachers.

The idea of Christian stewardship gradually transformed Church people's ideas of almsgiving during the post-Second World War era. Instead of sixpence in the plate on Sundays, congregations were encouraged to plan their giving according to their means, and to make regular generous donations to strengthen the work of the Church. This greatly reduced the sense of shock and innovation by the time it became necessary for parishes in Wales to make substantial contributions to the cost of their clergy, and to face the realities of maintaining their buildings.

6 WHEN THINGS WENT WRONG

During the early years of disestablishment the Church in Wales did its job well, within a rather narrow range of vision: it showed that it could stand on its own feet. Wales was still producing more clergy than it needed, many of the best of them going to English parishes. Britain was still an avowedly Christian nation. The liturgy was revised for the first time since 1661, the revisions of 1928 having been thrown out by the House of Commons. Unlike England, Wales retained much of the old magic of Cranmer's rhythmical, and thus memorable, prose. The bench of bishops masterminded the training and spiritual work of the clergy and of their lay supporters. The Constitution, like the Governing Body which devised it, was archaic in form, but in an essentially conservative institution the awkwardness which this imposed on getting things done, and in particular in introducing any changes, was accepted as a fact of life. It was not until the 1970s and 1980s that things started to go badly wrong, with a severe shortage of money as a result of inflation and with the cultural and social challenges of the 1960s beginning to bite. The old parish system, so long the bane of the Church of England, yet never seriously challenged, started to fall apart.

The forces of change which transformed Britain from a Christian to a post-Christian society during the forty or so years from 1960 to 2000 are not difficult to discover, although the details of the transformation leave plenty of room for discussion. Recruitment of clergy and the size and composition of congregations went into a seemingly inexorable decline, and were accepted with resignation by those who might, with courage and imagination, have cast out the nets on the other side. The reasons are complicated. The most obvious places to look for them are first to ask whether people no longer found it easy to believe what the Church taught, and secondly whether the Church as an institution was ill-fitted to teach its lesson, or in more appropriate language to convey the good news of Jesus Christ. I am not competent to write about doctrine, although I will hazard a few thoughts of a layman. But on the organisational or institutional side I feel strongly that the Church in Wales lost an opportunity to fit itself for the modern world.

William Temple, Archbishop of Canterbury from 1942 until his early death in 1945, summed up the essence of the Anglican Church: 'Our special character and, as we believe, our peculiar contribution to the Universal Church comes from the fact that, owing to historic circumstances, we have been able to combine in one fellowship the traditional Faith and order of the Catholic Church with that immediacy of approach to God through Christ to which the Evangelical Churches especially bear witness; and freedom of intellectual enquiry, whereby the correlation of the Christian revelation and advancing knowledge is continually effected.' But has that correlation been made relevant in the years since Temple died?

7 DOCTRINE

It is difficult for people nowadays to believe in the God of the Old Testament, who created the universe, whether the job was done incredibly quickly as in Genesis or incredibly slowly as in the view of some modern Christians. So, not believing in this God, they cease to be Christians. 'Mainline' Christians belonging to the larger and older denominations do not think nowadays of a God who actually created the world.

The Old Testament God was much in evidence in early Christian thought. The Jewish scriptures were still accepted, especially in the more Semitic areas of the ancient Near East, giving the early Christians the respectability of continuity. But then we also find a third-century Christian theologian challenging the story that God created the world in a week as 'stupid'. Most people assume that it was not until the time of Darwin that the Genesis story was widely rejected and they are correct: the contest between Huxley and Bishop Samuel Wilberforce, who ridiculed the idea that he might be 'descended from a monkey', were late-nineteenth-century affairs. Other ideas had been explored by learned people, especially after the early stages of geological discovery, but they were confined to a few thinkers. Canon William Buckland of Christ Church, Oxford was a geologist who advanced the concept of periodic global catastrophes, proposing that God's creation as we experience it had followed the last of these events, but his ideas did not catch on as Darwin's were to do.

Sophisticated modern ideas of creationists, stretched to accommodate the Big Bang and communication across billions of light years, with the requirement of 'intelligence' as part of its essence, is a barren one which begs the question 'What are we trying to prove about the power and nature of God?' The Old Testament God ceased to be the God of vengeance and retribution and became the God of Love, but He remained the omnipotent creator. Nowadays, in order to understand something of the nature of the Christian God, we have to concentrate our minds on the Good News delivered by Jesus; and we can ask ourselves what He said about a Creator. Search the New Testament and you will find that the answer is, if anything, very little indeed; in spite of the fact that it was taken for granted in the society He lived in that God had created the world. Of course, there are other things too which many people find hard to accept – including the reality of miracles and especially of the Resurrection. But how much help do they get from the parish clergy, who seem to be inhibited, rather as the Victorian upper class was inhibited over the discussion of wicked things in front of the children and the servants? I suggest that droves of 'ordinary' people, who are clever enough to dismiss the Genesis story, have deserted the pews by default.

Ever since the Reformation, all clergy have been obliged at their

The Church in Wales 1972–92

ordination to accept the Thirty-Nine Articles of Religion which constituted an ultra-severe test of doctrinal belief in a forlorn attempt by Henry VIII to stop the revolution he had started at exactly the point he wanted. At least since the eighteenth century it has been accepted by all, or almost all, concerned, that this does not demand a too precise adherence to the doctrinal niceties of the Articles, which themselves are far from lucid in meaning. Dr Johnson recorded that it was considered sufficient, both for the clergy and for devout laymen such as himself, 'not to preach against' the Articles, and I wonder whether this is true nowadays of the Creeds, especially the Nicene Creed, liturgically central since it is rehearsed by the whole congregation at the Communion service (or Eucharist, an original name revived), and beginning with a declaration of belief in the Old Testament God. Perhaps there are many Church members who privately regard it as merely 'not to be preached against'. Perhaps there are many who have rejected Christianity because they don't.

Whilst I was a member of the Governing Body the proposal to delete from the Creed the double precedence of the Holy Spirit 'from the Father and the Son' was periodically suggested, though in a rather half-hearted way, and set aside as being of little significance and thus not worth an argument. No other changes were ever suggested, which perhaps was just as well: for it may be best to retain the ancient text and apply William Temple's 'freedom of intellectual enquiry' to its interpretation. Is this generally accepted and understood by those who have voted with their feet? If not, why not?

One has to refer to the mainstream denominations (of which the Roman Catholic, Anglican and the Greek and Russian Orthodox are the largest) because an astonishing growth of Christianity is taking place in the newer and fundamentalist Churches where 'God is back', still the God who created the world in six days and rested on the seventh. But can the fruit of this mushroom-like growth survive? Perhaps mainstream Christianity has forgone its mass membership just because it seems to people that the Old Testament God is still there, and they don't believe in Him.

Anglican theologians (at least those in the limelight) in recent years have concentrated on – not to say have been obsessed by – New Testament criticism, some of which goes as far as to tell us that almost nothing in the four Gospels is definitely true. To them the Old Testament God has been brushed out of the picture many years ago, but is that the case with the average churchgoer, or, more relevantly, non-churchgoer? Studies of the Old Testament are mostly confined nowadays to scientific criticism, in which the question whether things are true or not is irrelevant. We used to have only two readings at the Eucharist: an Epistle and the Gospel. Now we have an Old Testament reading too. Some of the Old Testament readings are, to put the point mildly, peculiar.

This is not to say that the Old Testament is not important to students of Christianity. It reveals the background in which Jesus taught. It contains many wonderful stories, and in the Authorised Version it is a stupendous and inspiring collection of literature. But the odds and ends which have been stuffed into our Communion service can hardly help anyone who is trying to come to terms with Christianity in the light of William Temple's dictum.

8 INSTITUTIONS

Questions of faith are central to Christianity, although there has always been variety throughout Christendom. But in order to attract and retain adherents Christianity has to help enable people to realise that their faith makes an important difference to their lives. The extraordinary speed with which Christianity caught on in the early centuries may be a phenomenon we shall never see again. But there still has to be a way by which people can be captivated. There may be a critical stage in the decline of Christianity in Britain from which there is no return. Certainly very little has been done to 'cast out the nets on the other side'. The Church in Wales has suffered from an apparently endemic tendency to shiver on the brink, and never to accept the need for organisational change. This perhaps is as important a reason for decline as the loss of faith in what people suppose to be the orthodox God. Churches depend very much on their institutional structure for their long-term survival. This is why most of the thousands of nonconformist chapels throughout Wales are empty and redundant. Their congregations have simply died out. But can the Anglican Church use the benefits of its continuity – the Apostolic Succession – to enable its institutions to evolve with the times? For, after all, the Sabbath was made for Man, not Man for the Sabbath.

There have thus been virtually no doctrinal changes in the Church in Wales. Liturgical changes there have been. Modern versions of the Prayer Book were introduced with the object of making church services more normal and easier to understand. There may have been some beneficial results, but the Church was robbed of one of its greatest inheritances, the exquisite and memorable language in which acts of worship and mystical truth had been encapsulated in Britain since the Reformation and even since the very first translations into English. Ironically, this runs counter to Welsh cultural traditions, for Welsh culture has been handed down by word of mouth rather than by the written word, especially in the tradition of story-telling and most notably in ancient Welsh law. Law is not merely a set of rules, it is a reflection of a nation's customary life and its habits of thought. And the amazing thing about ancient Welsh law (which tells us so much about Welsh culture) is its memorability. In this respect, as far as the Prayer Book was concerned, and also with the rejection of the King James Version of the Bible, the baby was thrown out with the bathwater. Nobody remembers the banal phraseology of the modern liturgy or of the Bible in the form which ironically is intended to make it, as no doubt the devisors of the modern versions would put it, more meaningful.

More successfully, the atmosphere of services in parish churches became more friendly and welcoming, with an increasing sense of participation by the congregations. But the only radical change during these years was the ordination of women, which over the course of perhaps twenty years gained almost universal acceptance, and saved the Church from collapse. The institutional failure has been the lack of organisational changes aimed at transforming the parish system into an institution fit for purpose in the modern world. With the abolition of private patronage and of the parson's freehold, the disestablished Church in Wales was, for the first time, in a position to make radical changes. Never before in the course of a thousand years had the bishops been handed a clean slate. Yet, like the Anglo-Saxon church builders who imitated wooden poles in stone, or Herr Benz who designed his motor car like a horse-drawn carriage without shafts for the horse, the Church in Wales chose not to notice the opportunity.

Parishes developed in the early Middle Ages – indeed, in what used to be called the Dark Ages – from the need of every congregation to have a priest to lead it. The intention, from then until the time of motor cars, was to have a church and a priest within walking distance for every village, or of course every town. Town churches often multiplied in numbers because of particular congregations, notably guilds. Village churches, large or small depending on local resources, were built wherever a village could provide a congregation, which was usually where there was a lord of a manor, often not a lay landowner but the head of a religious foundation such as a monastery, to erect one. The resources to build the church and pay the priest (also supported by tithe) came from this patron. This is virtually the system which (in spite of noble Victorian efforts to modify it and provide new churches in growing commercial and industrial towns) survived intact until after the Second World War. Indeed, it survives, if not intact, to this very day.

In olden times when a village disappeared (most dramatically after the Black Death) its church fell into ruin. Recently many churches have been declared redundant, and either preserved by 'friends' in view of their architectural merit or converted to some other use. But the vast majority remain, many of them with congregations unable to sustain them. The response of the Church in Wales (and the Church of England) has been to make one priest responsible for two parishes. Or perhaps three, or four, or five. So the unfortunate clergyman, already isolated and discouraged and trying to make the best of a declining and ageing congregation, and attempting to be all things to all men, rather than being given help, support and encouragement, merely has his problems doubled – or tripled – or quadrupled. Had it not been for the advent of women priests to boost the numbers, the whole rotten institution would have collapsed years ago. As it is, it has been left to rot slowly. Who would opt to be a clergyman with this in prospect? The answer is: the very few noble souls who are so strongly called that they respond regardless of what lies ahead.

In the old days it was the parish priest of the strong congregation who was the vital influence in encouraging young candidates for ordination to come forward. But there are (almost) no strong congregations now; and a pathetic trickle of ordinands. The best priests also trained the clergy as their curates. Nowadays almost every parish is at best a one-man band, and at worst it can only claim a fraction of the work of a priest. No parish priest, however gifted and energetic, can answer every call: to baptise the infants, marry the few couples who apply, bury the dead, preach an interesting sermon, visit the sick and the elderly, instruct the children, lead the youth, teach the candidates for confirmation, counsel the bereaved or the stressed, and perhaps play the organ and mow the churchyard. There is, admittedly, more lay help than there used to be, mainly perhaps because people live longer, but there is

The Church in Wales 1972–92

nobody to share your concerns, except the next door parish priest who is suffering all the same problems.

It would not have been difficult for the Church in Wales to confront the problem and establish a smaller number of large parishes. The motor car which made the small parish unnecessary also makes it possible for every cleric in a strong team to reside as a vicar in a small parish, as used to happen long ago. A team of clergy under the supervision of an experienced priest selected for his ability as a leader could have transformed the whole life of the Church; provided only that he was given, as he would be given in every other calling, a reasonable measure of authority. One would have found parishes which made a real difference to the lives of their congregations, where service as a cleric was a joy and not a worry, and where young lay people, members of a dynamic congregation, came forward as recruits.

The Church both in England and in Wales has established 'teams' or 'groups' of clergy under various guises, but what is lacking is that every member of the team does more or less exactly as he or she thinks fit. In spite of having bishops, the Church cannot bring itself to give any select class of leaders at a lower level authority in a new type of parish. Not only was the isolated single professional in most walks of life an outdated concept by the second half of the twentieth century – because it simply did not work – but if it worked at all it was because of the highly specialised role of an individual, who was therefore essentially dependent for his usefulness on a larger institution or institutions. The Church in England was still restrained by a labyrinth of ancient legal rights and customs, but the Church in Wales was not. It did invent a new status for a few large parishes known as Rectorial Benefices, but ironically it used them for the specific purpose of giving those who would previously been known as curates the status of vicars, so that they could feel as if they were independent parish priests even if they were not: in other words the objective was diametrically opposite to what it should have been.

If the Church had wished to proceed by what appeared to be a more evolutionary process than simply abolishing old parishes and creating new ones, it could have taken hold of an ancient institution known as a rural deanery (now known more sensibly as an area deanery), which had long ceased to have any avowed purpose but provided a way in which a group of parish priests got together occasionally over a cup of coffee, presumably to moan about their problems – quite a helpful process, actually, as far as it went. The rural dean having virtually no surviving function, the members could elect any senior clergyman they wished, to make him feel good – or, at least, better; precisely as they still do in the renamed area deanery. He had (and has) no authority. The rural deanery could have been altered radically to turn it into a new type of parish, if that had seemed less radical. But the method would have been cosmetic, and anyway nobody was bold enough to contemplate such a change.

This idea was proposed to the Governing Body when the Board of Mission, egged on by the Archbishop, decreed that the 1980s would be a 'Decade of Evangelism'. The member who proposed the reorganisation of the parish 'system' forecast that such a vague evangelistic concept would never work without a radical change in organisation. His speech was received with a standing ovation, and a group was set up under a bishop to consider it in detail. The bishop called a few meetings, none of them with either agenda or minutes (evidently he had never come across such things) so nobody knew what, if anything, had been decided, and eventually the process ran into the ground. People who are deeply entrenched do not like to move.

Eventually, in 2012, the shortage of clergy became so desperate, in spite of the strength brought by the ordination of women, that the Archbishop felt obliged to establish a committee to propose larger geographical units to succeed parishes. Let's hope it isn't too late.

The Archbishop of Wales is elected from the existing bishops by an Electoral College, which also elects each bishop as vacancies occur. The College consists of the six bishops (to elect the Archbishop) or five (to elect the sixth of their number when a vacancy occurs) and of three lay and three clerical members from each diocese; except that the diocese for which a bishop is to be elected has six of each. The proceedings are secret. So far so good. But in the way it sets about its work it is the most archaic institution I have ever come across. No candidate can be proposed before the College meets. Any member able to find a seconder can put forward a candidate, but there is no method of ascertaining who the candidates will be, or of making inquiries about them, let alone seeking opinions from those who are likely to know them and to be likely to have formed sensible views. There is no question of taking up references, or of asking for reports or opinions (except those given verbally at the meeting of the College), let alone interviewing a candidate. The proposer has a chance to speak in support of the candidate, and there is an opportunity for anyone to speak in favour or against. The candidate's entry from *Crockford's Clerical Directory* (the *Who's Who* of the Church) is read, giving merely the bare bones of the proposed candidate's career. A ballot is held, and if the College cannot reach a conclusion during the first day, they have to stay overnight in isolation and try again.

In a small province, many members of the College are likely to know something of most of the candidates, but only a few will have more than a nodding acquaintance with them. I was a member for long enough to have had a part in the election of all the six bishops, and I suppose that the longer I was there the less incompetent I became, but I was not at all happy to undertake such a solemn duty more or less blindfold. We were there to seek God's will, but I couldn't help wondering whether ignorance was a useful qualification. Periodically members used to question the validity of the procedure, and on one occasion we had the opportunity to vote whether we thought any improvement on the system was desirable. Only two people (of whom I was one) thought it was: so there did not seem to be much point in arguing for reform.

The question therefore arises how well the procedure worked in practice. The opinions of the bishops were given a lot of weight, and the representatives of the diocese in which there was the vacancy had always done their homework and formed some idea of the person they wanted. I have to admit that on the whole the choices which the College made of diocesan bishops were good ones; perhaps as good as they would have been with a more normal and accountable procedure. But I cannot say the same of the choice of the archbishop, mainly because his colleagues felt that the senior bishop should be given a go. Poor fellow, it would have been hard on him were a more junior bishop preferred. This was disastrous. Two of the archbishops whose elections I attended were not really up to the job, and in each case the Church suffered under inadequate leadership. 'Buggins' turn' is not necessarily God's will. This is not to say that the choice was never right. The outstanding archbishop in my time was George Noakes, then Bishop of St David's, an inspired choice both as bishop (only recently he had been a mere parish priest) and then as archbishop.

George had the gift of tongues: he was a superb communicator, a man of radiant spirituality, one of those rare people who always has the right word or phrase at his command. He was witty and succinct and he used plain language. Rooted in rural Cardiganshire he had the instincts and assumptions of a Welsh countryman. He was the first archbishop to understand the potential of modern methods of communication. This meant of course that he had to be in Cardiff: that is where the media were. Provided that he was available, the press and the radio and television were always keen to ask his views on every social and moral issue. Since he was a very spiritual man whose daily devotions always came first, and since he lived some way off at Abergwili, the manifest tasks of the bishop of a large diocese together with the role of an archbishop who was willing to devote time and energy to being heard in public were too much for him, and he did not stay on beyond the normal age of retirement. But he had showed what could be done: if only the Archbishop of Wales lived near the capital.

The advantage of having an Archbishop who was Bishop of Llandaff, with or without an assistant bishop, or alternatively setting up a small diocese for him in the Cardiff area, soon became evident to the Governing Body, and they set up a working group to recommend what should be done. But, as usual, they drew back on the brink: for the simple but invidious, if not fatuous, reason that none of the other dioceses would ever again have the Archbishop as their own bishop. This was parochialism at its worst. The opportunity was lost, and was not going to be revived for some years.

I have argued that the Church in Wales as a province was of the right size: but the one objection was this parochialism which inhibited change, and perhaps cancelled out not only the advantage of being the right size to get things done, but also the freedom of action which disestablishment offered. It tended to invite the 'Buggins' turn' syndrome to operate at every level. Changes in parish structure, it was said, would deprive the clergy of their independence: yet at the same time these clergy were beginning to claim the rights of employees in secular institutions, thus wanting to have their cake and eat it. It was to be about thirty years before a system was painstakingly worked out in detail to give them 'normal' rights through their contracts of employment. And it was to be about thirty years, too, before things got so desperate that once more the province had to look at alternative structures – when, perhaps, it was too late.

9
Some Local Institutions

I THE FLINTSHIRE COUNTY COUNCIL 1970-74

After I had spent twenty years teaching in boarding schools, the last eight of them as a head master, my wife and I with our young family migrated to the old family home on the Welsh border at Hawarden in Flintshire. My father had died, aged nearly eighty, the previous year, and my mother was about to move to a newly built house nearby. I felt that I needed a sabbatical year before thinking about a new direction which my life might take. The family estate was complicated for its size, much of the property being ancient and in small units. The supervision of its management would have been enough to keep one busy; but being still in my mid-forties I knew that as soon as I had enjoyed a prolonged rest I would be in good enough shape to take on some additional work. I had the envious opportunity to consider what jobs I could do which might be both useful and enjoyable. Then, out of the blue, there arose an unexpected opportunity.

Michael FitzHugh, a county councillor, telephoned after the local elections to ask me whether I would like to join the County Council. The Conservative members of the Council would like to elect me as an alderman. He needed a decision within 24 or at the most 48 hours.

I did not know what an alderman was, although I vaguely associated the office wiith rather grand status in the City of London. However, I discovered that in all the County Councils in England and Wales the elected members could themselves elect a small additional number of members known as aldermen, and that this right was shared out between the political parties (and the independents) in proportion to the number of elected councillors. I accepted the invitation. It would enable me to get some experience of local government without having to take the trouble to get elected in the normal way.

This method of indirect elections was a residual survival of the old regime, the reform of which had begun in 1834 and had produced something like a modern County Council during the later years of the

Some Local Institutions

nineteenth century. The system had obvious merits. It enabled the people involved in local government to select a few members either with proven experience or particular expertise, and it enabled some of the older hands to be kicked upstairs, leaving the elected seats open for new blood to contest. It had some of the merits of a House of Lords without hereditary rights. But it did not fit with modern democracy and it was abolished four years later with the major reorganisation of local government in 1974. This provided me with a welcome escape route, for I had soon discovered that local politics were not my métier.

Flintshire was a small county, not much bigger than Rutland, with its northern boundary along the coast of Wales and the Dee estuary, from Rhyl in the west to the English border on the outskirts of Chester in the east, roughly rectangular in shape, about twenty to twenty-five miles long and ten to fifteen miles from north to south. It was the only county in England or Wales to be in two parts, or as it was expressed to have a detached part, marked on maps as 'Part of Flint' and known locally as The Maelor.

The western part of the county was much more Welsh in character than the eastern. Offa's Dyke, which runs through the county from north to south, was still something of a dividing line between the English-speaking and the Welsh-speaking areas, although English was widely spoken all along the coastal resorts and the strongholds of Welsh were really the rural areas. The western part of the county with Rhyl, Prestatyn and the tiny cathedral city of St Asaph were Conservative in politics, whereas the east was industrial and Labour. The Maelor was the only area still made up largely of rural estates.

The county takes its name from its magnificent but little known castle of Flint, one of the string of castles built by Edward I in the 1280s, all supplied by sea, to keep the Welsh in order. Mold, however, became the county town when Wales was divided into shires like English counties by Henry VIII in the 1530s. It is a pity that its old Norman name of Montalt had been shortened, as so many other Anglo-Saxon and Norman place names have been, because Mold sounds rather ridiculous and the Welsh name Yr Wyddgrug is not easy for English tongues.

Mold in the 1960s still had its own town hall, but as with so many other old county towns the local government offices had already spread into a number of disparate buildings and a grand scheme was set afoot to give it a new County Hall to accommodate all its departments in the

Some Local Institutions

town's outskirts. The Clerk of the Council (soon to be called the Chief Executive!) Haydn Rees, together with Armon Ellis, a distinguished solicitor and elder statesman of the Council, contrived that the Council should buy a smallish country house with about twenty-five acres of land to the east of the town and set about the construction in modular design of a modern office building of truly monstrous size (admittedly its several blocks look even larger than they are because they are tall and thin). To this new Shire Hall I was introduced as a member of the County Council in 1970. I found myself in an Alice in Wonderland world.

I had suffered a couple of culture shocks in my early life when I started at boarding school at the age of eight and when I joined the Navy at the age of eighteen, but it had not occurred to me that either of these institutions was unfit for purpose. The County Council, however, ushered me into a world where value for money was not a relevant concept and where decision-taking was not dependent on discussion. Since huge sums of money were involved, and since some of the decisions taken were important, this was to me to be quite unlike anything I had hitherto experienced as the 'real world'.

The Council had its strengths as well as its weaknesses. Haydn Rees was a capable administrator, and a negotiator of the first order, a quality which has perhaps become rarer in society since those days. He was patient, tactful, considerate, a good listener with an engaging personality, and he led a happy staff which, within its own terms of reference, was loyal and efficient. He was liked and respected both by his civil servants and the councillors, and he had a first-rate team of senior officers, men (they were all male) of rather a different stamp from what one finds nowadays, not least in that on the whole they expected to stay in post throughout their careers. This tendency ran throughout local government in Britain, and produced a civil servant rooted in his job and his locality. People did not expect to move from one local authority to another to take a small step up the ladder. The councillors, their colleagues, and the public who came in contact with them, liked and respected them. They knew their districts well and inherited and kept records going back perhaps for half a century, which helped them to make transparently fair judgements. They were professional but not bureaucratic. Reasonableness and common sense were more important than slavish adherence to petty rules. These qualities endeared them to the councillors who, although mostly of limited

Some Local Institutions

expertise and experience, went about their tasks in a civilised and good-humoured manner. Many of the councillors were of long standing, and they made newcomers feel welcome.

The Council operated by a system of committees, which were made up of members of the various political groups in proportion to their total representation. This was manifestly both fair and inclusive, although it did not work at all well if judged by results. Every member of the Council was thus included in its work, and had some choice as to which committees he or she would serve. The chairmanships were mostly, though not exclusively, in the hands of the political party or parties with a majority in the Council, and the weakness of the system was that all the detailed work had to be done by the chairman (and perhaps one or two others, vice-chairmen) and the senior officials, which in effect greatly limited the work of a committee itself. Much of what was presented to it was either *fait accompli* or a set of proposals requiring a vote yes or no, but the real trouble was that when a committee as a whole was entitled to make a decision the method was ludicrously inadequate. This applied especially to the making of appointments.

The power to select an individual for a job was the power which councillors most valued. In many cases it was the reward they expected for success in an election. Unseen forces running through the communities of Flintshire (and for all I know communities everywhere) formed this desire to decide who got the best jobs – and who didn't. Quite apart from their ignorance (or, to be charitable, lack of expertise) of the requirements of a job, inexperience in making selections, and what might (again charitably) be described as prejudice, the councillors who formed the selection committees were allocated an entirely inadequate opportunity to exercise their judgement, such as it was. For example, in appointing heads of schools, a short list of three candidates who had been screened by the chief officer (the Director of Education) and the Chairman and Vice-Chairman of the Education Committee was presented to the whole sub-committee of probably about fifteen members, together with three questions which each candidate must answer in a maximum of a quarter of an hour. Inevitably, in the circumstances, the questions were generalised in character and invited the kind of conventional answers which the committee members would lap up. How do you see the school fitting in to the community? What is your attitude to discipline? What part should parents play in the life of the school?

Some Local Institutions

If there was a local candidate, four times out of five he or she would get the job. Otherwise, whoever could lay on sentimental truisms with the biggest trowel would be selected, sometimes, as in a school headship, with disastrous consequences. On several occasions I found myself voting in a minority of two: Dr Liam Gavin and I seemed to ourselves to be the only members of the platoon in step. Eventually, however, the results seemed to justify our worries.

The members of the various education sub-committees could also expect to represent the County Council on one or more school governing bodies. This provided me with experience of a couple of governing bodies dominated by councillors, but in this case by more district than county councillors. Almost all of them appeared neither to know nor to care about education. It was a grim experience to sit through these meetings, comforted only by the patience and sense of resignation of the head teacher in the face of a system which he could not expect to change.

The main departmental committees were very large, because there were about eighty councillors (the Education Committee actually consisted of the whole Council) but the system could only be workable through a large number of much smaller sub-committees. Each councillor could expect to be a member of perhaps five or six of these. The alternative would have been to work with something more like a 'cabinet' system, with one councillor in charge of each department. This method has become much more popular nowadays, because it is rightly seen as being more efficient. But the trouble is that it makes most of the councillors (the backbenchers) even more powerless than they were under the committee system. This is the big problem with local government. You will not get capable people standing for election unless they are thereby going to be able to make some contribution to policy.

I have described my initiation into the County Council as a culture shock, but quite apart from that it took a long time to learn the ropes in order to be able to exercise any influence at all. The committee system provides continuity, which is one way in which local government was more efficient than national. Policy is based on committee minutes and can only be modified by minuted committee decisions. It is not easy to get a new topic on to a committee agenda because people cannot be expected to recognise its importance until it has been discussed. This militates against changes of policy and means that a newcomer to a

Some Local Institutions

committee cannot expect to have much effect; but at least he or she can have more of a say than the much more efficient but less directly democratic 'cabinet' system allows.

The powers of local councils have been remorselessly eroded since the Second World War as communications have improved, as the need for expert and technical knowledge has increased, and as the urge to centralise has become irresistible. Who would think of a County Council running its health service or its Police force or deciding the routes and designs of major roads? County Councils still have some influence in education, but their efforts have been so disastrous for many years that Parliament is now openly reducing their influence as a matter of policy.

This was already the position in 1970 and the erosion has continued. When Tony Blair became Prime Minister he promised a revival of local government but without being cynical I can point out that it was indeed a revival of the powers of local government provided that they did what the central government wanted them to do. After a great deal of argument about the cost of education the Government with much trumpeting provided the local authorities with an additional £300 million. It disappeared overnight. The local authorities had decided to use it for pay increases. The Government were furious and we heard no more about the revival. What we have heard since then from both a Labour and a Conservative-cum-Liberal Government is that schools are to be taken out of local authority control.

Councils used to be the largest employers of labour in their counties but their services provided without competition too often proved costly and inefficient. Twenty years ago I could joke that their only remaining function would soon be as dustmen – and this has turned out to be uncomfortably near the truth. And the problem is that as our dustmen they have to oblige us to follow quite tiresome regulations, which does not serve to increase their popularity. It must seem to some people that the main function of the Council nowadays is to prevent people from breaking petty rules. Whilst central government has relentlessly reduced local powers, it has also increased regulation. Health and Safety and Planning are two cases in which the general perception is that there are now too many rules, and it is 'the Council' which gets the blame. This was not the case to anything like the same extent in the 1970s. The problem then was a completely different attitude to money from what one would find in business or, indeed, in housekeeping.

Some Local Institutions

Planning is still in the hands of local authorities but the trouble is twofold: first, no councillor wants houses in his, or his constituents' or friends' back yards, and secondly that planning consent so vastly increases the value of land that the whole process is subject to the most elaborate, cunning and undesirable forms of persuasion, vulgarly labelled bribery. This has led to an elaborate code of rules which are often enforced by officials who are simply not up to the job, bringing long and stupid bureaucratic delays into an already complicated process. It is all very well to say that such contentious decisions should be in the hands of local people, but decades of frustration and an endemic national shortage of houses suggest to me that what is needed is a respected umpire, insulated from local pressures, who can bring both expertise and good judgement to the decisions which need to be taken. It is common sense that the high cost of housing is due to the excess of demand over supply.

It seems to be the custom to make radical alterations to the structure of local government approximately every twenty years. Each cycle starts with complaints that the units are too small, so the Government makes them bigger, as in 1974; then people grumble because the units are too big ('remote'), so the Government makes them smaller, as in 1996. We shall no doubt see them all getting bigger again within the next ten years, if indeed there is anything left for them to do. The changes of 1974, which mercifully released me from involvement, created larger units – actually for the convenience of Whitehall, which wanted a manageable number of Councils to bring to heel, but avowedly in order to remove small Councils because they were too 'parochial' in character. However, the whole process was spoilt in 1974 by simultaneously creating a lower level of District Councils which were not administratively linked to the County Councils and thus were a law unto themselves: so the overall remedy for pettiness was worse than the disease which it attempted to eradicate.

The late 1960s spilling over into the 1970s were the most extreme in the whole course of British history for Government expenditure as a perceived means both of stimulating economic growth and improving public services. Since 1945 Governments both Labour and Conservative had regarded incentives to spend, or not to spend, as the most important tool for controlling the economy, without much regard to the problems caused by inflation. The wartime economy, governed entirely by the cost of fighting the war, had inhibited normal manufacturing for

Some Local Institutions

six years and thus, with shortages of everything, there followed a long period of full employment accompanied by inflation. Inflation of around 5% (it was often higher) had come to be regarded as inevitable, or at least as the price to pay for full employment. The balance of payments (imports against exports) was negative throughout these years and was regarded, like inflation, as regrettable but, although this was not admitted, here to stay. Unemployment had been the nightmare of the 1930s and anything was better than that.

Conservative Governments reduced taxation to win votes and stimulate the economy, on the whole in that order of priority. Labour Governments increased taxation for the same reasons, in the same order of priority. Both policies were inflationary, but as they had the mandate of an elected majority the Governments' best efforts to limit both inflation and the adverse balance of payments could not amount to much. With full employment and very powerful Trades Unions always stoking wage-inflation their best efforts would be regarded nowadays as pitiful.

There was a lot of money sloshing about in local government, and the councillors made the decisions as to how to spend it. They seemed to be collectively rather like a poor person who has won a lottery: they had control of an amount of money which to a normal person would be unimaginable, and they spent it sporadically as if on a whim. There was no question of deciding priorities, or whether expenditure provided value for money. It was there to be spent, and that was that. A policy of high public expenditure was one thing; a policy of expenditure regardless of value for money was quite another. This was the unreal world in which I found myself, and it applied to capital expenditure as much as it did to income. Haydn Rees was expert at discovering how money was to be had. He built the Shire Hall (now called the County Hall) with money on a sixty-year payback loan! He also acquired the capital to build adjacent to it the County Library and to fill it with a superb collection of reference books: this of course was before the time of the Internet. I used to visit this library from time to time. Except on one occasion I was always the only person there, because it was in a hopelessly inconvenient location. There was also a large Record Library (that is, for gramophone records, before the day of CDs). The only drawback was that there was no money left to buy records, so this expensive building never performed a function.

Some Local Institutions

Also adjacent was the new Magistrates' Court, together with accommodation for the Crown Court, with the judge's lodging on the top floor: this was a useful building (except that it had a tiny car park, making it a nightmare for magistrates trying to arrive punctually, and worse still for the 'court users'); but perhaps that is just a grumble, as it would be to say that the jewel in Haydn's crown, the Theatre Clwyd, was too small to be viable, and has struggled from one financial crisis to another throughout its existence. Haydn was impatient to build this valuable cultural centre, but although he obtained huge sums, they were insufficient to achieve what he was determined to achieve. He went ahead nonetheless: perhaps he was right, for this period of extravagant public expenditure was soon to come to an end.

These were the early days of the quango and its cousins. A quango is a quasi-autonomous national government organisation established to control, encourage and regulate anything which a Government thought needed such treatment, but which itself is only quasi-regulated. The name has caught on and is casually applied to many other similar committees established locally or regionally, largely for cultural reasons, as a result of somebody having a bright idea.

Membership consisted of a few full-time or part-time professionals drawn from those who had climbed (by whatever means) into the ranks of the Great and the Good and of representatives of any relevant body which could be thought of, especially County Councils. Like many others I was a member of several of these, representing the Flintshire County Council, but I was not given any briefing as to what I might contribute. This was just as well, because these bodies were run by an inner core of people who took the decisions, the representatives like me being expected, on the whole, to perform the function of a medieval parliament 'to hear and consent'. I soon gave up attending their meetings, having other things to fill my time. I am not sure whether any of them still exist, but I am quite sure that nobody noticed, let alone regretted, my absence.

Councillors before 1974 were unpaid, but received their expenses. There were not therefore the 'professional' councillors who blossomed after that date, living on their pay without doing any other job, except insofar as large firms gave leave of absence to any of their employees who were councillors as indeed they did to magistrates and members of the Territorial Army. British industry was in decline, partly because of competition from the low-wage economies of the Third World, partly

Some Local Institutions

because of poor management often with a hereditary streak, and partly because of the over-mighty control exercised by the Trades Unions which was not acknowledged by the Labour Party until the time of Jim Callaghan when he recognised the inevitability of a 'sea-change' as Premier in the later Seventies. Nevertheless this was still the era of large factories, providing an ample pool of politically minded employees who would not have to make any financial sacrifice by becoming councillors. Perhaps this was the reason why the more able of the Labour councillors generally spoke more sense at council meetings than did Conservatives.

Not much could be said for the pronouncements of the most politically minded leaders of any of the political parties. I remember a function attended by the Conservative Secretary of State for Wales at which the leader of the Conservatives on the Council spoke. The Minister afterwards asked me 'Does he attract or repel?', to which I replied 'I don't know, but he repels me.' The problem was that these people were expert at working the system: they would comb through the committee minutes to find a fault which they could then criticise to win a point in debate. They spent a lot of time meeting the officials and mastering the details of the committees' business. On the other hand, many councillors either didn't have time or couldn't be bothered to read the minutes at all: they turned up at meetings with their brown envelopes containing the minutes and the agenda unopened. No wonder that the discussions were not of a high order.

The most serious problem was that hardly any of the councillors could understand a balance sheet, or had any inclination to do so. It was remarkable to me that the Labour Party, whose power and influence in Britain was primarily built up in local government in the years before it became a major force in Parliament, took no steps to give its councillors training. Much more would have been achieved if new or aspiring councillors had had the opportunity to attend weekend courses and discussions. As it was, as far as Flintshire was concerned, the County Treasurer, a civil servant of the old stamp, took the council through its annual accounts, explaining and simplifying lucidly without any hint of being patronising or condescending, and then answering questions. But it was only too clear that most of his hearers did not understand and had no idea how to work out for themselves the cost of the various measures for which they had voted, or indeed which they had opposed. The standard response to this

Some Local Institutions

criticism was that it was up to the officials to carry out what the councillors wanted.

The problem was exacerbated by the intricacies of local government finance. Only about one-fifth of the expenditure was funded by local taxation in the form of a property tax known as 'rates'. It was traditionally asserted that one-fifth was enough to concentrate the minds of the ratepayers, and the almost folklorist hatred of this tax (people 'paid their taxes with regret and their rates in anger') reinforced this view. Rates were simply based on valuations of property undertaken by district valuers, a laborious operation undertaken at long intervals of years (and even then postponed by Governments again and again as a political hot potato). The rate was simply the percentage of this value imposed as the local government tax, which needless to say had to increase with inflation in order to stand still. It sounds like a good, simple system, and so in a way it was; yet it produced manifest injustices. Nobody believed in it but nobody was willing to confront the problem and change it. Eventually Margaret Thatcher did change it, with politically disastrous consequences, substituting the 'poll tax' which obliged everybody (almost) to contribute.

Four-fifths of the revenue of local Councils were therefore subscribed by central Government, and the system of calculating the amount was subject to variation by no less than sixty 'indexations' devised, added to and modified over the course of many years with the object of making them fair. Understanding the purpose of each one of them must have involved a tedious and detailed study of their history. Only the most devoted practitioners knew how to apply them. Manipulation was a tactical, not a strategic exercise. Since, however, each local authority was free to set its own rate, eighty per cent of its income had to be provided willy-nilly by central Government using an arcane formula; a formula which anyone willing to take pains could apply, but which almost nobody fully understood. This was the root cause of the extravagant system of local government finance. It could have been dealt with by a rate cap, but this was not considered politically acceptable; and anyway, the policy of local extravagance went alongside the Government's policy of spending to stimulate the economy and of increasing public rather than private institutions. The worldwide financial crisis of 1974, when for the first time the oil-producing countries got together and hyped the price of fuel, was to deal it a severe blow; but by that time I had escaped. When the blow fell one of the remedies was to allow

Some Local Institutions

civil servants early retirement after thirty years of service with index-linked pensions based on their final salaries, which were deliberately hyped for their final year in order to make the package even more acceptable. It must have been obvious at the time that this policy could not be sustainable: but the time-bomb had to wait for more than thirty years before any Government dared even to try to defuse it. Capital expenditure was meanwhile encouraged by favourable payback conditions for loans. I have mentioned the repayment period of sixty years for the Shire Hall.

I have painted rather a grim picture of the County Council as I knew it in the early 1970s. Yet the people who worked in the Shire Hall were for the most part competent, helpful and, within the conventions of the Civil Service, conscientious. The conventions meant that they knocked off at 4 p.m. whether their work was finished or not, and that they defined their responsibilities very strictly so that they did not criticise or interfere with the work of their neighbours; and there were a few small dysfunctional offices tucked away where very little was ever achieved. The councillors, too, were almost all of them well-motivated people willing to give up time for public service, who went about their tasks in a sensible and civilised manner. There are bound to be clashes of personalities in any political institution, but good manners were very much to the fore in the Council at Mold, with the result that political differences did not spawn personal dislikes, making the Shire Hall a pleasant place to work.

2 THE MAGISTRACY, 1976–2000

I became a justice of the peace as a member of the Hawarden Bench in 1976. The township, licensed to hold a market in the Middle Ages, was the site of a very ancient Christian settlement and the modern parish had seven churches; and two castles, one of prehistoric origin and the other a Norman motte and bailey. By the 1970s the Hawarden Bench had ceased to use its own courthouse and was accommodated in the new building at Mold. The Bench covered the whole of the area later labelled 'Deeside' and had about twenty-four magistrates.

I have an abiding respect for the Magistracy, a medieval institution which has evolved over the course of centuries and nowadays settles more than nine out of ten criminal cases in England and Wales. Most of its sentences are in the form of fines or of so-called 'community service',

Some Local Institutions

which is officially regarded as an alternative and equivalent to a prison sentence; and it was empowered for crimes in the more serious categories to impose prison sentences of up to six months. In 'borderline' cases in terms of severity defendants can opt for trial by jury in a higher court: they quite often do so when their advocates think that they are more likely to be able to pull the wool over the eyes of a jury of twelve people than over three justices drawn from their own community. The vast majority of the cases which the magistrates' court settles are petty, including motoring offences, although many of these can now be dealt with by the Police or other authorities imposing standard penalties, provided that the accused does not appeal.

Three magistrates sit together, one of them acting as Chairman of the Bench, and they have to be unanimous in order to arrive at a verdict. For this purpose they retire to a private room, where their discussion is entirely confidential, after they have heard the evidence. If the decision is finely balanced, and they find themselves inclined to vote two to one, there is further discussion and the dissentient very often agrees to accept the view of his colleagues. In the unusual event that they cannot agree, there has to be a retrial.

The magistrates' clerk or the clerk's deputy (a qualified solicitor) is always present to provide technical legal advice if consulted by the Bench. Magistrates do, however, receive a very thorough training, and this is regularly updated. Most if not all the training is carried out locally, but some candidates can spare the time to go away for a residential course. Family cases are taken only by magistrates who have undergone a special course of training in preparation for this difficult and important work, the administration of which falls on social workers who, as far as public perception is concerned, have a rather thankless task in which only their failures are newsworthy.

In my day there was also a Licensing Bench which would sit specifically to grant or refuse licences to sell alcohol 'on or off the premises' and to decide the opening hours of public houses. This work, the result of Liberal legislation in the late nineteenth century in its endeavour to mitigate the curse of drunkenness, was gradually eroded and finally taken over as something of a formality by County Councils. The question how Government should, if at all, seek to limit and control the consumption of alcohol is as disputatious now as it was in Mr Gladstone's day, but with modern systems of manufacture, distribution and retail, plus the abolition of punitive (except for the rich) duties on

Some Local Institutions

imported wine when Britain joined the Common Market (now the EU), the old licensing laws became more or less redundant, even if the old and declining pub culture serving draught beer kept in its cellars in wooden barrels at about 52 degrees Fahrenheit tottered on until the abolition of smoking dealt it a final blow.

The majority of the work of the Magistrates' Court was dealing with petty criminal cases, and most of them were concluded without a formal trial. The Crown Prosecution Service did not exist. A Police inspector or sometimes a senior sergeant regularly attended court and did the work of the prosecutor, in my experience with great efficiency. This took up a good deal of Police time, but there was far less time wasted on 'paperwork' in the life of a policeman in those days than there is now, and the time spent on criminal cases was not wasted except insofar as the justice system bent over backwards (as it still does) to be fair, which led to rather laborious procedures and to interminable pleadings by long-winded local solicitors who evidently thought that the magistrates would not understand a point unless they made it at least three times. These small-time criminal solicitors were not the cream of the legal profession, but they had to be listened to patiently, or at least without a show of impatience.

Trials were interesting because one came across all sorts and conditions of men in the guise of the accused and of witnesses, the multifarious and sometimes extraordinary activities of which they were accused and the ingenious stories offered as evidence. Sentencing is notoriously the most difficult task with which the dispensation of justice is faced, but there were copious national guidelines, which were regularly updated. Magistrates built up experience and a judge was appointed to provide a fairly remote oversight and support for each Bench when needed. He presided over the annual swearing-in of new magistrates and on similar formal occasions and was available to offer help, especially perhaps on sentencing guidelines which did not *prima facie* appear to coincide with common sense. Two magistrates used to sit with the judge in the Crown Court, and although the judge's decision prevailed, he or she did take in to account the magistrates' views; but the main benefit of this system was to give the magistrates occasional experience coupled with some actual responsibility of the way in which serious crimes were handled.

In a Magistrates' Court custodial sentences were comparatively rare. Community Service seemed to be a soft option but was supposed

Some Local Institutions

to be an alternative. Fines were the commonest sentence but, in spite of guidelines, setting them at the right level was one of the most difficult tasks. For non-trivial offences they had to be painful but affordable, and could be paid by instalments over a period of up to six months. People often fell behind with instalments and had to be summoned and examined in an attempt to get them to agree reasonable rates of payment or to threaten or impose penalties for non-compliance. But it would be counter-productive to send an offender to prison simply because he or she could not pay. Knowledge of local circumstances was of particular value in setting an appropriate level of fines.

Each Bench elected a chairman annually, amongst whose tasks was to nurture new magistrates and sort out minor difficulties. The Bench Chairmen (of both sexes, of course) were people of high calibre capable of dealing tactfully but effectively with differences of opinion. The Lord-Lieutenant as Chief Magistrate in his ancient office as Custos Rotulorum (keeper of the court rolls or records) was called in very occasionally to join the Chairman of the Bench in dealing with the most difficult cases, where perhaps a JP's ability to form sensible judgements had deserted him or where he had conducted himself in an unacceptable manner, perhaps in a quarrel with a neighbour. But the calibre and standards of the justices was very high.

Justices were expected to devote a full day to court work once a fortnight, and schedules were prepared well in advance. This was the basic work, which governed the size of each Bench, and it was perhaps more demanding than it sounds because it took up the whole of a working day with inexorable regularity, although in the event one might occasionally be released early if a trial had taken less time than had been anticipated. One could exchange days with colleagues by private mutual agreement, which made it possible to arrange holidays or important engagements. As with all jobs, there is more to them than meets the eye. There were special courts, perhaps to remand an awkward customer in custody or perhaps because a search warrant or an arrest warrant was required urgently by the Police. There were training sessions and Bench meetings and committees to attend and lectures arranged by the Magistrates' Association. All these activities were of course unpaid, although modest expenses could be claimed. The honour of being a Justice of the Peace was considered to be a sufficient reward and, indeed, an adequate number of suitable candidates could be found, although it was not easy to maintain the various 'balances' which were considered desirable on each Bench.

Much of the work was tedious to professional or business people accustomed to making decisions without much beating about the bush, because of the legal constraints and procedures, including as I have mentioned listening with apparent patience to a slow-flowing stream of drivel in court. What made the work bearable was the congenial company of one's fellow magistrates and the court staff. This suggested to me that the size of the Bench was an important factor in the structure of the institution; one was working on the whole with people one knew and liked. One would expect to listen and to be listened to. This made disagreements relatively easy to resolve and difficult decision-taking a less unwelcome task than it often is in a profession or a business. One came across an interesting variety of people and circumstances, occasionally tragic or infuriating but more often intriguing and sometimes comical, even if this had to be met with a straight face. The character of a JP's work, or indeed the work of the Bench as an institution, was not understood by the people who were tasked with making the system cheaper and more efficient in the 1980s.

The inefficiencies of the system were by their nature intractable; especially the adjournments caused by lack of cooperation or, much more often, incompetence of those involved. If a witness failed to turn up, there was usually nothing one could do but adjourn a case. Witnesses had to agree to testify and the sanctions one could impose for their incompetence were limited; this might be the only occasion they would appear in a court of law, and even if they could be penalised this would not prevent similar problems occurring in the future. It was less difficult, but not easy, to refuse solicitors' requests for adjournments on perhaps doubtful grounds such as the possible emergence of new evidence. It was also difficult to forecast a timetable, so there was a good deal of expensive hanging about.

The size of each Bench determined the degree to which the justice dispensed by the Magistrates' Courts could be local, and the arguments in favour of 'local justice' were difficult to assess. Traditionally, the considerations were practical, but the days of the motor car were changing that. In the 1980s, a minority of court users had cars, and bus services were dreadful. Twenty years later that situation had changed, and with it all the equations of time and money, stress and convenience, time spent on travel as against time on the job. So one falls back on the

Some Local Institutions

theoretical benefits of local justice, which are easier to enunciate than they are to measure. Remoteness is often quoted (in my opinion often wrongly) as a reason for people's dissatisfaction with political decisions, but in the case of the Courts of Justice, the purpose of which is to try an individual fairly, provided that the Bench is drawn from all classes (if not quite all conditions) of men, then there is less resentment about Us and Them. Everybody concerned – not just the accused – is aware that judgements are made by a team of three local people, who are doing a difficult job without payment and who do understand local conditions, even in such trifles as knowing where a particular town or village lies and what it and its people are like. If a group of known rogues are accused of stealing metal from a large local factory then everyone knows whether or not they could have approached along the river bank or the railway line or over a farmer's field as the Police say they have, and they are no more likely to be convicted because they have a bad record than would be the case in a remoter court; but it is nevertheless easier to identify a tall story because little bits of evidence do not fit.

When it comes to imposing fines, a local court is more likely to understand an individual's financial circumstances than when centralised bureaucratic rules are the measure. A local court is moreover a better judge of witnesses than a remote one: it knows the probation officers better, and has a more accurate measure of their experience and judgement.

But then, how local is local? Wrexham, the largest town in North-East Wales, had a Magistrates' Bench of more than a hundred JPs and it worked well; but in country districts with villages and small towns, where the smallest Benches had already disappeared, over-enthusiastic amalgamation and centralisation destroyed the flavour of local justice.

Every magistrate in England and Wales was appointed by the Lord Chancellor as the head of the legal system, on the recommendation of the local Lord Chancellor's Advisory Committee chaired by the Lord-Lieutenant, which sought out candidates and selected those who were suitable. Only very occasionally did a minion of the Lord Chancellor bare his teeth, just to show who was who, by rejecting a candidate for some technical reason which more often than not was silly. The work of this Committee was interesting, partly because of the requirement to provide or maintain a 'balance' on every Bench. The balance required a mixed profile in sexes, politics, age, occupation, socio-economic category and area of residence. Thus in one particular Bench one might be looking for young female manual workers who supported the Conservative Party and did not live in – well, shall we say Buckley or Rhosllanerchrugog, the two most remarkable villages in our neck of the woods for their energy, personality, originality, and thus for having more than their share of the kind of qualities being looked for?

We explained to candidates at the outset that they might not be selected solely because they did not contribute to the balance of a particular Bench, although they would undoubtedly have made good magistrates. However, during the later years of my involvement in this work the powers that be decided that every rejected candidate had the right to be told the reason for his or her rejection. It had become part of everybody's right to be informed that they were too pompous or opinionated or prejudiced or incapable of drawing logical conclusions to be fit to serve on the Bench. The concept of openness in public affairs has its merits, but this did not seem to me to be one of them.

The selection process was thorough, and subject to detailed regulations, including the format of each of three interviews, one of which was held by a single member of the Committee at the candidate's home, and another of which involved detailed discussion of an imaginary trial. It was not possible to achieve all the criteria of the 'balance' all the time, but over the longer term we maintained them pretty well. The most difficult was to recruit a sufficient number of younger magistrates, until the whole system was wrecked by perhaps the most deplorable of all Lord Chancellors, Lord Irvine, whose sole qualification for office seemed to be that Tony Blair owed him a good turn: he decreed, presumably without giving the question one moment's thought, that 'ageism' should not apply, thus admitting the possibility that the whole Bench might be over seventy years of age! I think this came about because some high-powered candidate, probably a retired civil servant, complained personally to him that he had been turned down. Ironically, the Bench does not require high-flyers. They are not always good listeners to the opinions of lesser mortals.

In addition to the Lord Chancellor's Advisory Committee with its task of recruiting, there was the Magistrates' Court Committee which oversaw the organisation and administration of the Benches. This was a large committee on which every Bench was represented. In Margaret Thatcher's time it was subjected to an efficiency drive in the style of Marks and Spencer. The method was to appoint one bright spark to have a look at the organisation nationwide, and to make recommendations within forty days (why this Biblical period was selected I never discovered). The bright spark in this instance was a young (or youngish) civil servant described as a high-flyer named Le Vay. He decided that the Committees were much too large so the whole system of Bench representation was removed at a stroke. It was then pointed out that this destroyed the well-tried system of communication by which every Bench knew what the Committee was up to and, moreover, had a chance to make its opinion known if a proposal was disagreeable to it, a very important factor at a time when centralisation was often a route to efficiency, albeit at the expense of local input. Magistrates had a right to know what was being proposed and debated before it became a *fait accompli*, and provided that they had their say they were content to go along with the majority. The response of the Lord Chancellor's department to these objections was that in that case a new and different system of communication would have to be devised.

This is a good example of measuring efficiency in a very naïve manner and thus destroying an important characteristic of an institution, just as creating very large Benches to cover extensive areas made them less 'human' and diminished the sense of fulfilment which made the sacrifice of time worthwhile by people whose services were valuable to society and who had plenty of other demands on them. The improvements sought were solely economic and these were marginal. One does not have to look far in twenty-first century institutions to see that Big is not always Beautiful. It is easy to see the drift of David Cameron's concept of The Big Society without necessarily understanding its application in points of detail, but one of its most trumpeted characteristics is that it is made up of a lot of small bits; one might almost say that localism means not the bigger but the smaller the better. Local political institutions – County or District Councils – needed to be (but were not) large enough to attract good candidates, but this made no difference whatever with the Magistracy. Small – often very small – businesses are the salt of the nation's economy although they lack the benefits of scale which modern technology can confer. Their importance lies in the opportunities of fulfilment which they offer to countless individuals. 'Team-building' and all the blather that goes with it in big business cannot replace the motivation provided by individual independence.

Some Local Institutions

3 THE LORD-LIEUTENANT, 1985–2000

The Lord-Lieutenant (the title applies to both sexes) is the Queen's representative in each county throughout the United Kingdom. The appointment is a Crown appointment which means that it is made on the advice of the Prime Minister. There is a senior civil servant in No. 10 Downing Street responsible for identifying suitable candidates for these offices (which include bishops, regius professors and High Court judges) and consulting relevant people in order to be in a position to do so. I suppose that even in these days of 'open government' and 'freedom of information' he still goes about his task with the protection of confidentiality: certainly he used to. Amongst the criteria are that the Lord-Lieutenant must not be a party-political animal, although there are rare examples of former politicians who are appointed. The qualities required may become apparent as I describe the duties to be performed: they include those required in a justice of the peace and, indeed, the Lord-Lieutenant is also automatically appointed Custos Rotulorum, the Keeper of the Rolls, the person traditionally (that is to say historically) responsible for ensuring that the records of the courts of law were properly safeguarded.

The office of Lord-Lieutenant was invented by the Tudors in order to ensure that the Sovereign could call out the militia in times of riot or rebellion. Rather than hope for the support of local magnates as in the times of the Wars of the Roses, Henry VIII made it absolutely clear where authority lay, just as in later turbulent times Oliver Cromwell was to put the whole of England under eleven major-generals. Unfortunately these systems tended not to work very well on the rare and alarming occasions when they were needed, most notably when Bonnie Prince Charlie invaded Northern England with his army of Highland clansmen. However, during the French Revolutionary War, when Pitt had invented the Yeomanry in the form of volunteer cavalry regiments to stiffen up the militia, the authority of the Lord-Lieutenants was enforceable against a feared invasion.

A mounted regiment is a formidable instrument in crowd control and, having read the Riot Act, the Lord-Lieutenant called out the Yeomanry to quell a riot near Manchester in the discontents which followed the Napoleonic War: with the highly regrettable result that they killed a number of rioters in the Peterloo Massacre. That incident in effect brought the system to an end, but Lord-Lieutenants continued

Some Local Institutions

to be drawn from most assertive members of the landed gentry throughout Victorian and Edwardian times: men who used their income from rents to build grand houses and dominate local elections. Since the First World War, and even more so since the Second, the office has become gradually rather more representative, with some preference for those who have 'made their own way' rather than inheriting their wealth and standing.

As the Queen's representative the Lord-Lieutenant is best known nowadays as the person who organises visits to the county of the Queen and members of the Royal Family. This duty, though ceremonial in character, involves interesting work and makes one aware of the demanding duties of all the members of the Royal Family. The Lord-Lieutenant does his or her best to respond to requests for a royal visit either from official or from private organisations, often to perform a specific ceremonial function such as opening a new building – maybe a hospital or a school, or perhaps an office or a factory or a building provided by a charitable organisation; or to mark an anniversary. The day has to go like clockwork and careful planning is essential: fortunately most County Councils provide administrative and clerical help. I had the good fortune to be made Lord-Lieutenant of Clwyd and I had invaluable help from the Chief Executive's office in the Shire Hall.

It is not uncommon for the Chief Executive of the County Council to hold the office of Clerk to the Lieutenancy, probably to be appointed as a Deputy Lieutenant, and to assign one of his ablest assistants to do the administrative work. It is this availability of efficient clerical and organisational work which, in my experience, makes the work of a Lord-Lieutenant feasible. In 1974 Flintshire and Denbighshire were amalgamated to form the County of Clwyd which covered the whole of north-east Wales with a population a little less than half a million. Wherever one lived one could get to any part of the county by car in about an hour. The Chief Executives were Mervyn Phillips and then Roger Davies. The spadework was done by three people in succession ideally suited to the task, to whom I owe a big debt: Reg Evans, Norman Land and Ron Chamberlain.

The county could expect an average of five or six royal visits each year, some of them for very specific purposes when a member of the Royal Family was the patron or president of an organisation – for instance the Duke of Kent for the Lifeboats or the Duchess of Gloucester for the Order of St John. It was easy to invite them to undertake

Some Local Institutions

some additional engagement whilst they were in the county, very often to a charitable organisation or a progressive and ambitious manufacturing company. The Prince of Wales came often, usually but not always in connection with his own initiatives, most notably perhaps helping young people to achieve self-employment or to set up mini-businesses, or in connection with environmental issues. His idea of providing a small sum, perhaps a few hundred pounds, to enable an individual to buy equipment and thus obtain employment, was a brilliant one. His efforts to persuade Welsh sheep farmers to form cooperatives in order to market their products were less successful. Nick Archdale, a leading light in this field, gathered and hosted a group of them at my request to meet His Royal Highness; but one of them was frank enough to admit that the objective of most Welsh sheep farmers was to steal a march on their neighbours.

The Princess of Wales came several times, and one could immediately spot her star quality in this role. If she visited sick or elderly people, or when she came at short notice to visit the victims of the Kinmel Bay floods, she would sit down and talk to each individual or family for some time, showing a real understanding of their plight.

The Queen came twice during my tenure and of course these visits were very special occasions. She would usually fit four engagements into a day and it was an interesting task to work out the logistics for four events of different character, without any of them seeming to be hurried. On one visit at the County Council's request she opened the Bridge to Nowhere – the new Dee Crossing – on a wet and windy day with a rather disappointing public turnout. Another of the few less successful occasions was during her second visit, when she opened the new swimming pool at Wrexham. In spite of careful and detailed briefings and rehearsals the arrangements were altered by the staff at the last minute 'off the cuff'; but The Queen takes these incidents in her stride and the day was redeemed by a most entertaining visit to the village of Overton to celebrate the sixth centenary of its grant of a Royal Charter.

One of the Lord-Lieutenant's most difficult tasks was to remember the names of everybody who was entitled to be presented to Her Majesty at the beginning of each event. One got to know most of the prominent councillors in the County and District Councils but in most cases the mayor or chairman changed each year, and as far as the smaller councils were concerned it was quite likely that one would not have met them before the rehearsal. My worst experience in this context was

Some Local Institutions

when a chairman had already been presented at the first event of the day (celebrating, as it happened, seven hundred years since the foundation of Ruthin School) and then at the very last minute slipped into the line for the second event too. Reg Evans (and his successors) would ensure that everybody was in the right order but he was too late to remove this chairman, with the result that I was completely thrown!

The Lord-Lieutenant had to perform some ceremonial functions on behalf of the Queen including presentations of her awards for industry and export. These were most interesting occasions, giving one an insight into some small businesses founded by individuals of extraordinary ingenuity and enterprise. North-east Wales was one of the areas of Britain which suffered worst from the collapse of heavy industry in the 1970s and 1980s, notably coal-mining and steel. The biggest single disaster was the reduction of the John Summers steel works at Shotton (it changed names several times after 1945 with nationalisation, privatisation and renationalisation) from ten to two thousand employees. Many small firms dependent on it went under and thousands of its employees and eventually a whole generation of young people were unemployed. I have been critical of the old Flintshire County Council, but I must concede that the efforts made by the Clwyd County Council to alleviate this disaster were carried out with determination, persistence and, eventually, success. The area ceased to be a 'one-works' town and the Wrexham area too, losing its mines and heavy industry, began to prosper as one small business after another cropped up and grew. A surprising number of the Queen's Award winners were medical; and many of those who started these businesses were scientists who had been trained by Glaxo and had identified an opportunity to set up a specialised company to provide a treatment for some rare disease which, worldwide, had a substantial number of victims. Of the larger firms the most remarkable was Pilkington, whose main glassworks were at St Helens in Lancashire but who hived off specialised high-tech processes to semi-independent companies – making head-up radar displays for fighter aircraft, glass panels to protect spacecraft and even CDs for export to Japan. There was a Flintshire firm which made all the catalytic converters for Peugeot cars and another which exported millions of patented rivets worldwide. All these companies had applied for a Queen's Award and had undergone a rigorous process of selection. For several years running Clwyd achieved half the awards for the whole of Wales.

Some Local Institutions

Another ceremonial duty was to present the British Empire Medal on behalf of the Queen. This award was abolished by John Major on the mistaken grounds that it embodied some kind of social discrimination between those who received it and those who received the next senior award, the MBE. Actually the result of the abolition was to devalue the MBE and reduce the total number of awards made. The awards had been graded by the extent of the responsibility involved in the work of those who received them, just as are the OBE, the CBE and the KBE or DBE (and even the GBE which is a kind of extra layer of icing for those who already have the KBE and which would have been a more appropriate target for abolition). Maybe there ought to be only one grade – so that the lollipop lady could become a Dame alongside the Permanent Under-Secretary or the Admiral. But the idea of a medal for those who have worked long and nobly for some good cause at a comparatively humble level of responsibility was an admirable one and has now been revived. It was always much valued and appreciated by all concerned and the presentation ceremonies were a pleasure as well as an honour to perform.

The Lord-Lieutenant was invited to numerous special occasions by organisations large and small, and I picked up an idea from my neighbouring Lord-Lieutenant of Merseyside, who like a few others in metropolitan counties had almost a full-time job: namely that Small is Beautiful. It is often the smallest institutions which most value recognition. If they ask for a visit, then presumably they want one and they should get one. Rather as I was astonished to find so many small companies making specialised products I had never imagined, so there were small bands of volunteers devoting time and effort in a remarkable variety of ways to helping others less fortunate than themselves. One could not accept all the invitations and as with so many other voluntary jobs the work usually began after tea, just when one might have hoped to put one's feet up; but these visits were nevertheless enjoyable and rewarding. One was asked to become president or patron of many organisations.

Each Lord-Lieutenant has a large number of Deputy Lieutenants who do not have many duties but who value the right to put DL after their names. Their number is decided by the size of the population, in accordance with an elaborate scale. This is the only form of recognition which can be conferred locally, for although nominations have to be screened by Downing Street they depend on the Lord-Lieutenant to make them. The office, as I have explained, originates from the time when the lieutenancies were invented by the Tudors to reinforce their power throughout the country, especially in calling out the militia or raising an armed force in some other way. They created as their Lord-Lieutenants noblemen or gentlemen on whom they could rely, and deputies were needed to enforce the monarch's will immediately in all parts of a county. (It helped to have a castle.) Each Lord-Lieutenant inherits his or her predecessor's Deputies so it is a long-term project to adjust the Lieutenancy to the requirements of contemporary society. I inherited members of the diminishing generation who had warmly deserved to be made Deputies in recognition of distinguished service during the war. I did my best to add to them people from all walks of life who were performing some valuable public service and who were likely to be respected by those who knew them.

Deputies were people who could carry out the Lord-Lieutenant's duties if he could not be present himself, but the problem was that most people who invited the Lord-Lieutenant to a function did not want a Deputy. Nevertheless they could be very helpful, both as assistants and as advisers. One could establish something like a network of people who knew a lot about what went on in their patches and who could also help in the difficult task of recommending people for national awards.

The Vice Lord-Lieutenant was appointed by the Lord-Lieutenant personally and therefore had to resign on a change of office unless chosen as successor. This office did provide a single individual who was an acceptable substitute when the Lord-Lieutenant could not be present and I much valued the support of my own 'Vice', Michael Griffith, who had an astonishing record of service to Wales in many fields.

As Custos Rotulorum the Lord-Lieutenant was *ex officio* chairman of the Lord Chancellor's Advisory Committee. In Flint and Denbigh and then in Clwyd it was the custom also to elect him as chairman of the Magistrates' Court Committee. I thought that this was perhaps concentrating too much in one person's hands but I did not like to refuse the honour. This kept one in touch with what was happening in the criminal justice system in the county and to that extent it was an advantage. I was also made President of the Magistrates' Association, and attended most of their lectures.

The Police Authority consisted two-thirds of county councillors elected by the Councils themselves (both Clwyd and Gwynedd, because

Some Local Institutions

it covered all North Wales) and one-third of magistrates elected at Bench meetings, and since the powers and duties of these authorities were and are much misunderstood, and have subsequently, and most unfortunately, been abolished, I will add a brief account of the work.

Some members (notably some of the councillors) never grasped that the function of the Authority could not in theory trespass on the operational side of policing at all, which was the remit of the Chief Constable, but was solely concerned with finance and administration. Listening to the pronouncements of Members of Parliament and even Government ministers, one could be forgiven for thinking that they did not understand either; and that those who did understand had decided to fudge the issue and give the successors of Police Authorities 'teeth'. Police Authorities were often blamed for not exercising powers which, fortunately, they did not possess: so now the so-called 'Commissioners' can hire and fire the Chief Constable, with no other objective than influencing his or her operational activities. There could be no clearer example of politicians who are capable (as many are) of thinking clearly deliberately closing their minds. The time-honoured constitutional barrier preventing political control of the Police has been removed, as was done by Hitler, Mussolini, Franco and Stalin. A better solution would be to reform the Police, as proposed by Tom Winsor, and reduce the inhibiting power of the Police Federation, in order to recruit a larger number of potential senior officers, especially Chief Constables.

The system of finance was similar to that of a County Council in that a small proportion of the money was provided locally – by the ratepayers then, as now by the Council Tax – but most of it came (and comes) from Central Government. The Treasurer of the Police Authority was the County Treasurer of one of the two counties, the other county providing the Secretary. This was a good arrangement, considering that a similarly arcane system of funding applied to Local Government itself, with limits imposed by Whitehall.

The funds made available in the Authority's budget inevitably had some effect on the operational side of policing, so the theory that it had no operational role was blurred. The Chief Constable might ask for an extra sergeant or inspector, and the Authority, accepting his or her priorities, had to decide whether they could be funded or not. The development of helicopters with special equipment introduced a debate in the Authority which on the face of it ought to have remained beyond its power. However, the criterion was to decide how much money this would save in manpower and how effective it would be in reducing crime, which was an administrative exercise subject to the acceptance of expert 'operational' advice.

On the whole the Authority's decisions, steered by the Chief Constable and a few of his senior officers, were sensible, but the councillors tended to be too party-political for this work. One councillor got himself elected with the sole objective of obstructing the work of the Police and laboriously questioned and opposed every recommendation on the agenda – a most tiresome procedure for all concerned and a cross to bear for the Chief Constable. This was not by any means the case with all the councillors, but the magistrates played an important part in keeping political prejudice in its proper subordinate position. When it was decided by Margaret Thatcher's second Government that the Police Authorities were feeble, the remedy was to remove all the magistrates and to add some local business men instead. Results do not suggest that this has been a roaring success. The reforms revealed a misunderstanding both of the Authority's role and of the magistrates' important contribution.

None of the long-standing problems with regard to the political control of Policing in this country have been solved. They have become aggravated since the late years of the twentieth century by the increasing complexity and sophistication of criminal activities and the perception by the public in the age of the internet of its right to be consulted – and to criticise those in positions of responsibility – on matters of detail. The more important work of the Police in combating serious crime was and still is hidden from public view, so the curse of 'news' (that Good News is No News) falls more heavily on the Police than on any other institution: the good news, and in particular the skill, ingenuity and persistence which brought it about, simply does not get exposed to public view.

The difficulty is that a Police force – dare it be said? – requires much the same kind of structure as the Armed Forces do, but since it involves the relationships, in all their complexity, between a community and the treatment of crime and disorder within it in a democratic society, no way has yet been devised of reconciling calls for efficiency with those for 'freedom'. The Police themselves are heavily unionised by the powerful Police Federation, which prevented and still prevents the kind of gradual structural development needed by the Armed Forces, and the vested interest within the Police against any kind of officer entry or accelerated promotion still prevails. Lord Trenchard as Commissioner of the Metropolitan Police in the 1930s founded a Police College in Hendon, but his policy was quickly dismantled and during the war his empty college was commandeered for training the Home Guard in the grisly exercise of unarmed combat.

The Police Authority's budget indirectly affected operations, as did its task of appointing the most senior officers. Fortunately these powers were constrained by the rules that an Assistant Chief Constable could not be appointed to the top job in the force in which he was serving, and also that he must have attended the senior staff officers' course. The Home Office also had a veto, and thus effectively presented the Authority with a short list from which to choose. North Wales had two admirable Chief Constables in Sir William Williams and David Owen, but after that nobody with Welsh or northern roots could be found and finally in the early years of the twenty-first century the list of candidates was so thin that the North Wales Police sank to what the Inspector of Constabulary described as 'Alice in Wonderland' policing: 'Gilbert and Sullivan' would have fitted equally well.

HM Inspectors of Constabulary were *la crème de la crème*, selected from retiring Chief Constables. They worked from the Home Office and it was they who ensured that standards were maintained. I had the impression during the years in which I was a member of the Police Authority that there were just about enough candidates of adequate calibre to fill the office of Chief Constable, but below that there were serious shortcomings. Some police officers (I am not saying many) had risen to the rank of Deputy or Assistant Chief Constable who ought not to have been there. Unfortunately there was a sad example in North Wales, a senior officer who was unfit for the job and was not respected – indeed he was ridiculed – by his subordinates. In these circumstances the rot spreads quickly and David Owen was seriously let down. I know, because as Lord-Lieutenant I was very much a supporter and friend of the Chief Constable (who has a lonely job, especially if the Chairman of the Authority is not of the calibre to give him much support) and being myself a member of the Authority I got to know something of what was going on and was able to warn him.

Maybe this problem arose because the Authority made the senior appointments rather as the County Council did in its own sphere. With adequate candidates thin on the ground, it was essential to select the

Some Local Institutions

best, and to have a view furnished by experience, perhaps in other organisations, of the kind of qualities which were required. But alas, prejudice, ignorance and local favouritism played their part. An attempt was made by the Government to reintroduce Trenchard's idea of a graduate entry to the Police with a chance of accelerated promotion, but it was not well managed. The graduates were not welcomed into the closed-shop Police culture and were condemned for being theorists without common sense and lacking practical experience. There was no way the Police Federation was going to accept a system with any of the characteristics of an 'officer class'. There were and are variations in the possible method of getting sufficient capable people to the upper layers of the promotion triangle; but to judge by both public and political verdicts, they have not been successful.

At the bottom of the triangle the Police were overtrained and overpaid for the humbler jobs, so it was not possible to afford the necessary number of officers to do what was needed to prevent petty crime and disorder. Eventually, after I had retired, the Community Police were brought in: a step in the right direction. Part of the problem was the increasing requirement for 'paperwork' in a severely over-regulated society.

As Lord-Lieutenant and a member of the Police Authority I got to know a large number of Police officers in many roles and had a high regard for almost all of them. I also became more aware than otherwise might have been the case of the nature of some major undercover operations against cunning criminal gangs.

The Lord-Lieutenant held the office of President of the local Territorial Army and Volunteer Reserve Association, in which his official position was highly respected, although he no longer had the power, which survived until early Victorian times, to call out the Militia or the Yeomanry to quell a riot! The Army is intensely aware of a hierarchy of high-ranking officers, colonels of regiments and honorary colonels of regiments or battalions and so forth, and the Lord-Lieutenant was regarded as one of them. I turned up regularly at the TAVRA Committee meetings and was always warmly welcomed and entertained, and I attended celebratory events which were quite frequent, not least the St David's Day dinner – at the first of which my initiation involved swallowing the inevitable leek. The 3rd (Volunteer) Battalion of the Royal Welch Fusiliers was based at the Hightown Barracks at Wrexham, and had a corps of drums (a band of drums and fifes in layman's words) which added great style to ceremonial parades. The Battalion had companies in towns of North Wales: new headquarters were built at Colwyn Bay and at Queensferry during my time. The commanding officer and the adjutant were Regular Army officers, but all the other officers and the other ranks were volunteers. Morale was always high in this admirable institution, which provided at very low cost an Army reserve; but rather than serve abroad as complete units the Territorials were being used more and more as individuals to fill gaps in the regular forces, and they could provide men with a high degree of technical expertise in many fields.

The Royal Welch Fusiliers were proud of their 300-year record of service and were a Regiment of the Line recruited from the whole of North Wales, rather than being associated with a single county (or in a few cases a pair of counties) as in England. During the First World War they had provided the almost unbelievable number of forty-four battalions of infantry. This was an advantage to them during the long period of creating larger units, especially after the end of the Cold War, during which many of the English county regiments disappeared as single entities. Whenever the number of infantry battalions in the Army was reduced, the Regulars always preferred to sacrifice a Territorial battalion rather than one of their own, and in this they tended to get the backing of the generals, who came from the same stable. This was a mistaken policy, or at least it was pursued too keenly. The high cost of a Regular rather than a Territorial battalion meant that these funding crises, crying out for further reductions of manpower, recurred more frequently than they need have done.

There was also a strong Cadet battalion commanded by former Regimental Sergeant Major, by then Major, Hughes, an ideal choice for the role, with its base at Kinmel Camp, of which I was a very inadequate honorary colonel; and another such battalion in Caernarvon. There were Sea Cadets operating in a rather lower key (as might be expected, perhaps, of the Senior Service), and there were Air Training Corps units, notably the one based on the old RAF Hawarden which several times won the supreme national award. The cadet forces were supported financially by the Ministry of Defence, not specifically as aids to recruiting but because of the value of their training for young people from any walk of life. They did, however, have an indirect benefit to the Armed Services in the form of a 'footprint' – an awareness of the Navy, Army and Air Force in civilian families; and this, indeed was also one of

Some Local Institutions

the benefits to the Regular services which the Territorial and Volunteer forces themselves contributed.

The most remarkable of all the TAVRA units in north-east Wales was the Royal Engineers Heavy Recovery Company based at Prestatyn, which was as highly trained and skilled as similar Regular units, which were few and far between. This company, quite apart from providing individuals and small teams for the Regular Army overseas wherever they were needed, used to attend all the major training exercises undertaken by the Army, to move and repair heavy equipment, especially tanks. The least known of the voluntary units was the Royal Observer Corps who monitored Eastern Bloc radar and satellite communications during the Cold War. They had been founded to use binoculars to spot and identify enemy planes during the war and had gradually become more sophisticated in line with technological developments. They were disbanded not long after the end of the Cold War. All these various units requested the attention of the Lord-Lieutenant from time to time, as did the larger civilian institutions such as the Order of St John, the Red Cross, the Scouts and Guides and the Boys' Brigade. This last was by now a small organisation nationally, but as with so many voluntary institutions, one individual leader of genius was the secret of success.

Before the days of Lord-Lieutenants, High Sheriffs were powerful figures in their counties (my father as High Sheriff of Flintshire was the last to have to perform the statutory task of witnessing an execution) and had important functions in law enforcement, such as it was; but because they were returning officers for the Knights of the Shire, i.e. the two Members of Parliament for the county seats, and had been inclined to favour their own political allies rather than to pay much regard to the ballot (thus causing endless disputes), they were cut down to size by their tenure being limited to one year and by being selected by the King or Queen by 'pricking'. The story goes that Queen Elizabeth I closed her eyes and used her bodkin to make her choice. When (or before) the secret ballot was introduced by Mr Gladstone's first administration, the High Sheriff (already prevented from acquiring his office by merit or any other means, and then, when appointed and sworn in, from staying for more than a year) had no power left, and not much more than an honorary function. However, the office with its grand and venerable title still had not lost its prestige, and a list of candidates had to be formed. They were then 'pricked' in the strict order of the list annually by the Queen so that if there were five names on the list each one had to wait for five years before obtaining the office. In theory anybody could be put on to a list, but it had to be approved by the Lord-Lieutenant and then vetted by Number 10. I inherited an almost rigid system by which each High Sheriff could nominate one successor, whose name was placed at the bottom of the list and who thus obtained the office several years later. I enforced the system strictly, as I think most Lord-Lieutenants did, although I knew of at least one county list of ten candidates, and of a few other counties where the candidates did not automatically climb one step each year because the list was liable to alteration.

The High Sheriff was present at all the main ceremonial events of the year and was expected to provide entertainment for anybody who was anybody. It was customary that he or she should take an interest in the work of the Police and the Prison Service, and often launched or continued a project or charitable fund for a good cause, notably for the discouragement of criminality. I found it helpful if they were able and willing to entertain the High Court judges who sat occasionally in the county because, enjoyable as this duty was, I did not find it easy to fit it in with my other obligations.

The Lord-Lieutenant's role is a demanding one in that he or she is generally regarded as the most important person present, and whilst this does not exactly require that you are the life and soul of every party, it does place an obligation on you to say an appropriate 'few words' (as a speech is described in Wales, the most loquacious part of Britain) often without warning (other than Be Prepared, but not Too Prepared) and, even with warning, sometimes in an unexpected context. If something goes wrong, as it often does, you may have to try to plug a gap with a not too inane remark (and try to keep people smiling) as if all was proceeding like clockwork. And you have to look smart, often in quite a stiff kind of military general's uniform. On the grandest occasions you must wear your sword, which is not an ordinary infantry sword but a cavalry sword, which hangs loosely from its belt and is easily tripped over by yourself or, perhaps even worse, by somebody else. You may be accustomed to attending parties with light, or in some cases heavy, refreshments, and the need for three hands. But if nobody offers to take your hat and you need to hold on to your sword, then four or even five hands would come in useful. Nevertheless, even if your efforts to rescue a situation are not very clever, they tend to result in a detectable sense of relief; and the fact that so much of your work is involved with volunteers or dedicated professionals does make it rewarding.

Needless to say there is an Association of Lord-Lieutenants, which sent round very occasional circulars and met once a year in the House of Lords and later in the much more friendly surroundings of St James's Palace. In my early years this was a very stiff and formal affair under the chairmanship of Chips Maclean, but it was softened by his successor John Buccleuch and further so by Robin Kingsdown until, in the end, it was a pleasure to attend it. We were able to discuss problems in a friendly rather than the old intimidating atmosphere. On appointment one received some very detailed printed information, mainly regarding protocol, especially in relation to the Royal Family. The essential principles of one's responsibilities in the magistracy and the Armed Forces were also defined. But apart from that, one of the merits of the office was that no guidelines were laid down and each of us had wide discretion to do what seemed to be most worthwhile and what in some contexts coincided with one's own particular interests. I had already become aware as Chief Scout of the little differences in idiom, custom and approach between every county of Great Britain, and it is my opinion that these diversities of culture add flavour to the richness and diversity of the United Kingdom. Minor local variations are being eroded as communications grow. The differences in dialect between individual villages have mostly gone as older generations have disappeared. The continuation of this process is inevitable. The old diversity will be replaced by other forms of cultural recipe – just as recipes for cooking have lost their local features, but acquired multiple new sophisticated ones.

For anyone to be chosen as Lord-Lieutenant is an honour, not least because the office is respected by many people who know little about it, just as it is by those who are involved in one way or another with the Lord-Lieutenant's duties and activities. It opened attractive opportunities and the hard and sometimes difficult work which it involved was amply recognised and rewarded, especially perhaps by the interesting people one met from many walks of life. Moreover, the Queen gave a reception in Buckingham Palace which included our spouses, and both Margaret Thatcher and John Major invited us to 10, Downing Street. As in so many roles, the early years were in one sense the less rewarding, when one was greeted with a faint whiff of uncertainty as 'The New' Lord-Lieutenant, rather than a familiar and friendly piece of endogenous furniture. But equally in my experience (although not in that of all my colleagues) there came a time when one began to get stale and, as happens to any talker, one's voice began to sound to oneself like an old, worn gramophone record, to use an appropriately outdated simile. A retirement age of seventy-five was introduced just before my time, and regardless of one's individual physical or mental state I felt that after fifteen years perhaps enough was enough.

Dramatis Personae

Alington, Cyril, Head Master of Eton, 26, 45
Allen, Tony, 175
Alston, John, 129–30
Annan, Noel (life peer Baron Annan, 1965), 10
Asquith, H. H., 1st Earl of Oxford and Asquith, 204

Babington Smith, Harry, 25
Baden-Powell, Robert, 1st Baron, 122, 149, 150, 151, 152, 153, 160–4, 172–3, 174, 187, 188, 190, 191, 192, 194; widow Olave, 153, 192
Baden-Powell, Robert, 3rd Baron, 184
Baker, Revd Tom, 133
Bancroft, Donald, 141, 142
Bannister, Sir (1975) Roger, 103
Barker, Alan, 112
Barstow, Lieutenant-Commander George, RN, 85
Beasley-Robinson, Claude, 25
Beeston, John, 146
Bendell, Mr, Eton School Clerk, 36
Benz, Karl Friedrich, 231
Birley, Robert, Head Master of Eton, later Sir, 108–9, 120, 121, 123, 125
Blair, Tony, 242, 254
Blake, Robert, life peer (Baron Blake) 1971, 98–9, 100
Blakiston, C. H., 138

Blunt, Wilfrid, 26
Bourne, Bobby, 116
Britten, Benjamin, 130
Brocklebank, Tom, 31, 116
Brown, Laurence, 142
Browne-Wilkinson, Nicholas, 145
Browning, Oscar, 40
Buccleuch, 9th Duke of, 269
Buckland, Canon William, 228
Bué, Henri, 11
Burd, Sub-Lieutenant Oliver, RN, 90, 91
Butterwick, Cyril, 19, 29
Buxton, Tommy (Sir Thomas, 6th Bt, 1945), 14

Caesar, Julius, and Gallic War texts, 8–9
Callaghan, James, Baron, 2
Callender, David, 122
Cameron, David, 255
Campbell, Bill, 198
Campling, Revd (later Very Revd as Dean of Ripon) Christopher, 129, 131, 132, 140
Card, Tim, 109
Carl XVI Gustaf, King of Sweden, 199
Carlyle, Thomas, 3
Carpenter, Richard Cromwell, and son Richard Herbert, architectural work at Lancing, 128
Cecil, Lord Hugh (Baron Quickswood 1941), 47

Dramatis Personae

Chacksfield, Air Vice-Marshal Sir Bernard, 183–4
Chadwyck-Healey, Charles, 145
Chamberlain, Christopher ('Monkey'), 138
Chamberlain, Neville, 17
Chamberlain, Ron, 257
Charles I, King 201, 214
Chataway, Sir (1995) Christopher, 103
Chaucer, Geoffrey, and author's School Certificate, 24
Churchill, E. L. ('Jelly'), 26, 39–40,
Churchill, Sir Winston, 6, 35, 47
Claret, Alf, 43, and raft hands Charlie and Froggie, 43
Claret, Frank (son of preceding), 118
Clark, Christopher Storm, 141
Clarke, 'God', 31–2
Cooper, Arthur, 138
Corlett, John, 12, 13
Cory, Christopher, 182
Cory, Raymond, 225

Dancy, John, later Professor, 129, 130, 132, 133–4, 135, 136, 141, 148
Davies, Roger, 257
de Havilland, R. S., 116
Deacon, Tom, PT instructor, Lancing, 147
Dovell, Bill, 139
Dundas, Robin, 100–1

Edinburgh, HRH Prince Philip, Duke of, Award, 124, 174
Edward VII, King, 150
Eisenhower, General Dwight D. (later President), 9
Elizabeth II, HM Queen, 157, 179, 183, 201, 258, 259, 260, 269

Elliott, (Sir, 1958) Claude, Head Master of Eton, 26, 37, 38–9, 48, 108–9
Ellis, Armon, 239
Ellis, Glyn, 223
Evans, Reginald, 257, 259
Evetts, Lieutenant General Sir John, 136, 146

Fagents, Sergeant, 12, 14
Feiling, (later Sir) Keith, 97
Fielding, Bernard, 138–9
FitzHugh, Michael, 237
Foulkes, Trevor, 135
Freeman, Clifford, 145

Gabr, Malek, 189
Garnier, Captain, Royal Marines, 57–8
Gavin, Dr Liam, 241
George VI, King, 29
Gibbon, Edward, 3, 22–3
Giffard, Miles, 15
Gladstone, (Sir) Charles Andrew, 6th Bt (author's father), 6, 15, 16, 17, 32, 149, 237; and wife Isla Margaret (author's mother), 6, 15
Gladstone, Peter (author's brother), 15, 29
Gladstone, W. E., 36, 94, 95, 98, 99, 127–8, 204, 205, 206, 249, 267
Gloucester, HRH Duchess of, 257
Gorbachev, Mikhail, 2
Graham-Campbell, David, 112, 113
Griffith, Michael, 261
Griffiths, Tom, 146
Guest, Harry, 141

Haig-Thomas, Peter, 117

[274]

Dramatis Personae

Halsey, Patrick, 138
Harris, Chris, 220
Harris, George, Oxford boatman, 102
Hayden, Ted, 158, 159, 196
Headington, Christopher, 141
Headlam, G. W., 'Tuppy', 111
Henry VIII, King, 201–2, 229, 238, 256
Herbert, John ('Bertie'), 25
Heseltine, Michael, MP, later life peer, Baron, 173–4
Higginbotham, John, 142
Hilder, Alan, 13–14
Hillcourt, William, 192
Hitler, Adolf, 17, 35; forged diaries, 98; 99, 262
Hope Jones, William, 25
Houston, Ordinary Seaman Bill, 56
Hughes, Major, Cadet battalion Royal Welch Fusiliers, 266
Huskins, John, 158, 159, 169
Huxley, Thomas Henry, 228

Ireland, Walter Anthony von Simunich, 32
Irvine, Derry, Baron Irvine of Lairg, Lord Chancellor, 254

Jagger, Sam, 134
Jenkins, Canon Claude, 97, 100
Johnson, Dr Samuel, 229
Jones, Dr Glynne, 226
Jones, Graham, 223
Jones, W. R., 223
Joseph, Keith, Baron, 2

Kent, HRH Duke of, 257
Kermode, Terry, 138
Keynes, John Maynard, 1st Baron, 175

Kingsdown, Robin Baron (life peer), 269
Kinnaird, Arthur, 11th Lord, and football, 115

Land, Norman, 257
Lawson, Sir William, 145
Le Vay, Julian, 255
Lestock-Reid, Lt Cdr William, 184
Ley, Henry 'Daddy', 26, (and wife) 36, 45
Lloyd George, David, 1st Earl Lloyd-George of Dwyfor, 204
Lockwood, Lieutenant, RN, 90
Lockyer, Roger, 141

'Ma Bub' and daughter Rosie, Scaitcliffe, 14–15
McIntyre, David, 223
Maclean, Sir Charles ('Chips'), 11th Bt, Chief Scout, 151, 152, 154, 179, 184, 269
Maidment, Ted, 141
Major, Sir John (KG 2005), 269
Marsden, H. K., 25, 29
Marten, Sir (1945) Henry, 23, 111
Martineau, Richard, 22
Masterman, Sir (1959) J. C., 101
Matthew, Colin, 99
Montgomery of Alamein, Field Marshal 1st Viscount, 9, 186
Morford, Mark, 142
Mount, Ferdinand, 3
Muna, Solomon T., 197

Nagy, László, 188–9, 190, 193
Nicholson, Archie, 116–17
Noakes, Rt Revd George, Bishop of St David's, later Archbishop of Wales, 235–6
Noble, Sir Marc, 178
'Nurse Minor' and 'Nurse

Dramatis Personae

Minima', Scaitcliffe (sister) matrons, 14

Olden, Jack, 186
Owen, David, Chief Constable North Wales Police, 264
Owen, Denis, 8, 13

Pahlavi, Mohammad Reza, Shah of Persia, 194
Passey, Mr, gardener at Lancing, 146
Pears, Sir Peter, 130
Pemberton, Roger, 11
Perkins, Ordinary Seaman, 56
Perkins, Petty Officer 'Polly', 63
Perkins, Revd Jocelyn, 16
Phillips, Mervyn, 257
Poppett, Ordinary Seaman, 56
Pound, Captain (RN) George, 182

Ranfurly, 6th Earl of, 184
Rees, Brian, 112
Rees, Haydn, 239, 244, 245
Reeve, Robin, 141
Richardson, Charles, RN chaplain (later vicar of Rowmarsh, Yorkshire), 90
Roberts, Field Marshal Earl, 161
Robinson, Robbie, 159
Rockwell, Norman, 192
Routh, C. R. N. ('Dick'), 112
Rowallan, 2nd Baron, Chief Scout, 150
Rowlatt, Charles, 37

St Aubyn, Hon. Giles, 112, 113, 114
Sanderson, Revd Dr R. E., 138
Sellers, Peter, 172
Shakespeare, William, and auhor's School Certificate, 24

Shaw, Revd Cuthbert, 129
Shearwood, Ken, 134, 139, 140
Shelmerdine, David, 160
Sisman, Adam, biography of Hugh Trevor-Roper (q.v.), 99
Slim, Field Marshal 1st Viscount, *Defeat Into Victory* (1956), 121
Smith, Adam, 3
Smith, G. B., 31, 32
Smith, Sub-Lieutenant Laurie, RNVR, 90
Smythe, Revd Paddy, 132–3
Somers, 6th Baron, Chief Scout, 150
Spanoghe, Peter, 31
'Starchy Ethel' (Scaitcliffe), 14, 15
Stayt, Robin, 184
Stevens, Ken, 157–8, 159, 178, 185, 190
Stuart, Charles, 95, 100
Surplice, Alwyn, 11, 12

Tait, George, 19
Taylor, A. J. P., 97
Temple, Archbishop William, 227, 229
Thatcher, Margaret, Baroness, 2, 4, 95, 98, 247, 254, 263, 269
Thorold, Revd Henry, 131, 139, 140–1
Tooley, Ordinary Seaman, 56
Trenchard, 1st Viscount, 264
Trevor-Roper, Hugh (life peer 1979, Baron Dacre of Glanton), 97–8, 99–100
Twine, Derek, 160, 178
Tydd, Bill, 145–6, 147–8

Vaughan, David, 225
Vickers, Ronald (Scaitcliffe), 7ff
Vickers, 'Ma Bub', second wife of

[276]

preceding, and daughter Rosie,
  14–15
Villiers, Hon. Arthur, 125
Vollmer, Gustavo, 198–9

Wales, Charles, HRH Prince of,
  258
Wales, Diana, HRH Princess of,
  258
Walker, Captain Johnnie, RN, 78
Walton, Lieutenant (E) Kevin,
  90–1
Warre, Revd Dr Edmond, Head
  Master of Eton, 28–30, 40–1, 44,
  45, 46, 116, 124

Watson, Steven, 95, 100
White, Hon. Luke (later 5th Baron
  Annaly), 11, 13
Whitfield, Brian, 19, 20
Wilberforce, Bishop Samuel,
  228
Wilkinson, Denys, 19
Williams, Archbishop Gwilym,
  220, 221, 222
Williams, Charles, 156
Williams, W. W. ('Fishy'), 37–8
Williams, Sir William, 264
Wood, Frank, 147
Woodard, Nathaniel, 127, 128,
  137–8, 144, 148